Contents

KT-562-426

ReadMe.first **17**

Introducing Email **19**

The growth of email	19	Copy to field	31
The uses for email	21	Blind copy field	32
A social tool	21	Subject field	32
A business tool	23	Message field	32
How email works	25	Attachments	33
Email servers	26	Send button	34
Setting up an email account	27	Methods of receiving email	34
The anatomy of an email	30	Computer	34
The toolbar and menu bar	30	Mobile telephones	35
Recipient information	30	Handheld computers	37
Address book	31	Television	37
To field	31	The future	39

Email Programs *41*

Available programs	41	System requirements	56
Microsoft Outlook & Outlook		Installing email programs	56
Express	42	Through your ISP	56
Outlook	42	With a CD-ROM	57
Outlook Express	43	From the Web	58
Eudora	44	Upgrading programs	58
Eudora modes	45	Using more than one email	
Sponsored mode	45	account	59
Paid mode	45	Setting a default program	61
Light mode	46	Importing addresses and messages	62
Eudora features	46	Opening emails with different	
System Requirements: Windows	47	programs	63
System Requirements: Macintosh	47	Using a different program for	
Netscape Messenger	48	a new account	64
Pegasus	50	Menus and toolbars	65
Obtaining Pegasus	51	Menus	66
Installing Pegasus	52	Toolbar	68
Features	54	Additional views	70

Finding Contacts *73*

Setting up contacts	73	Address books	76
Obtaining email addresses	74	Viewing details	77
Asking people	74	Searching for contacts	77
Recording addresses	74	Creating contact groups	78
From business cards	75	Contact information	80
Email directories	75	Editing contact information	81

MAKE THE MOST OF EM@IL

in easy steps
.compact

NICK VANDOME

in easy steps and **in easy steps.compact** are imprints of Computer Step
Southfield Road . Southam . Warwickshire CV47 OFB . England
Web site: http://www.ineasysteps.com
Email: books@ineasysteps.com

Notice of Liability

Every effort has been made to ensure that this book contains accurate and current information. However, Computer Step and the author shall not be liable for any loss or damage suffered by readers as a result of any information contained herein.

Trademarks

All trademarks are acknowledged as belonging to their respective companies.

Printed and bound in the United Kingdom

ISBN 1-84078-108-4

Editing groups	83	User details	85
Finding items	83	Finding people on the Internet	86
To find a message	84	To use an email directory	
To find contacts	85	on the Web	87

Sending and Receiving *89*

The basics of sending and receiving	89	Draft messages	104
Setting options	91	Checking a message has	
General settings	91	been sent	106
Send/receive messages	92	Replying to emails	108
Connection	96	Replying to a group	109
Send	98	Forwarding emails	109
Message icons	101	Dealing with junk email	110
Writing offline, sending online	103		

Formatting *111*

Formatting possibilities	111	Signatures	132
Plain text	112	Creating a vCard	134
Rich Text Format (RTF) and HTML	113	To attach a vCard	135
Formatting toolbar	114	Spelling and grammar	135
Formatting the background	123	Copying and pasting text	136
Stationery	124	Importing text	137
Font settings	129	Digital certificates	138
Opening and closing conventions	130	Encryption	140

Including Attachments *141*

The technical side of attachments	141	Images files	151
The benefits of attachments	141	A digital camera	152
Using attachments carefully	144	Scanners	161
Size issues	144	Photo CDs	162
Program compatibility issues	146	Portable Document Format (pdf)	163
Transmission of viruses	148	Saving attachments	166
Types of attachments	150	Printing attachments	169
Program files	150		

Organising Emails *171*

Reasons for organising	171	Archiving or backing up	180
Folders	172	Rules for incoming email	182
Folder notation	173	Blocking senders	189
Creating folders	174	Organising messages	190
Deleting folders	176	Mailboxes	192
Renaming folders	177	Using a different email account	
Moving folders	178	with a new identity	194
Moving, deleting & copying messages	179		

Email Services *195*

Web-based email   195
What is a Web-based email
  account?   195
Finding Web-based email
  providers   197
Web-based email options   198
Creating an account   200
Accessing an account   203

Information misuse   205
Email good practice   206
Forwarding services   209
Other email forwarding
  services   211
Electronic cards   212
Email to fax   216
Electronic invitations   218

Outlook *219*

Attributes of Outlook   219
Latest features   220
System requirements   222
Outlook Bar   223
Menu bars   224
File   225
Edit   227
View   229
Go To (sub menu of View)   230
Tools   231
Actions   233
Help   233

Email/Inbox   234
Composing   235
Sending and receiving   236
Address book entries   239
Adding a signature   240
Calendar   241
Viewing options   241
Creating appointments   242
Viewing other users' calendars   243
Contacts   244
Tasks   245
Notes   246

Eudora *247*

Eudora modes	247		Mailboxes	282
Sponsored mode	247		Styled Text	284
Paid mode	248		Spell checking	285
Light mode	248		Auto-Completion	286
Features	248		Date Display	287
Menu bar	249		Labels	288
File menu	249		Getting Attention	288
Edit menu	252		Background Tasks	289
Mailbox menu	255		Automation	290
Message menu	256		Extra Warnings	290
Transfer menu	258		MAPI (Messaging Application	
Special menu	259		Program Interface)	290
Tools menu	262		Advanced Network	291
Options	265		Auto Configure	291
Getting Started	265		Kerberos	291
Checking Mail	266		Miscellaneous	291
Incoming Mail	267		Window	293
Sending Mail	270		Help	294
Internet Dial-up	273		Creating a new message	296
Replying	274		New message toolbar	297
Attachments	275		Receiving messages	299
Fonts	277		Working with folders	
Display	278		and mailboxes	300
Viewing Mail	279		Signatures	302

Netscape Messenger *303*

Creating a profile	303	View	318
Menu bar	305	Go	320
File	305	Message	321
Edit	308	Communicator	322
Preferences	309	Toolbars	323
Appearance	309	Viewing options	325
Navigator	310	Composing messages	326
Mail and Newsgroups	311	File	326
Roaming Access	317	Edit	327
Composer	317	View	328
Offline	317	Insert	329
Advanced	318	Format	330

Pegasus *331*

Menu bar	331	Message settings	341
File	331	Toolbars	343
Edit	333	Message	344
Addresses	334	Folder	346
Tools	335	Window	348
Options	337	Help	349
General	337	Creating a new message	351
Reader settings	338	Adding attachments	354
Hyperlinks	339	Sending	354
Signatures	340	Address books	355
Reporting	340	Mail folders	356
Sending mail	340	Signatures	357

Netiquette *359*

Composing with care	359	Avoid shouting	364
Reply promptly	360	Do not expect confidentiality	365
Check your Inbox regularly	360	Be careful with humour	365
Do not hassle people for a reply	361	Take your time to respond	366
Be concise	361	Avoid flame wars	367
Avoid sending huge attachments	362	Using emoticons	368
Edit your responses	363	Using abbreviations	369

Email on the Move *371*

WAP	371	Computing sites	380
The beginnings of WAP	372	Corpex	380
How WAP works	373	LCI Technology Group	380
Drawbacks of WAP	374	JumpingDuck	380
WAP resources	377	Siteloft Wireless AS	381
Business sites	378	Haloplayers.com	381
Wapetite	378	Wap Planet	381
WAP NAWEB	378	xebec mediafactory	381
BlueCycle Auctions	378	Mdj's Computer Guide	381
VipWap	378	Email sites	382
Hughesmedia	378	Quick Access E-mail	382
Bandwidth Telecommunications	378	Mail and News	382
ITIL	379	WAP 0	382
Agilic	379	WAP Machine	382
Minutehand.com	379	M-Minimail	382
Uplands	379	E-Search	382
Vesti Mobile Service	379	Financial sites	383

Mobile Invest 383
Jagnotes 383
UBS Quotes 383
money.pl 383
Wiener Börse 383
moneyeXtra 384
Stock Smart 384
Stockpoint 384
Entertainment sites 385
UK Entertainment Centre 385
Sessami 385
Breathe 385
Rock Nights 386
Hitchhiker's Guide to the Galaxy 386
Games sites 386
BetMart 386
Hangman 386
wapscallion.net 387
WAPCasino 387
Space 387
News sites 387
BBC 387
Newsvendor 388
News Unlimited 388
CNN 388
The Tuck Shop 388
Interpuntonet.it news 388
Shopping sites 389

Homepages.co.uk 389
1-800-MOBILESInc. 389
Battery Outlet 389
Camera Sound 389
Candlescape.com 389
Cellpoint Corporation 389
Cool Sports Equipment, LLC 389
Flowers On Command 389
Gadget Universe 390
Getcellular 390
Pinelli's Flowerland 390
Metrolabels 390
D M Merchandise Company 390
Top Dog Entertainment 390
A-1 T-Shirts 390
Young Pharmaceuticals, Inc. 390
Sport sites 390
WAP a Result 390
Arsenal Wapsite 391
Manchester United Wapsite 391
I Golf The World 391
Travel sites 391
CitiKey 391
Italy Hotel Reservation Online 392
The Hotel Catalogue 392
Personal Travel Mart 392
BCN WAP 392
GIN 392

IRLWap	392	Handspace	396
Malaysia Search	392	Interactive Investor	397
Shefon.com	393	Leek Computers and Comms	397
Wonderful Copenhagen	393	Limahl	397
worldroom.com	393	Loot	397
Giroscopio	393	Mapquest	397
Hotelguide.com	393	Mobile Invest	397
2PL	393	NCB Direct	397
UK miscellaneous sites	394	News Unlimited	398
Advanced Telecom PLC	394	PR Newswire	398
All The Recipes	394	Rebus Electronic Business	398
Alternative QPR Wapsite	394	Rishworth School, Yorkshire, UK	398
Autolocate	394	Scoutnet	398
Bigger Deffer	394	Search UK	398
BlueSky	394	Sedbergh School, Cumbria, UK	398
BookBrain.co.uk	395	Swanage Lifeboat Crew	399
Brighton and Hove Albion FC	395	Swindon Town FC	399
Bullivants Garages	395	TV2000	399
Chess Corner	395	Under One Roof	399
Clockwork Orange	395	United Kingdom Music Coverage	
Curryhouse.net	395	(UKMC)	399
CurryPages	395	Unmissable TV	399
E Loan	396	Wolverhampton Warriors FC	399
ents24.com	396	Worldof.net	400
Flowerwap.co.uk	396	4 Clubbers	400
Frazer and Orr	396	WAP search directories sites	400
Freedom Phones	396	Ajaxo	400
Gillingham Football Club	396	AusWAP	400

Babelserver	400	WAPJAG	401
FAST Search	400	WAPjump	401
M-Central	400	Wapmore	402
Oracle Mobile	401	WAPscan	402
Pinpoint	401	Wapwag.com	402
wannaWAP.com	401	Webcab	402
WAPAW	401	Yahoo!	402
Wap.com	401	2thumbsWAP.com	402

Junk Email *403*

What is junk email?	403	Combating junk email	414
Types of junk email	404	Opt-in emailing	418
The cost of junk email	411	CAUCE	419
The cost to the user	413	Other Web sites	420
Spam and newsgroups	414	Newsgroups	422

Security and Viruses *423*

Security	423	Viruses and the Mac FAQ	424
Computer virus resources	423	Hoax and chain letters	425
Frequently Asked Questions (FAQs)		Charles Hymes' New Hoaxes	425
sites about computer viruses	424	CIAC (Computer Incident	
Computer Virus FAQ for		Advisory Capability)	425
New Users	424		

Internet Chain Letters: how to
recognize a new chain letter,
what to do   425
Command Software – Virus Hoaxes
                                             425
Computer Virus Myths home page   426
Data Fellows – Hoax warnings   426
IBM antivirus online – hype alerts!   426
ICSA – Hoax Information   427
iRiS Software's Virus Lab –
Virus Hoaxes   427
McAfee – Virus Information Library
– Virus Hoaxes   427
Network Associates – Virus
Library – Hoaxes   427
Sophos Virus info – hoaxes
and scares   427
Symantec AntiVirus Research
Center (SARC) – Virus Hoaxes   427
Virus Databases   427
Central Command – AntiViral
Toolkit Pro Virus Encyclopedia   427
CIAC Virus Database   427
Command Software – Virus Alerts   427
The Joe Wells Virus Encyclopedia   428
Computer Associates –
Virus Encyclopedia   428

Data Fellows F–Secure Virus
Info Center   428
Dr. Solomon's Virus Central   428
IBM antivirus online – virus
information   428
McAfee – Virus Information Library 428
Proland Software – Virus
Information   429
Trojan Horses   429
Sophos Virus Information   429
Symantec AntiVirus Research
Center   429
Trend Micro – Virus Encyclopedia   429
Virus Bulletin – The Project
VGrep Home Page   429
IBM antivirus online   429
Virus Bulletin list of anti-virus
Web sites   429
The Original J and A Computer
Virus Information Page   429
Virus organisations   430
EICAR (European Institute for
Computer Anti-Virus Research)   430
ICSA (International Computer
Security Association)   430
Virus Bulletin   430
The WildList Organization
International   430

Anti-Virus Products 430
Aladdin Knowledge Systems 430
Central Command, Inc. 431
Command Software Systems, Inc. 431
Computer Associates
  International, Inc. 431
Data Fellows Corporation 431
Dr. Solomon's Software Inc. 432
iRiS Software Ltd. 432
McAfee 433
Network Associates, Inc. 433
Norman Data Defense Systems 433
Proland Software 433
Sophos 433
Symantec Corporation 434

Trend Micro, Inc. 434
Online articles 434
Flash in the Pan? 434
The NORMAN Book on Viruses 434
Various Papers at Command
  Software Systems 434
Various Papers at Dr. Solomon's 435
Various Papers at SOPHOS 435
Various Papers at Symantec
  Antivirus Research Center 435
Don't Spread that Hoax! 435
How to Hoax-Proof Yourself 435
Newsgroup sites for viruses 436
Mailing lists 436
Denial of service 436

Mailing Lists and Newsgroups *439*

Options 439
Mailing lists 439
Finding mailing lists 440
Subscribing to a mailing list 440
Quality of lists 441
Newsgroups 442
Newsreaders 442
Configuring a newsreader 443
Outlook Express 444

Messenger 445
Accessing newsgroups 446
Outlook Express 446
Messenger 447
Removing yourself from a
  newsgroup 448
Outlook Express 448
Messenger 448
Participating in newsgroups 449

Newsgroup messages   450
Flame wars   451
Finding newsgroups   454
Newsgroup directory   456
Alternative groups   456
Recreation groups   466

Society groups   473
Talk groups   477
Computer groups   478
UK groups   481
Miscellaneous groups   484

Jargon Buster **487**

Index **497**

ReadMe.first

For anyone who uses email on a regular basis, it is hard to think of life without it. It has become such an integral part of so many people's lives that it is becoming as generally accepted as items such as the telephone and hard copy mail. However, despite its amazing rise in popularity, it is something of a novelty to find someone who has been using email for more than 10 years. But for all its youth, any history of the late 20th century will undoubtedly give more than a passing nod in the direction of the communication phenomenon that began life as electronic mail but quickly became universally known as email.

In some ways, email was the application that transformed the Internet from a geeky hobbyist tool into a truly global communication medium. Initially it was seen as a bunch of computer enthusiasts, or netheads, tinkering around with computer code and sharing in-jokes that were deemed too superior for the general populace. Then email began to filter out to the waiting world and all that changed. A computer program or application that dramatically alters the environment in which it operates is known as a killer application or a 'killer app' for short. Email was undoubtedly the killer app for the Internet, and in many ways it still is. As soon as people realised that they could actually do something that was useful to them on the Internet, i.e. send messages around the world quickly and cheaply, the non-computing community woke up to the potential of the Internet in all its forms. This not only included email, but also the World Wide Web (WWW), newsgroups (which are an extension of email) and chat rooms. It took a few years for this initial trickle to become a flood; but when the dam broke, there was not a corner of the globe that was unaffected.

In many ways, it was the widespread availability of email that kick-started the global spread of the Internet

Although the name email was designed to convey the origins of this medium, i.e. mail messages that are delivered electronically, the term no longer does it full justice. Due to considerable advances in email technology, it is now possible to send any document or program created on a computer to anyone else in the world. These are known as *attachments* and they can include anything from a digital photograph of a new baby to a fully-fledged computer program. In addition, email services can send cards and invitations and emails can be formatted to look like professionally-produced documents and even pages for the Web.

As well as being able to send an increasingly varied range of items via email, it is also now possible to access email in a variety of ways, not just through a desktop or a laptop computer. The advent of wireless technology means that we do not have to be tied to a machine that is connected with cables and plugs. The Internet has been liberated from its wired attachments and is now ready to move on to the next stage of its development. Currently there is a crop of devices through which the Internet can be accessed and emails sent and received. These include mobile phones, electronic personal organisers and digital televisions. As the technology progresses some of them may even be more popular for accessing the Internet than a standard computer.

Despite its numerous advantages, there are some drawbacks with the use of email. It can cut down on traditional one-to-one communication; it can be used to spread computer viruses; it can lead to legal battles following misuse or harassment via email; and there is no such thing as a completely confidential email. These considerations should be kept in mind when using email but do not let them put you off. Email is very much here to stay and it can justifiably lay claim to being the most successful killer app of all time.

Introducing Email

The growth of email

Every era has at least one form of communication that proves to be revolutionary and genuinely transforms the way in which we interact with each other: be it the telephone, the postal service, the wireless or even the pony express. Each new development is quicker and more efficient than its predecessor and relies more heavily on technology. The end of the last century and the beginning of the current one have seen the latest in the long line of these developments and it is potentially the most significant to date. Electronic mail, or email as it is now universally known, is the means of sending electronic information via computers. It is quick, cheap and can carry a variety of data including plain text, images, sound and even video.

Email is one of the four elements that make up the Internet, the other three being the World Wide Web (WWW), newsgroups and chat rooms. The Internet is the infrastructure of computers, cables, modems and servers that are linked together to form a global network through which information can be shared. The World Wide Web is the collection of pages that individuals and organisations create so that they can be viewed by anyone who has access to the Internet. The Web is not the whole Internet; it is just one element of it, as is email. Email is an integral part of the Internet and if you have access to the Web from your own home computer then you will almost certainly have your own email address too.

Initially, when the Internet was being developed in the 1960s, it was thought that it would just be a network for the US military and academic institutions and that it would be of little commercial worth. However, this could not be further from the truth and the Internet has become one of the fastest growing phenomena in history. As the technology has advanced, more and more people have become convinced that the Internet is, and will become increasingly more so, a vital part of our society. From business to the social user, there is virtually no area where the Internet does not have a role to play today. Email is at the forefront of this revolution as users around the world begin to fully appreciate the benefits that can be gained from this deceptively simple yet effective tool.

One of the great advantages of email is that it is non-platform dependent. This means that an email that is sent from a PC can be received and read on an Apple Mac computer, or a UNIX system, and vice versa. This has removed a problem that has long troubled the computer industry. As far as email is concerned, there are no barriers, either of the geographical kind or those of a technological nature.

Email has recently moved on from its first major stage of development, when it was accessed through desktop and laptop computers, to its second stage. This has seen email being provided on a variety of different devices e.g.:

- mobile phones
- handheld computers
- televisions

Telecommunications companies are currently investing millions of pounds on devices and systems that can provide a mobile platform for email and so open up the resultant opportunities to a vast number of people who do not have their own computers. This is going to be an enormous growth industry in the future and it is proof that email is no flash in the pan and that it is here to stay.

The uses for email

Most new technological systems start off with the basics and then develop from there and this was true with email. In the early days of the Internet it was considered a major achievement to send a plain text message from one computer to another: numerous problems could be encountered along the way and this seemingly simple process took up an enormous amount of computing power and could take several hours to complete. Now, it is commonplace for emails to be sent in a matter of seconds and contain an array of multimedia content.

Do not be limited to thinking that email can only be used for textual correspondence. Almost anything that is created on a computer can be sent by email.

A social tool

For the social user, email offers a greater number of options than a conventional letter. Items such as digital images, sound clips and video clips can be attached and sent to friends and family around the world. Images can be captured with a digital camera or a scanner and digital sound clips can be created using the type of sound recording program that comes as standard with most operating systems on consumer computers today. Video clips have to be captured with a digital video camera and although these are relatively expensive the prices are falling as the technology improves. Once the effect that you require has been created it can be selected from your computer and attached to an email. This creates larger emails than just plain text ones but the impact can be dramatic.

Email can also be used to contact a group of people at the same time. For instance, you may want to invite a dozen people to a family celebration or a dinner party. This can be done by selecting the recipients from your email address book, writing your message and then sending it to everyone with one click of the mouse.

Other social uses for email include:

- Messaging services, where the sender of an email is sent a message automatically if you are unavailable to access your emails.
- Remote access, where you can have your emails read to you over the phone if you are away from your computer.
- Automatic invitations, where a Web site automatically emails specified individuals and invites them to a certain event. This is similar to doing this yourself with a group of recipients, but the automatic service also collates responses and sends reminders to people who have not replied.

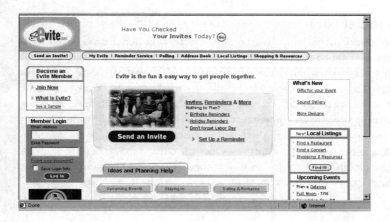

A business tool

In some ways, email has had an even more significant impact in the business world than in the arena of personal usage. In addition to being able to send global emails via the Internet, internal networks, known as intranets, can be used to send emails within an organisation. While this may not have delivered the Holy Grail of the paperless office it has certainly increased the speed at which employees can communicate with each other.

The advantages of business email are obvious: commercial decisions can be reached more quickly, business documents can be sent to the other side of the world in a few minutes and virtual communities can be established within businesses that have offices in widespread geographical locations. However, there are drawbacks to using emails in a business context:

- It can be seen as being impersonal. Sometimes face-to-face contact can resolve a situation more effectively than a raft of emails.
- It can lead to information overload. Because of the facility to send the same message to large groups of people some workers find that they are swamped under a mountain of electronic messages and this adversely affects their working routine. It is undeniable that some workers get a little too 'trigger happy' with email, with the result that they cause more work than they are saving. Email should be used thoughtfully and other methods of communication should not be forgotten.

One of the newest causes of stress in the workplace is employees having to read dozens, or hundreds, of emails every day. If you are sending a message, make sure that you really need to do so and that email is the best format.

- Viruses can enter office networks via emails. These are usually in the form of attachments that are activated when the user opens them. They can then destroy information on the network computers or disable the system by sending multiple emails until the central computer cannot cope. In some cases, even the risk of receiving viruses has been enough for some major organisations to shut down their entire email systems until the threat has passed.

- Misuse of email. Business email is subject to the same conditions that apply to other forms of communication i.e. it should not be used to send material that is in any way inappropriate. This generally applies more to internal email networks and there have been numerous cases of employees who have been dismissed for email offensive material.

- There is no such thing as a private business email and once it has been sent there is no guarantee as to who will then see it in the future. This was demonstrated most notably in the anti-trust case undertaken by the US Government against the software giant Microsoft, who were accused of creating an unfair monopoly. As part of the evidence the US Government produced a number of internal emails that had been sent by Microsoft employees and since been forwarded on to other individuals. It is worth remembering that every email that is sent leaves some form of electronic signature.

Once you have sent an email, you have no control over what happens to it. It could be forwarded on to your best friend, your boss, or even dragged up and used in court.

How email works

Millions of people who use email every day have no idea how the technology works and they probably care even less, just as long as it does. This is a bit like people who have no interest in what happens under the bonnet of the car, just as long as the machine gets them from A to B. But in the interests of thoroughness, here is a quick overview of how an email gets from one computer to another.

When an email has been composed and the writer hits the Send button a series of digital signals pass from the computer to the modem. (This can either be external or internal but it does the same thing wherever it is situated.) Modem stands for MOdulator/DEModulator and this is the device that translates the digital signal from the computer into an analogue one that can then pass down standard telephone cables. When all telephones and cables are digitised there will be no need for modems. When the modem has translated the email it then has to send it to the computer of the company that is hosting your email account. This will almost certainly be the same company that provides you with your Internet connection and it is known as an Internet Service Provider (ISP). The ISP's computer is known as a server and this is where the email will be sent initially.

There are dozens of Internet Service Providers and they are all desperate for new customers. Because of this, most of them offer various deals on registration fees (a lot of them charge nothing) and also call costs for while you are connected to the Internet. Shop around to try and find the best deals.

However, when an email is faced with the journey to the ISP's server, it has a huge array of possible routes from which to choose. Since some of them will be in use at any given time, the data does not have to travel down one particular combination of cables. This allows the email to pick the quickest available route to the server. To make the operation even quicker, the email is broken up into small segments (known as packets), which are given unique identifiers in sequence and then left to make their own way to the server. When all of the packets have reached their destination they are reordered in sequence to reconstitute the email.

Once the email has reached the sender's ISP, the address of the recipient is read and it is then sent to the recipient's ISP. This follows the same procedure as above, with the email being split into packets for its journey between servers. When the data reaches the recipient's ISP it is stored there until the recipient sends a message to check whether there are any new emails awaiting them. If there are, these are then sent to the recipient's computer using the well-worn packet method. This ensures that emails are not lost even if the recipient's computer is not turned on when the message is sent.

Email servers

Email programs work by using specific programs, or protocols, that are recognised as the standard for transmission of email on the Internet. This means that messages can be sent between any computers, regardless of type. ISPs have email servers that are configured for the different email protocols, which include separate ones for sending and receiving messages.

The two most commonly used protocols for receiving messages are POP3, which stands for Post Office Protocol, and IMAP, which stands for Internet

Message Access Protocol. Some ISPs provide servers for both of these protocols, but POP is the most commonly used one. If you need to configure a new email account you will need to know which type of server you are using and its address e.g. 'pop.beeb.net'. (See the 'Email programs' chapter for more on configuring an email account.) If you are using the email program that was provided by your ISP, it will almost certainly be configured using the information you provided during the registration process – the server details will have been entered for you.

The most commonly used protocol for sending mail is SMTP, which stands for Simple Mail Transfer Protocol. As with the protocol for receiving messages, your email program will have to know the address of you SMTP server, but this will probably be included during the registration process.

Although it is perfectly possible to spend a lifetime sending and receiving emails without even knowing of the existence of POP, IMAP and SMTP servers, it is worth looking at the options for your program just so you can see

If you change to a different email program from the one your ISP provided, your configuration settings may automatically be adopted by the new one.

what they are called and where they are located. If you decide to use a new program you may need to configure these settings.

Setting up an email account

In the UK there are dozens of companies who will provide email accounts and also access to the other elements of the Internet. When the Internet was first becoming available to consumers, companies were able to charge a monthly fee for connection to these services. However, in 1998, Freeserve became the first company to offer free access to the Internet, with the only cost being that of the telephone charges. Since then other ISPs have followed suit, with the result that it is now possible to choose between a wide range of companies offering free access to the Internet and an email account. Some companies do still charge a monthly fee for what they call an enhanced service but unless they are providing something that you need and cannot get elsewhere you will be just as well sticking with a free access provider.

Some of the ISPs that offer free access to the Internet and an email account include:

- BBC at *www.beeb.net/*
- BT ClickFree at *www.btclickfree.com/*
- Free-Online at *www.free-online.net/*
- Freeserve at *www.freeserve.net/*

- TescoNet at *www.tesco.net/*
- Zoom at *www.zoom.com/*

Other companies that charge a subscription for their Internet access service include:

- AOL at *www.aol.com/*
- BT Internet at *www.bt.com/* (One option that they offer is unlimited, and unmetered Internet access in the evenings and weekends for £5.99 a month. If you use Freeserve as your ISP, this is available for £4.99.)
- Cable and Wireless at *www.cwcom.co.uk/*
- Demon Internet at *www.demon.net/*
- NTL Internet at *www.ntl.com/*

It is worth shopping around for an ISP, particularly as more companies are exploring options for free Internet calls as well as free connection. The digital television companies, such as OnDigital and BSkyB are also immersing themselves in the email revolution and this is one way to get email access without even having to buy a computer. It is possible that, in the near future, direct payment for surfing the Web and sending emails will be a thing of the past.

Internet addresses of ISPs (and all other sites on the Web) begin with 'http', which stands for HyperText Transfer Protocol. Although this is part of the Web address, it does not have to be entered when you are typing it in since the browser recognises the format and knows that 'http' should be included. (If a Web address does not include 'www' then the 'http' will have to be entered to let the browser know that it is a Web address.)

The anatomy of an email

For something as deceptively simple as an email there are actually a number of different elements that go into its construction.

The toolbar and menu bar

This is the group of menus and icons that appears at the top of an email program. They enable the sender to choose from a variety of options, which cover areas such as who the email is being sent to, how the email looks, and settings for sending and receiving messages. All of the most common functions of the toolbar and the menu bar will be looked at throughout the book.

Recipient information

This is the address of the person to whom the email is being sent and it is inserted at the top of an email once the New button has been clicked to begin a new message. The recipient's email address can either be typed directed into the To box or it can be selected from an address book (see later). If the first method is used, then the whole email address will be visible; if it is the second method then you may only see their first name or a predefined name that you have already chosen for them to be identified by. Either way, a recipient's email address will take the format similar to: 'ian.someone@ISP.co.uk'. The first part of the address is the recipient's name, followed by the 'at' symbol @ and then the ISP's name and then usually the location where the ISP is based. (There can be a variety of suffixes at the end of an email address: '–.com', '–.net', '–.org' or '–.ac'. These help identify the type of organisation or individual to whom the email is being sent: '–.com' and '–.net' are usually commercial organisations, '.org' represents a charitable or voluntary organisation, and '–.ac' is for an academic organisation.)

Address book

An email address book is an electronic version of a traditional hard copy diary or filofax. This is where email addresses are stored. When a message is composed a name is selected from the address book. Address books can contain individual names or groups of people. An email group is given a title, such as 'Family member' and people's names and email addresses are added to the group. When you want to send an email to all of these people at once, it is simply a case of selecting the group name and everyone in it will receive the message.

To field

This is usually the first field that is filled in on an email. It contains the recipient's details. This can either be done by selecting a pre-entered item from the address book or by typing in someone's full email address. (It is also possible to enter your own details in the From field, but since this is displayed automatically in the recipient's In box when they receive the message, it is largely redundant.)

Copy to field

The Cc field underneath the To field enables a message to be copied to people other than the main recipient. This is used most frequently in business communications when several interested parties may need to be kept informed

The To Field is like the address on the front of a hard copy letter. If you make a mistake with this then there is no chance of an email getting to its intended destination.

about something that they are not directly involved with. Using this option can require a certain amount of sensitivity since the main recipient may wonder why you are copying what they see sd an email for them, to other people.

Blind copy field

The blind copy field is similar to the copy one, except that the recipient does not see the blind copy information when they receive the message. This option should be used with care, because if the recipient does discover that you have sent a blind copy to someone (and this does happen, thanks to that old fashioned device, word-of-mouth) then they may be suspicious of your motives and conclude that at best you have something to hide and at worst you are being underhand.

Subject field

This is the field into which a line of text is inserted, giving a brief description of the content of the email. This will appear in the recipient's In box when the email is delivered. The information in the Subject field should be as concise as possible: if it is too long, there will not be enough space to display it all in the user's In box.

Message field

This is the area where the body of the email is created and is the large white area underneath the field information. Email can contain a few words or run to several pages in length. If the amount of text is greater than the visible area in the message field, the page will wrap downwards i.e. it will move down to accommodate the amount of text that is being entered. Text in an email can be formatted using various styles and these will be looked at in the 'Formatting' chapter.

Attachments

One of the great benefits of email over conventional forms of mail, is the option for attaching items other than plain text messages. This can include

One of the great benefits of email is its tendency towards brevity. Try not to get too carried away when you are writing a message – keep it short and simple if possible.

documents from other software programs such as Word or Excel documents, HTML files or PDF (Portable Document Format) files, digital images, sound files and even video clips. Attachments can be added to an email by clicking on the attachment button (which is usually a small paperclip symbol) and then selecting the relevant file from the hard drive on your computer or an external source such as a digital camera. The two main points to remember with attachments are:

- They invariably increase the size of the email. A digital image takes up a lot more disc space than plain text and video clips are usually larger still. This will increase the amount of time for both sending the message and the recipient downloading it onto their computer.
- If you are sending attachments in a variety of file formats then it is important to ensure that the recipient has the relevant software to open these files. There is little point in sending someone a video clip if they do not have the means to open and play it on their computer. Also, if you email an attachment that was created in a specific software package, such as Word, make sure the recipient has a version of the program that is up-to-date enough to read the file: many people have been caught out

by sending a file created in the latest version of a program, only to find that their friend or colleague does not have a compatible version on their machine.

Send button

Once an email has been created, and checked, it can be sent to its destination by clicking on the Send, or Send and Receive, button on the toolbar. At this point you should not be connected to the Internet i.e. you should be offline. This is because there is no point in being online and paying telephone charges while you are composing a message. Once you select the Send option, your email program should recognise that you are offline and ask you if you want to send your message now or save it until later. If you select the latter, the message will be saved into a Draft folder, to be accessed and sent at a later date. If you elect to send the message immediately, your program will connect to the Internet through the modem and once a connection is established, send your message on its way. When the recipient turns on their computer, the message will either be downloaded automatically or they will have to send a command asking for this task to be performed. There are various settings for controlling how programs handle Send and Receive commands and these are looked at in the chapter entitled 'Sending and Receiving'.

Methods of receiving email

Email is no longer just something that can be used on a computer: in addition to this, there are a range of options for sending and receiving electronic messages:

Computer

Currently, the most common way to receive email is via a computer. This can either be a desktop or a laptop but the principles are the same: the messages are downloaded through a modem and then accessed onscreen using an email program. The messages can then be stored on the computer's hard drive, or saved onto a disc.

One of the great benefits of email is that it is generally platform independent, which means that it can be sent on one type of computer, say a PC, and received on another type, say an Apple Mac. It is also possible to send and receive messages between UNIX and LINUX systems. So there is no need to worry too much about your computer system as far as email is concerned.

One area of debate about choosing a computer is whether to go for an Apple or the more ubiquitous IBM compatible PCs. As far as email is concerned, there is little difference: Apple have some high specification machines, such as the G3 series and the iMac while PCs are increasingly more powerful and constantly falling in price. Both types will be more than adequate for your email needs and you should base your final choices on other considerations.

Mobile telephones

Telecommunications companies are currently spending millions of pounds on the development and expansion of the wireless Internet. This means that emails and the Web can be accessed over a mobile phone. The technology behind this is known as Wireless Application Protocol (WAP) and some analysts have predicted that within the next five to ten years this method of

Although computers are facing increasing competition from other devices for sending and receiving email, they are still the most versatile and efficient method for this form of communication.

sending and receiving emails and surfing the Web will have a higher usage than access through a computer. Whether this is the case or not remains to be seen, but this technology is already in the marketplace and being used and it is an area with huge growth potential.

In Japan, companies such as NTT DoCoMo are developing what they hope will become a new worldwide standard in mobile phone technology, called Wideband Code Division Multiple Access (WCDMA). This is based on the iMode wireless technology that is used in Japan and some analysts are predicting that it could be more widely used than WAP, even if its name is not so snappy.

Handheld computers

In an attempt to try and get the best of both the computing and the telecoms worlds, some manufacturers have produced handheld computers that can send and receive emails and access the Web. In addition, they can also perform some traditional computing tasks such as basic word processing and creating spreadsheets and databases. It is possible that this type of computer will be made redundant by increasingly sophisticated WAP-enabled mobile phones but they currently have a place for those people who want to have a bit more than just a mobile connection to the Internet.

Email telephones are another way to send and receive emails. These are standard telephones that have an email screen attached. Amstrad and BT currently have these available.

Television

Several cable television companies have recently introduced email through the television, as part of their packages to try and win customers. This works through a basic keyboard and the message appears on the television screen. It can even be set up so the message is written on top of whatever is being broadcast at the time. This is aimed at capturing people who do not own computers but who still want to have access to email and the Web. There have been some doubts expressed at whether this will catch on, based primarily on the argument that watching television is a relaxing pastime and people may not want to spoil it by writing emails or surfing the Web. However, it is a step towards integrating different technologies into a single monitor and it is conceivable that in years to come we will be accessing all of our computing, telecommunications and television requirements through a single screen.

Some of the companies involved with email and digital television include:

- BSkyB at *www.sky.com/skydigital/*
- OnDigital at *www.ondigital.com/*
- Telewest at *www.telewest.com/*

The future

The future of email and the Web is an exciting one, which is advancing rapidly. Virtually every day there are improvements with the technology and the methods of distribution so that a much wider audience is being introduced to the possibilities of the Internet. For many people, email is now the tool of choice for both social and business communication and this is only going to develop further as more people get access to email through different devices.

If you want to use email through your television, you will have to subscribe to one of the digital television companies that offer this service.

One of the big developments with email in the next few years is likely to be the way we access our messages — having to be tied to your own computer is going to be a thing of the past. There are currently numerous start-up companies that are looking at ways to deliver a whole range of communication services to the new generation of wireless mobiles phones. This includes email, voice mail and faxes and it is an area that has an enormous potential for the

Do not get too stuck in your ways with the email technology you are using today: in a year's time, it may be out-of-date and be replaced by something new.

business user. The idea of the mobile office is no longer a mere concept: forward thinking companies are already putting it into practice.

In a lot of ways this communication revolution is still very much in its infancy and in ten years time we will probably look back with horror at the archaic practice of sending plain text messages between computers. The Internet is not going to stand still, so the users have to make sure they move with it into the future.

Email Programs

Available programs

In the early days of email, it was sufficient for products to offer a service that transferred a simple message from one computer to another. But both the technology and the user expectation have moved on from there and email programs are increasingly sophisticated packages that not only send messages but also help organise the items you send and receive and integrate with other programs.

Although the market for email programs (or email clients as they are sometimes known) is dominated by three companies (Microsoft, Netscape and Eudora) there are dozens of options to choose from. These range from free programs, some of which are surprisingly powerful, to those that have to be paid for and generally offer additional features. The first thing to decide before choosing an email package is what you want it for. If it is for emailing family and friends then one of the free programs will be more than adequate for the task. However, if you want to use more advanced email and organisational features then one of the more powerful programs may be required.

If you want to find some email programs of your own, enter 'email programs' or 'email clients' into your favourite search engine on the Web.

Microsoft Outlook and Outlook Express

www.microsoft.com/

Outlook

As befitting the world's largest software company, Microsoft has a major hold on the email market, in the form of Outlook and Outlook Express.

The full Outlook program comes integrated with Office 2000 and it is a powerful messaging and organisational tool. It is designed primarily as a business tool and in addition to sophisticated email facilities it also has facilities for organising information with tools such as calendars, contact lists, task management and miscellaneous notes. It can also import data from other email programs, such as address books, making it easy to migrate from comparable email clients. Outlook is a serious contender if you want a program to handle the following:

- Advanced email and discussion group facilities
- Powerful personal management tasks

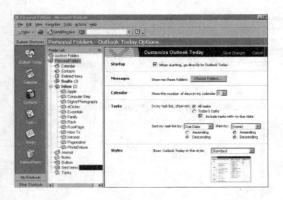

Outlook Express

Outlook Express does not have the advanced management capabilities of Outlook but it is nevertheless a highly efficient and effective email program. It comes bundled with Microsoft's Internet Explorer browser (version 4.0 and above) and it is available for both the PC and the Macintosh platforms. Outlook Express offers excellent service for standard email functions and it also has powerful features for formatting messages and filtering items into specific folders when they are received. In addition, the interface ensures that it is easy to use, particularly if you are familiar with other Microsoft products, and it is designed to integrate with all of the major email protocols on the Internet. Unless you require the more advanced features of Outlook, or a similar program, Outlook Express is more than adequate for the private user who is not going to have a large amount of email traffic.

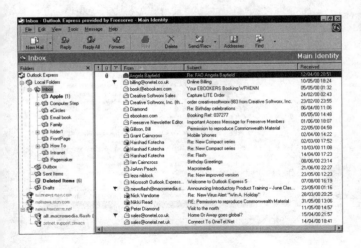

Eudora

www.eudora.com/

Eudora, named after an author who wrote a book about living in a post office, is one of the leading email programs, with over 20 million users worldwide. It was first developed in 1988 and later distributed over the Internet as a shareware product. When Eudora first appeared it had two distinct advantages: it had a user-friendly interface and it was able to send and receive attachments. The Internet community soon embraced Eudora and the user feedback has played an important part in the subsequent releases of the program. In 1991, QUALCOMM purchased the rights to the program and then launched it as a consumer product.

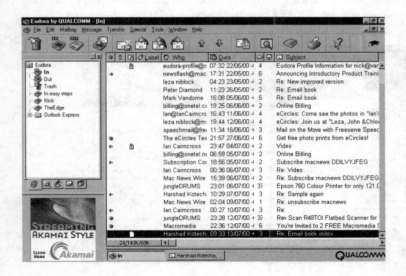

Eudora modes

When Eudora was first marketed as a consumer product there were two versions of it: a light version that was free and a full version that was paid for. However, in 2000 three new versions, or modes, of the program were released:

Sponsored mode

Sponsored mode provides the full-featured Eudora desktop email program at no charge, and includes free technical support (up to six calls per year). The one slight drawback to this generous offer is that small advertisements are displayed while the program is open. However, these do not appear within the actual email workspace and they are generally unobtrusive. If the program is downloaded from the Web, it is in Sponsored mode. This can be done by downloading it directly from the Eudora Web site.

The advertisements in Eudora Sponsored mode are very unobtrusive and are unlikely to make you want to part with hard cash for the paid version.

Paid mode

Paid mode provides the same email program and facilities, except that there are no advertisements. If this option is chosen, the user has to fill in a straightforward online form and then authorise payment, and then the program will be downloaded.

The retail price for the paid mode is $49.95.

Light mode

Before Eudora introduced the three modes for its email program there was a paid for version and a free version. The free version was named Eudora Light and users who have this program can upgrade to the Light mode of the new program. This is free and does not include advertisements. However, it has fewer features and email management tools than the other two modes.

Eudora features

The Sponsored or Paid modes have a large number of advanced features:

- Enhanced filters that enable you to select sources from which you do not want to receive emails. This type of feature can be particularly useful when there are known email viruses in circulation.
- Powerful searches that enable you to search for words or files within your email system.
- Spell checking.
- Multiple signatures that can be used to specify specific identities for different users.
- Formatting of text.
- Import option – (Windows only) Import settings, mail and address books from Microsoft Outlook Express 5.0 (or older) or Netscape Communicator 4.0.
- Multi-tasking which enables you to do other tasks while your emails are being sent or downloaded.
- Multiple personalities that enable you to use different identities for different email accounts.
- Automatic name completion that recognises the first few letters of a name and then enters the appropriate email address.
- User-configurable toolbar.

- Message preview pane which enables you to see a preview of the selected email message in your Inbox.
- HTML-styled text and formatting which enables you to insert images and hyperlinks to other files, or pages on the Web.
- Attachment forward and redirect that enables you to include attachments when you send an email you have received on to someone else. In some programs, if you forward or redirect an email that contains an attachment, only the text of the message will be sent.

System requirements: Windows
- PC with Microsoft Windows 95, 98 or NT 4.0 or greater.
- An Internet Service Provider account with POP or IMAP and a network connection modem or TCP/IP to access mail accounts via PPP dial-up.
- CD-ROM drive or Internet download capabilities for installation.

System requirements: Macintosh
- Macintosh OS 7 or newer.
- An Internet Service Provider account with POP or IMAP and a network connection.
- Modem or TCP/IP to access mail account via PPP dial-up.
- CD-ROM drive or Internet download capabilities for installation.

For a detailed look at the workings of Eudora, see the 'Eudora' chapter.

All Macintosh computers which are currently on sale, including the iMac and iBook, are installed with the operating system OS8.5 or later, which is easily capable of running Eudora.

Netscape Messenger

www.netscape.com/

Netscape Messenger is the email program that comes with Netscape Communicator. This is based on Netscape's popular browser, Navigator, and the email program is included with the package and integrates closely with the browser. The Communicator package is free and can be downloaded from the Netscape Web site (the latest version is 4.73 but version 6 is being tested at the time of writing). Alternatively, CD-ROMs that accompany most computer magazines have a variety of free software and you should be able to find Communicator on one of these. Messenger is usually used by people who are familiar with Netscape and the Navigator browser and it is also a popular choice for businesses that already have these products. Messenger is a full-featured program that supports all of the major Internet standards and also offers an integrated newsreader.

Some of the features of the latest version of Messenger are:

- Sends and receives email from virtually any other Internet mail application. Support for all of the main email Internet standards such as IMAP4, SMTP, POP3, MIME, UUENCODE, and BINHEX.
- Checks spelling before sending messages.
- Organises and prioritise incoming messages with filters.
- Accesses messages from multiple locations and computers.
- A three-pane user interface for simplified message management.
- Provides a new two-pane address book interface that supports multiple address books and improved list management.
- Enables fast and accurate addressing with Pinpoint Addressing.
- Finds email addresses from multiple personal address books or a corporate directory.
- Imports messages, mail folders, address books, and preferences from other email programs such as Eudora and Outlook Express.
- Supports standards-based MDN Read Receipts so you can find out when your messages have been delivered.
- Enables participation in secure discussion groups with a new three-pane interface.
- Creates reusable message templates.
- Supports standard data encryption, which protects messages as they are transmitted over the Internet, and digital signatures, assuring your recipients that you are the author of the message.

For a more detailed look at Messenger, see the 'Netscape Messenger' chapter.

Pegasus

www.pmail.com/

Pegasus is something of a rarity in the increasingly commercial world of the Internet. It is a program that is effective, popular, free and, more surprisingly, it has managed to avoid being swallowed up and produced by a large company. In addition to this, it is very neat, is quick to download, takes up less disc space than most other email programs and it does not even have advertisements.

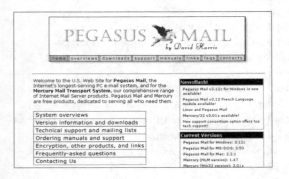

Pegasus was developed by a university worker, David Harris, in Dunedin, New Zealand and it sent its first message in 1989. The only reason Harris had started working on the program was because his department had spent their IT budget on other equipment and they could not afford to buy an email program, which in those days were still relatively expensive. When the program first appear it was greeted with enthusiasm, so Harris decided to make it available on the Web. This too proved to be a success and users flocked to download this new, free, email program. By 1993 the demand was so great that Harris gave up his university job to work on Pegasus full-time. Although the program itself is still free, the manual can be purchased and this helps to pay for the development of the software. In many ways, Pegasus is a reminder of the way the Internet was when it was first being expanded to a worldwide audience. Knowledge sharing and helping others on the Web were generally considered to be more important than making a profit and these ideals have been held onto by Harris and his program. His belief is that communication should be a right, not a privilege and it is commendable that he has held on to these principles in the face of the commercialisation of the Internet. Thankfully, there are still some idealists operating in cyberspace.

Pegasus may not look quite the same as other email programs, but it is powerful, easy-to-use and packed full of features.

Obtaining Pegasus

Pegasus is probably the best email program for obtaining and downloading quickly from the Web:

1. Visit the Pegasus Web site at www.pmail.com/ (there are other sites it can be downloaded from too, but this is one of the easiest to remember).
2. Select the Version Information and Downloads button on the Home Page.
3. On the download page, select the version that is appropriate for your operating system.
4. Select the geographical area where you are located.

5. Select the version of Pegasus that you want to download i.e. 3.12 for Windows or 3.5 for DOS.
6. Click on the program name for an overview of its features.
7. Return to the downloads page and select Download next to the version of Pegasus that you want to install.
8. Select to download the file to disc and select a location on your hard drive where you want the file to be downloaded to.
9. Pegasus files are small for programs of this type (the largest version is just over 3 MB) and the downloading process takes approximately 15 minutes over a 56K modem.

If you are downloading an email program from the Web, check its file size and the downloading time. Try and download when it is the cheapest time for call charges.

Installing Pegasus

When the downloading process is completed, the Pegasus program file will have been placed in the location that was specified in step 8 above. Locate this file and double click on it to open it. It is a program file, so it will have an '–exe' after its name. You will then have to follow a few steps to configure the program:

1. When the installation process begins there are half a dozen dialog boxes that ask for general information about installing Pegasus. Unless you have a good reason not to, leave the default information as it is and select Next for each dialog box.

2. The installation will be performed automatically when you have moved through the dialog box.

3. A dialog box will appear when the installation is finished. Select Finish.

When you first open Pegasus (go to the folder that was specified during the installation process) you will be asked for settings for how you want to send and receive email. (These settings have to be entered manually and can be obtained from your existing email program. To obtain these settings you should have an email account already set up with an ISP. Once Pegasus has been configured you will then be able to use it with your existing account.)

1. In the 'Setting up mailboxes' dialog, specify who is going to be using the program. If it is a single user, select the first button; if it going to be used by more than one person on the same computer, select the second button; and if it is going to be used on a network, select the third button.

2. Once you have set up your mailbox(es) you have to tell Pegasus how to connect to your email server, or ISP. This information is entered in the Mail Options and Preference Settings dialog.

3. Enter your email address.

4. Enter the name of your host POP3 server that will be sending you your messages. (POP stands for Post Office Protocol and it is one of the standard Internet protocols for receiving email.) If you do not known the POP3 address, it can be obtained from an existing email program such as Outlook Express:

   • Select Tools>Accounts from the menu bar.
   • In the Internet Accounts dialog, select the Mail tab and select Properties.
   • In the Properties dialog box, select the Servers tab. This will contain details of your incoming and outgoing server. The POP3 server will be in a format similar to 'pop.myisp.co.uk'

5. Enter your name and password. The name should be your user name, or account name, rather than your actual name. This will be displayed in the Properties dialog box with the POP3 server name. The password will be the one that you gave when you first registered with your ISP. However, since you can usually log-on to your ISP automatically you may not use your password regularly enough to remember it. If this is the case, contact your ISP for advice. The password will probably be case sensitive, so try a few different versions if the first one does not work.

6. Enter the name of the SMTP server. This is so incoming messages can be downloaded. SMTP stands for Simple Mail Transfer Protocol and it will appear in the same dialog box as the POP3 name above. It will also be in a similar format, with 'smtp' replacing 'pop' in the address.

7. Select whether you will be using a Dial-up connection i.e. through a modem and a phone line, or a network one.

8. Once these settings have been added, Pegasus is ready to use.

Features

Pegasus is continually being developed and improved and the latest version, 3.12, contains some of the following features:

- Mail filtering. Pegasus has some of the best filtering options available in an email program and this is a good way to cut down on junk or unsolicited emails.
- Mail Merge for sending letters to multiple recipients.
- Support for all major Internet mail-related protocols.
- Improved distributions lists.
- Support for multiple "identities" – easily-selectable groups of preference settings.

- Support for multiple users on the same machine as well as on networks.
- Powerful message editor with full formatting capabilities.
- Full support for the Internet MIME protocol.
- Improved address book facilities, allowing for nicknames and complete user details.
- The ability to read and compose your mail while you are not connected to the Internet.
- Time saving features such as lists of recently used items.
- Spelling checker.
- Messages can be highlighted with different colours.
- Sort your mail by date, size, sender, subject, colour or thread, in ascending or descending order.
- View attachments directly from within the program.

A thread is a connected conversation in a newsgroup, where several people comment on a topic that has been raised. A new thread can be started with a new topic.

- Can confirm when messages have been delivered and read.
- Frequently used items of text can be generated by assigning them to a single keystroke.
- Advanced encryption facilities for added security.
- Noticeboards for controlling newsgroup postings.
- Toolbars that can be customised according to individual preferences.
- Numerous preference settings to make the program look the way you want it.

- Facilities for creating hyperlinks, even in non-HTML messages.
- Expanded online help.
- Improved drag and drop facilities.
- Facilities to send the same message to successive people in turn.

System requirements

Windows, 32-bit version:
- Windows 95, 98, NT or 2000
- 4MB disk space
- 2MB RAM above minimum system requirements.

Windows, 16-bit version:
- Any version of Microsoft Windows v3.1 or later
- 4MB disk space plus whatever is required for mail storage
- 2MB RAM above minimum system requirements

Installing email programs

Email programs can be installed in three main ways:

Through your ISP

When you connect to the Internet through your ISP. This will invariably be done through a CD-ROM that is inserted into your computer. This will then run automatically or there will be instructions included about how to begin the installation process. Once the CD-ROM is running a Wizard will take you through the installation process for connecting to the Internet and also setting up an email account. When it comes to the email account it will suggest a name for you to use for your email address. This will probably be a combination of your name that will have been entered at an earlier part of the installation process and the name of the ISP.

When the installation has been completed you will probably have to restart your computer and there will be a message prompting you to do this. Then you will be able to access your email account. This is usually done by double-clicking on the mail icon (probably an envelope of some description) that has been placed on your desktop. This will then connect you to the Internet and open your email program.

When this has been completed, you will probably be met with a welcoming email from the manufacturers of the email program. Most ISPs use Microsoft for their Internet products, so if you obtain your first email account in this way then it will almost certainly be:

- Microsoft Outlook

Or:

- Microsoft Outlook Express

With a CD-ROM

Through a stand-alone email CD-ROM. If you buy a hard copy of an email program, it will invariably come on a CD-ROM. This can then be inserted and run as above and a Wizard will take you through the installation process. This method could be used if you want to try a different email program from the one that is provided by your ISP.

CD-ROMs that are attached to the covers of computer magazines are an excellent source of free software, including email programs. Have a browse before you buy because the contents of the CD-ROM are usually listed on the front.

From the Web

By downloading it from the Web. Several companies offer users the option of downloading their email programs from the Web, either free or for a fee that is paid online. This can be done by clicking the button for downloading, filling in an online registration form and then following the instructions for downloading the program onto your computer. In most cases this is a straightforward operation but the downloading time can take approximately one hour, depending on the size of the program and the speed of your modem. This is another option for when you wish to try another email program: if you can download a program this means you already have access to the Internet and so you will have a default email program that has been supplied by your ISP. However, there is no reason why you should not have more than one email client.

Upgrading programs

If a new version of your email program is issued you can upgrade to it in a similar way to installing the program in the first place: by using a CD-ROM or downloading the upgrade from the manufacturer's Web site. This is usually a quicker process than loading a program for the first time because only the updated files have to be added, rather than a whole new program. If your email program you are using was free then you almost certainly will not have to pay for the upgraded version. If you have paid for your program then the upgrade will either be free or a proportion of the cost of the full program – you should not have to pay the same amount again for an upgrade.

If you want to keep up to date with the latest technology and ensure that you have got the most modern email program possible, then make a point of regularly checking the Web sites of the makers of your email programs to find out the latest developments. Also, if you obtain a program by downloading it from the Web, there will generally be an option asking if you want to be updated by the company about their latest products. If you check this on then you will be emailed whenever there is a new version of one of the company's products available. This is useful for alerting you to new and upgraded products but it also means that you will probably be sent a stream of emails for items that you are not the least bit interest in. However, the benefits of keeping up-to-date outweigh this minor inconvenience – and most people like to get email, particularly when they have only recently set up an account.

Using more than one email account

When you first register with an ISP and are given access to the wonders of the Internet, the last thing on your mind will be the company that is providing your email program. The main concern is that there is an icon to click that delivers your cyber messages to your desktop. For a lot of people an email program is like a bank: they stick with the one that they first join, even if they are not 100% satisfied with it all of the time. It is human nature to stick with what you know, rather than having to go through the hassle, and potential uncertainty, of moving to something new. With email accounts people are reluctant to make any changes for two reasons:

1. They do not want to change their account because it will mean obtaining a new email address.
2. As for changing the program through which the account is accessed, a lot of users are not even aware that this can be done.

The first of these points is a valid reason for keeping the same email provider and account: if you have given out your email address to a lot of people you will be reluctant to change it. In addition to the work of letting people know your new email address there is always the fear that emails will be sent to your old address and you will not be able to access them.

If you are unhappy with the service you are receiving from your ISP it may be worth changing to another. Make sure you are organised about updating people about your new address.

The prospect of changing your email program is different from changing your email account. This is just the means by which you access your account and it is like watching the same television programme on a different set – the program is exactly the same regardless of the means by which you are viewing it.

This is the same with different email programs: if you install a different program on your computer you can still use it to access your existing email account. In this respect, email programs are the same as any other items of software in that there are a number of choices that can all perform similar tasks.

It is possible to have multiple email programs installed on one computer and you can then choose which one you want to use each time you send and receive messages. However, this does involve specifying a few settings for your default email browser and also importing addresses and messages from another email program.

Setting a default program

When you install your first email client on your computer, this automatically becomes the default email program i.e. the computer's first choice for this option. However, if you have more than one email program installed, you will need to tell the computer if you want to change the default program.

When an additional email program is installed, the installation process should not impinge on any existing programs that are on the hard drive. But when you first open the program a dialog box may appear, alerting you to the fact that this is not your default email program and asking if you would like to change it to the default. If you select Yes, the program will be made the default, and if you say No, the existing default will remain and the message will appear each time you open this program, unless you turn it off. Other than this dialog

You can install as many different email programs as you like and use all of them to test them for speed, ease-of-use and the program interface. However, if you download messages with one program, you will not be able to download the same messages with another client. (If you want to view them in another program, some of them have an option for importing messages.)

box, it makes little difference which program is your default one and it is possible to change the default and then change it back again if you want. Whichever is the default, it does not alter the functionality of other programs.

Importing addresses and messages

More important than setting the default is the ability of an email program to import addresses and messages from other programs. If you are looking for a new email client, make sure that it has this facility. The import function transfers the addresses and messages from one program to another program. They also remain in the original program and they are also available in the new program. This is an invaluable option because it means you do not have to reconstitute all of your addresses if you change programs.

There are two ways to import addresses and messages into a new program:

- When the program is first opened it may ask if you want to import information from another program. If you select Yes, a dialog box will appear asking you to select a program from which to import the information. Select the other email client, or clients, on your computer, which should automatically appear in the list of options because your new program will recognise other email programs that you have installed. Once the program has been selected, the addresses and messages from here will be imported and placed in your new program,

An email address book is the location where you store all of the email addresses that you collect. Folders are the location where messages are stored.

under a folder named after the program from which they were imported. So, if you import addresses and messages from Outlook into Eudora, there will be an Outlook folder placed in your folder list in Eudora. This will contain all of the messages from your Outlook folders.

- Using the Import command. If a program is capable of importing information from other email programs, it will have an Import command that will probably be accessed through the File menu. This can be used at any time once the program has first been opened and it is best to do this as soon as you feel confident with the new program. If you do not import your addresses, you will have to re-enter them into your new program and this can be a time-consuming process, and also an unnecessary one if your program has an import facility. To import items from an existing email program, select File>Import and then select a program from which to import messages and addresses. If any other details are required, you will be prompted for them during the Import process. This should not take more than a couple of minutes and it can save a great deal of time and effort.

Opening emails with different programs

If you have more than one email program installed, it is possible to open new messages with any of the programs at your disposal. However, once a message has been opened by one program it will not automatically be available in the other ones. For instance, if you use Outlook Express to download your emails from your ISP then they will not be visible in Eudora as new messages. In order to see them in the second program, they have to be imported from the program that originally downloaded them. This can be done as above, but it can get a bit confusing if you are continually switching between programs and then having to import messages that you have recently downloaded in another program.

In the interest of consistency, experiment with different email programs to see which one suits you best, then set this as your default and use it for sending and receiving all of your messages. Try not to switch between programs on a regular basis as you may lose track of which messages you have where.

Using a different program for a new account

When a new program is first opened, you may be asked if you want to use it with an existing account or create an entirely new email account. Unless you have a good reason not to, select the option for using an existing account. This will then enter you current email settings that you have already provided to your ISP and your new program will be configured accordingly. This means that your new program will be able to communicate with your ISP and access your email account.

If you choose to set up a new email account this could affect some of the settings for the program and if you want to do this, you should contact your ISP for their advice. In reality there is little reason to set up a different account since most ISPs offer at least five different email addresses for each individual account, which is enough for most avid emailers.

If you want to contact your ISP, try doing it by email rather than the telephone helpline, as these can be very expensive (50 pence a minute in some cases).

Menus and toolbars

Although individual email programs have their own specific interfaces and functions, the most popular ones share many common features that can be found within the toolbars and the menus. These may differ slightly as to where they are located in different programs but the following is a general guide to the commands that you can expect to find in one of the top email clients.

By default, menus and toolbars appear docked along the top of the screen. However, it is usually possible to drag them to a new location by clicking on an area of the menu or toolbar that does not contain an active element i.e. an empty area, usually at the top or far left-hand side.

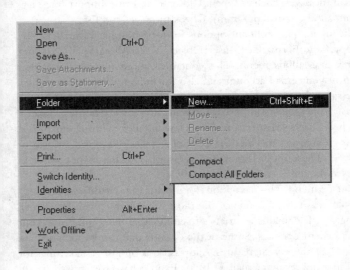

Menus

The menus for email programs are located at the top of the program. There are usually at least half a dozen standard menus, which each have a textual tile. If you click on the main heading this will access the items on the menu. If a menu item has a right-pointing arrow next to it, this indicates that there is a further menu attached to this item. This is known as a submenu. The following is a general overview of the types of menus that appear in email programs and the general options they contain. The exact detail will differ from program to program and even between different versions of the same program:

- File menu. This contains a number of commands for manipulation of email messages, such as Open, Close, Save, Print, Import (messages from another email program), Check messages and Exit.
- Edit menu. This contains options for formatting tasks such as Cut, Copy, Paste, Format Text, Insert Objects, Select All and Spell Checking.
- View or Mailbox menu. This contains options for viewing folders within your email account and also for moving between individual messages. Some of the options are for moving between the In, Out and Wastebasket folders and also for creating new folders. Some programs, such as Outlook Express, use the View menu for sorting emails that have been received. This can be by Subject, Date Received, Priority or Sender. These options can also be accessed by clicking on the equivalent bars at the top of the In box window.
- Transfer menu. This has options for moving items to different folders.
- Tools menu. This is one of the most versatile menus in any email program. It contains a variety of settings that determine how your email client operates. Some of the options that can be included are Filters, Stationery, Signatures, Address Book options, and settings for sending and receiving mail. Outlook Express has a particularly useful

option within the Tools menu. This is Add Sender to Address Book and if this is selected the sender of the currently open message will have their email address automatically entered into your address book. This is a great time saving device and one that ensures no mistakes are made when typing in an email address. At the bottom of most Tools menus, there is usually an item called Options, which has a number of submenus coming from it. This is where you can determine a number of important settings in regard to how your email program operates. Some of these include: sending and receiving options, connection options, formatting options, auto-completion, labels, security and site maintenance. The Options settings cover several aspects of email such as how they look and operate.

- Special/Message menu. These contain options for creating new messages or forwarding or replying to ones that you have received. They also have options for filtering out unwanted messages.
- Help menu. This contains options for the online help that is provided with the program. This usually consists of a table of contents and an index, along with additional items such as a tip of the day, information about technical support and details of the release version of the program you are using.

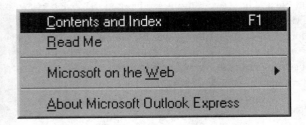

Toolbar

This is generally situated directly below the menus. Most programs have at least one toolbar, while some have a standard and an advanced toolbar. In addition, the layout of the user interface can also be altered by selecting various ways to view the onscreen details . Some of the general functions of the toolbar are:

- New Mail. This is selected whenever you want to create a new email message.
- Reply, Reply All, Forward. These options can be used when you have received a message and you want to either reply to the person who has sent it or forward it onto someone else. Reply To All can be used if you have been sent an email as part of a group and you want to send your reply to the whole group.
- Send and Receive. These commands can be used to send messages that have been completed and also to download messages that are waiting to be downloaded from your ISP's server.
- Previous and Next. These two buttons can be used to move between messages to view the content more quickly. In some programs, such as Outlook Express, this option is only available once an initial message has been opened. In other programs, such as Eudora, the Previous and Next buttons are available in the In box and they automatically open the selected message.

- Print. This can be used for printing email messages that have been received.

Email is designed to cut down on the need for paper and so the printing of them should be avoided if possible, unless it is for reference during a meeting or something similar.

- Delete. This removes the selected item to the Wastebasket, which is another folder within the program. To delete a message permanently, select it in the Wastebasket and delete it again or close down the program once the item has been placed in the Wastebasket.
- Find. This can be used to find items within your email system. This can include folders, messages, names and subject. Some programs have more advanced search facilities than others.

These are the more general commands that are found on email program toolbars. Most programs have additional icon buttons that can be added by customising the toolbar. This can usually be done using the options in the View menu or the Tools>Options command on the menu bar:

Additional views

As well as the menus and the toolbar there are additional ways to arrange the interface within an email program. These consist of extra panes within the program's main window, which displays a variety of information. All of these views can be visible, or hidden from view. Some of the additional views that are include in email programs are:

- Preview pane. This is one of the most popular options for viewing messages. It works by splitting the In box window into two. The top pane contains the header information about the email: Sender, Subject and Date Received. When the message is selected (by clicking on it once) a preview is displayed in the bottom pane. This contains the same header information and also the text of the message. This is a quick way to see the content of a lot of messages without having to open them individually and then return to the In box each time. However, it does take up more space on screen and if you are reading a long message it is probably best to turn off the preview pane so there is as much space as possible for viewing the selected item.

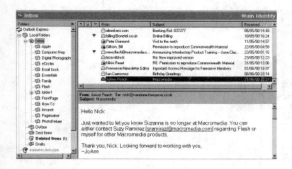

- Status bar. This appears at the bottom of the screen and it contains details such as whether you are working online or offline (i.e. connected to the Internet or not) and whether keyboard functions such as caps lock or number lock are active.

If you are connected to the Internet this will be denoted by two computer icons on a PC or a flashing apple symbol on a Mac.

- Folder bar. This informs you about which folder you are currently in, i.e. the Inbox, Out box, Drafts etc. It usually appears underneath the toolbar at the top of the screen.

- Folder list. This is a pane that lists all of the folders that are in your email program. These include the system folder like the Inbox and Outbox and also any folders that have been created by the user. It is always a good idea to create different folders for different types of messages, such as from family, or on work related subjects. The folder list is usually situated at the left-hand side of the screen. Creating and using folders is looked at in more detail in the 'Organising Emails' chapter.
- Contacts pane. This is a pane that contains the email addresses that have been entered into your address book. This can be a useful way to

quickly access individuals when you are sending them messages, but it is worth remembering that the more panes that are open on screen, the less room there is available for reading and composing messages. The Contacts pane usually appears below the folder list at the left-hand side of the screen.

- Cascading and tiling. Some programs have an option for viewing multiple mailboxes at the same time. This can be done with the cascade or the tiling commands. Cascade arranges the mailboxes one on top of another, so the top bar is visible and the mailbox can then be accessed by clicking on it. Tiling can be done either horizontally or vertically and this places the mailbox windows next to each other, according to the option selected.

Mac computers, such as the iMac and the iBook, now come bundled with Microsoft Outlook Express, version 4.5. In general this is the same as the PC version, although some of the commands are accessed through slightly different routes. Contextual menus can be used for individual items by selecting the item with Ctrl+click.

Finding Contacts

Setting up contacts

Without anyone to communicate with, email is virtually useless; like sending a letter with no address on it. However, as the email culture takes a firmer grip in society more and more people have email addresses and it is becoming commonplace for these to be distributed in a similar manner to household addresses and telephone numbers. These can then be entered and stored within your email program, for easy access whenever you want to send someone an email.

When you first start setting up email addresses you may find it hard to believe that you will reach the stage where you begin to lose track of the contacts you have entered. But after a few months use, you may find that you have the equivalent of an overflowing diary. Thankfully, email programs have facilities for organising and storing numerous email addresses, so there should be no excuse any more for not being able to find a contact.

The following examples are based mainly on Microsoft Outlook Express, since this is by far the most widely used email program. However, in other programs, such as Eudora, similar principles apply and each of the other most commonly used programs – Outlook, Eudora, Messenger and Pegasus – will be dealt with in individual chapters. Since Outlook Express comes with the Microsoft Internet Explorer Web browser and this is the one most commonly used by Internet Service Providers (ISPs) this is therefore the most widely used email program.

Obtaining email addresses

There are several ways to obtain email addresses, for entry into your online address book:

Asking people

If someone has an email address they are usually more than willing to let other people know about it. In many respects email addresses are more secure than giving out telephone numbers or house addresses: unlike telephone numbers there is no way for an individual to identify someone's home address from their email address (unless perhaps they are an experienced hacker, but most people of this nature have more important things on their cyber minds). Ask people at parties, family gatherings or at work for their email address. Make sure you have a pen and paper handy because, due to their frequently convoluted style, email addresses are not always the easiest to remember.

Also, when you are given an email address, make sure you enter it into your computer as soon as possible. Otherwise you may lose the piece of paper it was written on, or find it several months later and wonder who on earth it belongs to.

Print your own email address on labels or business cards. These can then be given out as requested and there is no chance of anyone writing down your address incorrectly.

Recording addresses

Whenever you receive an email enter the address of the sender into your address book. This can be done by opening the email and then selecting File>Properties from the menu bar. This should then display a panel with information about the email including the sender's email address. This can then be added to your address book.

From business cards

Email addresses are becoming a standard item on business cards and this is a good way of collecting contacts. If someone you know or meet has a business card, ask them for it and keep it until you have a chance to enter their email details. This can be neater than having dozens of pieces of paper stuffed into your pockets.

Email directories

Just as with telephone numbers, there are a number of online directories that list individuals and their email addresses. Each company has its own way of compiling these lists and there is not always a consistency of approach. Some email directories to try are listed at the end of this chapter.

Email directories are still very much in their infancy and most users are unaware of their existence or of the uses to which they can be put.

You do not lose anything by obtaining and entering as many email addresses as possible, even if you think you may never use some of them. They take up virtually no disc space on your computer and you can always delete the ones that you never use. Also, be careful when entering email addresses on your computer. Double check your typing, particularly with long addresses, as a typo discovered at this stage will save a lot of time and hassle at a later date.

Address books

When you have obtained an email address you should enter it into your email program's address book as soon as possible. Once it has been entered, all you have to do when you want to email that individual is to select their name from a list, rather than having to type in their entire email address.

To enter an email address:

1. Open your email program.
2. Select Addresses from the toolbar.
3. Select New from the toolbar in the dialog box and select New Contact.
4. In the Properties dialog box enter the contact information for the individual. This can include First, Middle and Last names, Title, Nickname and Display, which is the name that you want displayed in the address book. (If you enter the first and last name, this is perfectly adequate.)
5. Enter the email address in the E-Mail Address text box.

6. Select OK. This contact should then have been placed in your address book. When you compose an email and select this person's name the information that was entered in the Display text box in Step 4 will appear at the top of the message.

In addition to entering an individual's basic items such as name and email address, it is possible to include more detailed information such as home address, business details, personal details such as birthdays and general miscellaneous items. These can all be accessed by selecting the relevant tabs in the New Contact>Properties dialog box.

Viewing details

It is possible to view the information you have stored for any of the entries in your address book. From the main toolbar, select Addresses and then click once on the name whose details you want to check. Then select Properties from the Address Book toolbar. The selected individual's details will then be displayed.

Searching for contacts

As your list of contacts grows you may find it harder to locate certain individuals, particularly if you do not contact them very frequently. This can be partially solved by creating different folders for separate groups of people i.e. family, friends, work colleagues and business associates. Alternatively, you could place all of your contacts in one folder and then use the search facility to find particular contacts. To do this:

1. Select Addresses from the main toolbar.
2. Select Find People from the Address Book dialog box toolbar.
3. In the text box, type in the name of the person you are looking for.

4. If the person is in the address book, their details will appear. (If nothing is found, try putting in variations of their name, in case it has been entered under a different combination.)

Creating contact groups

In addition to being able to create contact details for individuals, it is also possible to create groups of people, to whom you may want to send a single message or messages. This is a great time saving device, because instead of having to select each name one at a time, you only have to select the group name and all of the contacts it contains will be entered into the To box of the email. Group contacts can be created for family members, people who have a shared interest, business contacts or a mailing list for either personal or business use.

Entries can be added to, or deleted from, contact groups. Make sure you keep your groups up-to-date, so that all of the correct people get the intended messages.

Creating a contact group is similar to the process for creating an individual email contact:
1. Select Addresses from the toolbar.
2. Select New from the Address Book dialog box.
3. Select New Contact from the menu. This will take you to the group properties dialog box.
4. In the Group Name box, type in a name for the group. This could be anything from 'In-laws' to 'Railway Group'. This is the name that will appear in the address book when you compose a new email message.

5. If you want to select someone whose details have already been inserted into your address book, click on Select Members.

6. In the Select Group Members dialog box, select the name of the person you want to add to the group and click on Select. Their name should now appear under Members on the right-hand side of the dialog box.(Another way to select the contact is to double click on their name. However, make sure the name appears in the Members box, otherwise it will not be inserted into the group.) Select OK.

7. To add a new contact to both your address book and the group you are creating, select New Contact. Enter the details for this contact in the dialog box in the same way as you would if you were adding a single contact into your address book i.e. enter a first and last name and an email address. Select Add to include this entry as a single entry in your address book and also as part of the group you are creating. Select OK to return to the group properties dialog box.

8. To add a new contact to the group that is not included as an individual entry in your address book, enter their name and email address at the bottom of the dialog box and select Add.

9. When all of the contacts have been added to the group, select OK. This group should now appear in your address book, with the name that was assigned to it in Step 4. Check this by selecting the Addresses button on the main toolbar. The newly created group should appear in your address book with its group name.Groups in the address book are identified by having a button next to them showing two heads, and the group name is in bold.Also, the Email Address column is blank since the group will contain more than a single address.

Contact information

As with postal addresses, people can change their email addresses and contact details with great frequency. Even though an email address is a portable item, unlike a postal address, if people change their ISP they will require a new one. It is not possible to transfer your email address from one ISP to another in the same way as you could transfer your telephone number if you moved house. It is therefore important to keep your records of email addresses up-to-date. One way to do this is to hope that people let you know when they obtain a new email address. However, human nature being what it is, this does not always happen for a number of reasons, the primary one being forgetfulness.

If people send you a couple of emails and they are not delivered then they may not bother again. Always tell people in good time if you are going to change your email address.

Another way of identifying whether someone has a new email address it to look at the properties of messages they send you. This does not have to be done every time you receive a message, but if you suspect someone may have changed their ISP then it is worth looking to see if they have a new email account. One way by which you may be alerted to someone changing their email address is if you send them a message and it is returned undelivered. This could just mean that there is a problem with the server that is processing your contact's email, but a more likely reason is that they have moved from that account and it is no longer active.

To check the address of an email that has been sent to you, to see if the sender's address is different to their contact details in your address book:

1. Right-click on the message details in your Inbox.
2. Select Properties from the contextual menu that appears. (A contextual menu is one that is accessed by right clicking on an item on screen. If there is a menu that contains options that are specific to this item, it will appear as a result of the right click, and is known as a contextual menu. It takes its name from the fact that it applies specifically to the context in which it was accessed, rather than the program as a whole.)
3. Select the General tab to view general details of the email, including the sender's email address.
4. Select the Details tab to view more specific details of the email, including the exact time it was delivered and the issuing server.

Editing contact information

If you discover that one of your contacts has changed their email details it is possible to edit the relevant entry in your address book so the next message you send them goes to the correct location.

1. Select the Addresses button on the main toolbar.
2. Select a contact in your address book and select Properties from the Address Book toolbar or double click on the name itself.

3. In the Properties dialog box, select the Name tab. This will display the contact information entered when this contact was first created.
4. Select Edit, to change the email address of the contact.
5. The current email address will become highlighted. Overtype the new email address and select OK.

Other information about a contact can also be changed in this way. For instance, if someone in your address book gets married, their surname can be altered from their maiden name to their married one. Also, this can be amended in the Display box, if this is the information that is displayed as the address book entry.

An email address book can be used to store all of the personal details about your contacts. Make sure you back it up onto a disc though, in case your hard disc crashes.

Another way to insert a new contact into the address book is to right click on an email in the Inbox. From the contextual menu, select Add Sender to Address Book. This will add the sender's name and email address into your address book, in exactly the format in which it was sent e.g. if the sender's name appears in your In box as Joe Potatohead, this is how it will be entered into your address book.

This is a useful option for updating email addresses, but if you do this, the old email address will remain in the address book. So the next time you compose a message to that individual, there will be two entries for them. To avoid confusion, it is a good idea to delete the old email address as soon as the new one has been inserted. To do this, selected the Addresses button on the main toolbar, select the entry to be deleted and click on the Delete button, which is denoted by a large black cross. Alternatively, right click on the entry in the address book and select Delete from the contextual menu.

Editing groups

As with individual entries, group entries also have to be kept up-to-date and edited as necessary. To do this:

1. Select the Addresses button on the toolbar.
2. Locate the group name in the address book.
3. Select the Properties button on the Address Book toolbar, or right click on the group name and select Properties from the contextual menu, or double click on the group name.
4. Click on the entry in the group that you want to edit and access its Properties dialog box using the same methods as in the previous step. (Properties button, right click and select Properties, or double click.)
5. Edit the contact's details in exactly the same way as if you were doing it for an individual entry. In effect, this is what is happening because an amendment will be shown in the contact's entry within the group and also their individual entry in the address book.
6. Select OK to update the contact entry within the address book and also in the group.

If an individual entry is a part of group and it is deleted from the address book, it will also be removed from the group. Bear this in mind when you are deleting entries from a group.

Finding items

In Outlook Express it is possible to look for messages and also individual contacts.

To find a message:

1. Select Edit>Find>Message from the menu bar.
2. In the Find Message dialog box, select the folder where you want to search for a message. By default, this is the Inbox.
3. Enter details in the From, To, Subject and Message boxes. This will set down the search criteria for the message you want to find. You can enter details for one of these items, or all of them, if you know them.
4. Enter details for when the message was received, if you can remember. This takes the form of specifying if it was before or after a certain date.
5. There are also two boxes that can be checked on to specify whether a message has an attachment or has been flagged.
6. Once you have entered all of the details you know about the message you want to locate, select the Find Now button.
7. Any messages that match your search criteria will be displayed in the Find Message dialog box, in a pane underneath the searching details.
8. Double click on a message that has been found to open it.

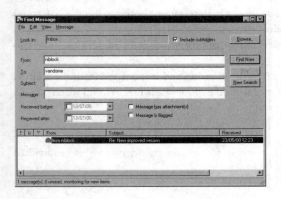

To find contacts:

1. Open your address book by selecting the toolbar Addresses button.
2. Select Edit > Find People from the Address Book dialog box menu bar.
3. Select the address book where you want to search for a contact.
4. Enter the name, email address, address, phone number and any other information about the contact you want to find. Only one field has to be completed, but the more information you can include, the better the chance of a positive search being returned. Also, it will help to narrow down the number of matches.
5. Select the Find Now button to look for the required contact.
6. Any matches will be displayed in a new pane of the Find People dialog box.
7. Double click on an entry to display that individual's contact details.

Use the Advanced Find function for a more sophisticated search for both messages and contacts.

User details

The information that is entered when a new contact is made is known as their user properties i.e. their own personal contact details. User properties can be accessed to see what information they contain and also to edit them. To do this:

1. Select the Addresses button from the main toolbar.
2. Select a contact by clicking on their name once in the address book.
3. Select Edit > Properties from the Address Book dialog box menu bar or click on the Properties button on the toolbar.

4. The current details of that user will be displayed under the Summary tab in the Properties dialog box. To edit the contact details, click on one of the other tabs (Name, Home, Business, Personal, Other, NetMeeting and Digital ID) to edit the current information. These details will then be updated under the Summary tab.

Finding people on the Internet

In addition to looking for contacts within your own personal address book, it is also possible to search for any individual or business who has an email address, anywhere in the world. This is done through email directories and it can be useful if you want to see if a long-lost friend has an email address. Outlook Express has several built-in directories which you could use, or you could access more directories through the Web. Although email directories are not as commonly used, or as extensive, as telephone directories, they are growing in popularity and are likely to continue to do so. To use an email directory through Outlook Express:

You have to actively put your name into an email directory by notifying the company who hosts it. Addresses are not entered automatically.

1. Select the Address button on the main toolbar.
2. In the Address Book dialog box select Edit>Find People from the menu bar, or select the Find People button on the toolbar.
3. In the Find People dialog box, select a directory from the drop-down list in the Look in box.

4. Enter the details for the person you want to locate, in the same way as if you were looking for someone in your own address book.
5. Click the Find Now button. Outlook Express will connect to the Web; any matches will be displayed in a new pane in the Find People dialog.
6. Select the Web Site button to connect directly to the selected email directory.

If you are searching for someone with a common name, you will probably be faced with numerous possibilities. Look at the email address for hints i.e. '–.co.uk' for a UK address.

To use an email directory on the Web

Email directories can be accessed directly on the Web and some to look at are:

- Four11 at *www.four11.com*
- Bigfoot at *www.bigfoot.com*
- Infospace at *www.infospace.com*
- Switchboard at *www.switchboard.com*

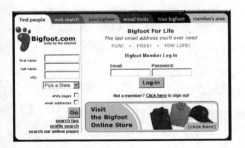

Once you have accessed one of these sites, you can search for an email address in the same way as you would within your own address book: enter information about the person you are looking for, then wait and see what search results come up — the more search information you enter, then the more specific the search will be.

Information about directory services can be accessed in Outlook Express by selecting Tools>Accounts>Directory Services from the menu bar.

Sending and Receiving

The basics of sending and receiving

One of the essential elements of email is the ability to send and receive messages. This involves connecting to the Internet through your computer and then instructing your email program to send messages that you have written and download those that are waiting to be accessed on the server. Each program has default settings for how this is achieved, but it is possible to customise these so that the sending and receiving functions are best suited to your own needs. The first thing to do is to configure your email program so that it knows how to connect to the Internet for sending and receiving messages. If you have already registered with an ISP you will probably have a fully configured version of Outlook Express but if you need to configure it:

1. Select Tools>Accounts from the main toolbar.
2. In the Internet Accounts dialog box, select the Mail tab and then select the Properties button.
3. Select the Servers tab. This contains information about the protocols, i.e. computer languages, used to send and receive mail.

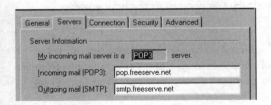

4. In the My incoming server is a xx server box, there will be a name for the type of email server that is used for delivering your messages. It will almost certainly be a POP3 (Post Office Protocol) or IMAP (Internet Message Access Protocol) server, which are the two most commonly used types, with POP servers being more popular.

5. In the Incoming mail box, enter the address for your incoming server. If this is not already entered, you may need to contact your ISP. It will take the format of POP and then the last part of your ISPs email address i.e. 'pop.freeserve.net'

6. In the Outgoing mail box, enter the address of the server that is used to deliver your messages. This will probably be a SMTP (Simple Mail Transfer Protocol) server and will be similar to the POP one except it will start with SMTP i.e. 'smtp.freeserve.net'

7. Enter the Account name, which is not your actual name, but your user name that is specified when you register with your ISP. It will take the format of the part of your email address following the @ sign.

8. Enter your password which you used when you registered with your ISP. If you have forgotten this, you may need to consult your ISP.

If you cannot configure your email program to send and receive mail, try switching over your user name and account name, as they can sometimes be entered in the wrong place.

In Outlook Express the send and receive settings can be determined in the Options dialog, which can be accessed by selecting Tools > Options from the menu bar. This contains a number of menus that are tiled one on top of another. To access each menu, click on the relevant tab at the top of the Options dialog box. The menu will then be displayed.

Setting options

General settings

The first menu to be displayed is the General one. This has a number of options for settings that affect (among other things) the sending and receiving of messages. Each of these can be checked on or off by clicking in the small box next to it. Click once to either insert or remove a tick, depending on whether you want that option to be active or not.

- When starting, go directly to my Inbox folder. This defines the mailbox that Outlook Express displays when it opens. It is best to tick this option on for opening the Inbox, because this is where any new messages will be downloaded.
- Notify me if there are any new newsgroups. Check this box on if you want to be told if any new newsgroups have been added to the list that

is viewed by the newsreader in the program. Newsgroups are groups of people with a shared interest who communicate over the Internet with email messages that are posted for everyone in the group to see. There are tens of thousands of newsgroups on the Internet and you can subscribe to as many as you like, free of charge. Once you have subscribed to a newsgroup you can send messages for the other members to see, reply to messages that have already been posted or simply read the messages from the other members of the newsgroup. There is no obligation to post any messages yourself. Newsgroups are looked at in more detail in the 'Mailing Lists and Newsgroups' chapter.

- Automatically display folders with unread messages. If this option is checked on then any folders that contain a message that has been received but not accessed will be displayed. This is regardless of the layout option you have selected for Outlook Express.

Send and receive options
The General settings for the send and receive messages options are some of the most important for organising your email procedure and ensuring that you use your time as efficiently as possible in terms of only being logged onto the Internet for the shortest time necessary as far as sending and receiving messages is concerned. If you get these settings right then you will not have to worry about inadvertently being connected to the Internet while you are composing a message.

With Internet connection charges coming down all the time (and in some cases they are free) it is not the end of the world if you are connected for a bit longer than you intended.

You only have to be online for the process of sending and receiving a message. It is good practice to write messages while you are offline and then connect to the Internet to send them once they are completed. Similarly, once you have downloaded a message you should disconnect from the Internet before you open it and read it (unless you intend to reply to it almost immediately). A good rule to follow in respect of this is, 'Compose offline, send online'. The send and receive options under the General menu are:

- Play sound when new message arrives. If this option is checked on, a sound will play whenever a new message is downloaded onto your computer. This is usually in the form of a tinny chime, but is does let you know that you have something to look at. If you have set the program to open in the Inbox folder then the new message should also be displayed here. It will be depicted by an unopened, yellow envelope next to it. This changes into an opened, white envelope once the message has been accessed.

In most programs you can change the sound that plays to alert you to new mail. You can even create your own custom sound or spoken message.

- Send and receive messages at startup. This is an important option because it determines how Outlook Express reacts when it is first opened up. If this option is checked on the program will automatically connect to the Internet when it is opened. Once this has been established it will download any new messages from your mail server. The plus side of this is that you will be able to see if you have mail as soon as you open the program, without having to do anything else. The downside is that, if the first thing you see when you open the program is a new message, you may become absorbed in this and forget that you are online. If this option is checked off the program opens in its offline mode. If you then want to connect to your mail server, you can do so by clicking on the Send and Receive button on the main toolbar. The advantage of this is that you can choose when you want to access the Internet and check for new mail, thereby, perhaps, being more aware about being online. The disadvantage is that is can be mildly frustrating having to click an extra button if you want to access your mail as soon as you open Outlook, particularly if you know it can be done automatically. Try both ways and see which one best suits your own method of working.

- Check for new messages every xx minute(s). This is a useful option if you are expecting an email but you do not want to stay online while you are waiting for it and so run up a considerable telephone bill, particularly if it is during peak times. If this box is checked off, then the options that are associated with it are greyed out which means they cannot be activated. However, if the Check for new messages box is checked on, two further option boxes became available. The first one is for entering the time limit you want the program to wait before it returns to the email server and looks for new messages. The default is 30 minutes but this can be set as high or as low as you like. The second option is for what happens when the time limit has been reached and it is titled, 'If my computer is not connected at this time:' There are three further options for this, which appear from a drop-down menu if the arrow at the right hand side of this box is clicked:

- Connect even when working offline. This means that your computer will connect to the Internet and your email server, even if you have specified to work offline. (Working offline is normally a safeguard against being connected to the Internet without knowing it. To ensure you are offline, for instance while you are writing an email, select File>Work Offline from the menu bar. Then, when you next try and connect to the Internet i.e. go online, a message will appear telling you that you are offline and asking whether you now want to go online. Click OK to connect to the Internet.)

Make sure you know what your connection settings are. You do not want your computer to connect to the Internet automatically when you are not there and then stay online.

- Connect only when not working offline. This means that your computer will only connect to the Internet if you are working online. It is possible to be working online even if you are not actually connected to the Internet. It means that you have slightly quicker access when you do want to achieve a connection.
- Do not connect. This means that you will not be connected, whatever option has been previously set.

The Check new messages command is best used sparingly, or if you are waiting for an urgent email. Otherwise it can become annoying if your computer is trying to connect automatically to the Internet every few minutes.

Connection

There are only two options relating to email in the Connection tab but they both play an important role:

- Ask before switching dial-up connections. If this is checked on, then a warning box will appear if you change your dial-up connection from the default. The dial-up connection is the means by which your computer is connected to your ISP and if you change the default, for instance if you join an additional ISP, then you will be alerted to the fact that this is a different one from normal that you are using. It is perfectly possible to do this and some people have several ISPs and email accounts. If this applies to you, then you may want to check this box off so that you do not have to read the same message every time you use a different ISP, if you are using more than one.

Some telecommunications companies offer a free second phone line. This is worth looking at if you spend a lot of time on the Internet while others want to use the phone.

- Hang up after sending and receiving. This is an important option for ensuring that you do not remain connected to the Internet by mistake once you have downloaded and sent your messages. Not only will this run up your telephone bill, but if you only have one telephone line it will not make you very popular if there are other people in the household that want to use the phone. (If there is a heavy demand for the phone and you want to spend time on the Internet, it may be worthwhile investing in a second telephone line, so that one can be used for conversations and the other for the Internet. Most telecommunications companies offer a second line and some of them do not charge for this if you are a new subscriber to their service. The main drawback with two telephone lines is that if they are both in use at the same time it could mean a bill that is double in size.) If this option is checked on Outlook Express will automatically disconnect from the Internet once all of your messages have been downloaded or sent. However, if you regularly reply to emails as soon as you receive them, you may want to check this option off to save having to reconnect immediately after accessing a message.

If you do not select the above option for disconnecting from the Internet, you will have to do so manually. To do this:

1. Select File>Work Offline from the menu bar.
2. A dialog box will appear asking if you want to hang up the modem before you go offline. Click OK. (Being offline is not necessarily the same as disconnecting from the Internet. It just means that no messages will be sent to your email server.)

Or:

1. Double click on the Internet connection icon that appears at the bottom right hand corner of the monitor (on the status bar) while you are connected. It is usually in the form of two computers that are linked together.
2. Select Disconnect from the dialog box that appears.

Make sure the two linked computers have disappeared. If they have, the connection to the Internet has been broken. They will also disappear if something unexpected disconnects you from the Internet while you are online.

The other option that appears in the Connection dialog box is for changing Internet Connection settings. This includes changing the default dial-up connection settings and also various settings for viewing the Web through your default browser, which will be Internet Explorer unless it has been changed.

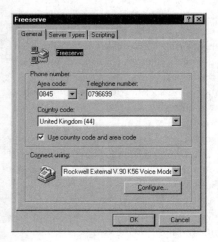

Send

The Send tab has options for sending messages and also for formatting them:

- Save copy of sent messages in the Sent Items folder. This creates a backup of emails that you have sent by placing them in one of the folders that are automatically generated by Outlook Express, Sent Items. This is a good way to keep a record of what you have sent and it is worthwhile to have this option checked on as there will always be times when you will want to check what messages you have sent to certain people and what you said.

- Send messages immediately. If this box is checked on, outgoing messages will be sent whenever the Send and Receive button is clicked.

- Automatically put people I reply to in my Address Book. This is a useful way to add email addresses to your list. If this option is checked on, every time you reply to an email (i.e. send it back to the sender with your own comments added to it) this person's email address will automatically be added to your address book. This saves you from entering it manually and it can always be deleted at a later date if you decide you do not need it.

- Automatically complete email addresses when composing. This is a function by which Outlook Express memorises the email addresses that you have entered previously when composing messages, whether they have been placed in your address book or not. So when you compose a new message, all you have to do it type in the first two or three letters of a person's email address and the program will add the rest for you. If it is an entry in your address book, that contact's Display details will appear in the Inbox i.e. the name that you have specified in the address book that will display when their name is selected. This option is an effective shortcut if you do not want to access names through your address book, or if you have emailed someone previously but you have not entered their email address. As long as you have sent your message to them from the same computer the program should be able to retrieve their email address. The one drawback with this option is if you have several people with a similar name. For instance if you have four contacts with the first name 'John' then you will need to enter at least five or six characters (until the beginning of their surname) until this option can determine which address it is.

If you want to reply to a very long message, consider editing it before you include it in the reply. The recipient may not want to see the whole of their original message.

- Include message in reply. This is an option for use when replying to an email that has been sent to you. This can be done by opening the message and clicking on the Reply button on the toolbar. If the 'Include message in reply' box is checked on, the recipient's original message will be sent back to them, along with your own message. If this box is checked off, only your message will be sent by way of a reply. The default is for this box to be checked on, because most people like to see what they said when an email reply is sent to them. If both messages are together, it can save the recipient from having to open up their original message to see what they said.

- Reply to messages using the format in which they were sent. One of the developments in email in recent years is the ability to send messages in formats other than just plain, unformatted text. This includes Rich Text Format (RTF) and Hypertext Markup Language (HTML) which is the language used when creating Web pages and it gives a greater degree of flexibility when sending messages. If this option is checked on, a reply to a message will be in the same format as the one in which it was sent. Compatibility should not be an issue, since the message was sent in this format in the first place.

- The formatting options that are available in the Send dialog box refer to emails created in either HTML or Plain Text and newsgroup entries created in the same way. Formatting of email messages is looked at in greater detail in the 'Formatting' chapter and the rest of the options are dealt with in their relevant chapters.

Message icons

When new messages are received there are several icons that can appear beside them, denoting a number of factors, such as level of importance or whether they contain any attachments. The icons that can be assigned to email messages are:

- A closed yellow envelope. This denotes a message that has been received but not opened.
- An open white envelope. This denotes a message that has been received and read.

- An open white envelope with a left pointing purple arrow on top of it. This denotes a message that has been opened and a reply sent to the sender of the original message.
- An open white envelope with a right pointing blue arrow on top of it. This denotes a message that has been opened and then forwarded on to one or more people.
- An envelope with a paper clip attached to it. This denotes a message that has an attachment with it.
- An envelope with a red exclamation mark next to it. This denotes a message that has been sent with high priority.
- An envelope with a blue, down pointing arrow next to it. This denotes a message that has been sent with low priority. (It is rare for people to use this with their emails as most people think their messages are of high priority, particularly in the business world.)
- An envelope with a sheet of paper icon on top of it. This denotes a message that has been placed in the Drafts folder. This is a folder that is automatically generated by Outlook Express and it is used for items that are not finished or ready to be sent.
- An envelope with a red and yellow rosette on top of it. This denotes a message that has a digital signature attached to it.

If your email program tries to connect you to the Internet when you are composing a message, disconnect by double clicking the two-computers icon at the bottom right hand corner of your screen (on a Mac, click the Apple symbol in the top left corner) and select Disconnect. If prompted, select Work Offline from the dialog box which appears.

- An envelope with a blue rosette on top of it. This denotes a message that has been encrypted. Digital signatures and encryption are looked at in greater detail in the 'Formatting' chapter.

Writing offline, sending online

Since an email can only be sent once the whole message has been written, there is no point in being connected to the Internet while you are composing it. This just wastes your telephone bill and ties up a telephone line unnecessarily. However, depending on the settings that have been specified in the General Options dialog box for 'Send and receive messages at startup', Outlook Express

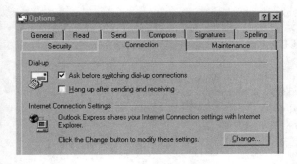

may connect to the Internet once the program is opened up. If the 'Hang up after sending and receiving' option is not checked on in the Connection Option dialog box then you will still be connected to the Internet once you have downloaded any messages that are waiting on your email server.

If this is the case, then you should disconnect before you start composing any messages of your own. The exception to this is if you are sending a very short message that will only take a minute or two to write. To disconnect, use the same procedures as described under the Connection section earlier in this chapter:

1. Select File>Work Offline from the menu bar.
2. A dialog box will appear asking if you want to hang up the modem before you go offline. Click OK. (Being offline is not the same as disconnecting from the Internet. It just means that no messages will be sent to your email server.)

Or:

1. Double click on the Internet connection icon that appears at the bottom right hand corner of the monitor (on the status bar) while you are connected. It is usually in the form of two computers that are linked together.
2. Select Disconnect from the dialog box that appears.

Make sure the two linked computers have disappeared. If they have, the connection to the Internet has been broken. They will also disappear if something unexpected disconnects you from the Internet while you are online.

Draft messages

Sometimes, if you are writing a long message, or one that you want to get the wording exactly right on, you may not want to send it as soon as it is finished. Or you may want to write some of it and then go back to it later. In this case, the message can be stored in the Drafts folder rather than the Inbox or the Outbox. This is displayed in the Folders list pane that appears at the right hand side of the screen. If it is not showing:

1. Select View>Layout from the menu bar.
2. Check on the box next to the Folder list in the Basic section of the Layout dialog box.

The Drafts folder is located within the Local Folders, which contain all of the folders within your email account. Double click on the Local Folders folder to view its contents, which should contain the Drafts folder. This is depicted by an envelope with a pencil over it. To save a message into the Drafts folder:

1. Open a new message and select a recipient and subject heading.
2. Compose part or all of the email text.
3. Select File>Copy to Folder from the menu bar. (There is also an option for Send Later on the File menu. Although this sounds as though it would place the message in the Drafts folder, it in fact places it in the Outbox, ready to be sent the next time you select the Send and Receive option.)
4. In the Copy dialog box, navigate to the Drafts folder.

5. Select the folder by clicking on it once.
6. Select OK.
7. Click on the Drafts folder in the Folder list pane to check that your message has been saved there. If it has there should be a blue "1" in brackets next to the Drafts folder. This indicates that there is one unopened message stored there. This notification is used for all folders that contain unopened items.

Checking a message has been sent

Whenever you send an email message, the first thing you want to know is whether it has been sent successfully or not. This can be done by checking in the Sent Items folder, which is located in the Local Folder, the same as the Drafts folder. To check that a message has been sent:

1. Click on the Sent Items folder.
2. Depending on how the folder is organised, the most recently sent message will appear at either the top or the bottom of the list. Double click on it to check that it is the right message and contains the content that you put into it.

Don't forget you can also view the contents of an email simply by selecting it and inspecting it in the Preview pane.

If you receive an email that annoys you, take your time to reply. Do not send a stinging reply as soon as you read it. This can lead to what is known as 'flame wars'.

If an email is not sent successfully, an error message will appear in your Inbox alerting you to the fact. There could be several reasons for this:

- The email address has been entered incorrectly.
- The recipient has changed their email address and the one that is being used has been discontinued.
- There is a problem with either your ISP's mail server or that of the recipient's.

If you do receive an error message, try sending it again and if it persists contact your ISP.

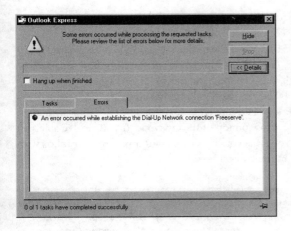

Replying to emails

How often have you received a letter and wished you could just scribble a few lines of reply on it and then send it back to the person it came from, without having to write a new letter and send it in a new envelope? Well, with email it is possible to do this with the Reply function. To do this:

1. When you receive a message that you want to reply to, open it and select the Reply to Sender button on the toolbar (this is depicted by the figure of a single individual, with a left pointing arrow pointing towards them). This automatically inserts the sender's email address details into the To box.
2. Enter the text of your message, which appears above the original message you received.
3. Select the Send button on the toolbar to send the message back to its original author. (By default, the sender's message is also sent back to them, although this can be changed by checking off the 'Include message in reply' box in the Send options box.)
4. When an email has been replied to it appears in the Inbox with a left pointing purple arrow on top of the envelope. If you receive an email that is a reply to one that you have sent it will appear in your Inbox with the prefix 'Re' in the subject box.

If you forward a message, it is polite to let the original author know about this. Therefore they will not be surprised if someone else contacts them about their original message.

Replying to a group

If you receive an email as part of a group, i.e. the sender has sent the message to two or more people, it is possible to send your reply to the whole group, rather than just the original author. This is done in the same way as replying to an individual, except that you select the Reply to All button rather than the Reply to Sender one. The Reply to All button is depicted by two people with a left pointing arrow pointing towards them. If you choose this option, check the names in the group to make sure that you want to reply to all of them. If not, you will have to select the recipients individually.

Forwarding emails

In addition to being able to reply directly to the sender of an email it is also possible to forward a message on to someone else. This could be if the sender has asked you to let other people know about a certain event or if it is a business item that needs to be distributed to other interested parties. To forward a message:

1. Open the email to be forward by double clicking on it in the Inbox.
2. Select the Forward icon from the toolbar (this is depicted by a figure of a single individual with a right pointing arrow pointing towards them).
3. In the To box, enter the address of the person, or persons, that the message is to be forwarded to.
4. Select the Send button on the toolbar.
5. When an email has been forwarded it appears in the Inbox with a right pointing blue arrow on top of the envelope. If you forwarded an email to someone it will have the prefix 'Fwd' in the subject box.

Dealing with junk email

Junk mail is the bane of many people's lives and, unfortunately, email is as susceptible to this as postal mail. Whenever you conduct any kind of online transaction, whether it is buying something on the Web or registering for an online service, you will be asked for your email address. Once this has happened you will then be subject to junk email. This is usually in the form of marketing information with the company that you have already done business with and any other organisations that they have given your email address to. It is impossible to have any kind of online existence without, sooner or later, being subjected to junk email, since with most online transactions the disclosure of an email address is a required element. As with other forms of junk mail, junk email, or spam as it is sometimes known, is generally little more than a mild irritation but there can be some more sinister aspects to it. However, there are ways to avoid disclosing your own email address and also for blocking junk email before it reaches your Inbox. The issue of junk email is looked at in greater detail in the chapter entitled 'Junk Email'.

Formatting

Formatting possibilities

In some people's eyes, email is purely a functional device and it does not really matter what it looks like, as long as the message is there and it is delivered quickly. While this is true to a certain extent, developments in email programs have led to a far greater flexibility as far as the look and formatting of emails are concerned. Rather than just having unformatted text in a single font it is now possible to create emails that have coloured backgrounds, formatted text and even hyperlinks to pages on the Web.

With the increasing number of formatting options that are available there is now no reason why emails have to be functional or dull. However, this does not mean that it is advisable to go overboard on the design front and use every available option for every message you send. When considering the design and formatting of an email there are some points to take into consideration:

- Not everyone will share your views on what is a compelling design. The more complex the formatting then the greater the chance that the recipient will find it a little too much to take.

- Business people are busy people who usually just want to obtain the information they are looking for. So if you are sending a business email then it is better to make it functional, and to the point, rather than try adding too many bells and whistles to it. By all means use simple formatting options such as italics and bold but steer clear of some of the more all-singing, all-dancing techniques.

- The more complex the formatting, the larger the file size of the email. This could have a negative effect on the recipient if they feel your beautifully designed and formatted message takes too long to download.

But these points do not mean you should not try and make your messages as appealing-looking and professional as possible.

Plain text

As the name suggests, this is the option for producing messages with the most basic text. There is little in the way of formatting options available if you are composing a message in plain text, but it does produce functional messages and small file sizes. When using plain text, the message will be composed using the default font setting on your computer. So if this is Times New Roman, then this is what will be used for your email text. To set plain text as the default for formatting messages:

1. Select the New Mail button on the main toolbar.
2. Select Format on the New Message menu bar.
3. Click on Plain Text so that a black dot appears next to it.

When you compose the message, there will not be any formatting menus or toolbars available.

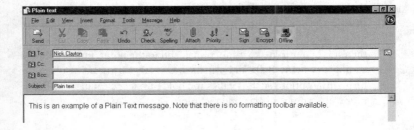

Rich Text Format (RTF) and HTML

If you are looking for more versatility than can be offered by plain text formatting, then the Rich Text Format (RTF) should be selected. This is the default setting and it also allows for the use of HyperText Markup Language (HTML) formatting to be applied to an email message. HTML is the method that is used to create pages that are displayed on the Web and it consists of a set of codes that instructs a browser to display the content of a page in a particular way. If HTML is applied to an email then the same instructions tell the recipient's email program to display the message in its HTML format. In order for the recipient to be able to view the message in this way they must have an email program that supports the MIME (Multipurpose Internet Mail Extensions) standard. If they do not have this then the email will appear with an attachment that can be opened through a Web browser and read in this way. Most recent email programs support the MIME standard and so using HTML formatting should not be a problem in most cases.

Email messages can be made to look more like Web pages by using HTML formatting. They can also have hyperlinks to pages on the Web inserted.

To set HTML formatting for all messages that are composed and sent:
1. Select Tools>Options from the main menu bar.
2. Select the Send tab.
3. Check on HTML in the Mail Sending Format section.

To set HTML formatting for a single email message:

1. Create a new mail message.
2. Select Format from the New Mail menu bar.

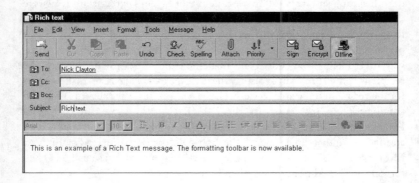

3. Click on Rich Text (HTML) so that a black dot appears next to it. This will enable the relevant formatting options.

Formatting toolbar

If the Rich Text (HTML) option has been selected it is possible to use the formatting options that are on the Formatting toolbar. If this is not visible:

1. Select View>Toolbars from the New Message menu bar.
2. Check on the Formatting Bar option. (Most of the following options can also be accessed from the menu bars.)

The options on the formatting bar are (in the order in which they appear, from left to right):

- Font. This is a box with an arrow at the right hand side. The default font is displayed in the box. Click on the arrow for a drop-down list of the other fonts that are installed on the computer and available for use in formatting. (If you select an unusual font or one that you have added to the system fonts, then the recipient will not be able to view the font unless they have the same one installed on their system. If this is the case it will be replaced with the nearest available substitute.)

Do not use too many different fonts when you are composing a message. Keep it to two, or three at the most, otherwise the message may begin to look over-designed.

- Font size. This also has an arrow to access a drop-down list. The available options are between 8 point and 36 point. (When choosing a font size, bear in mind the age of the recipient of the message. As we get older, out eyesight deteriorates, so a point size of 8 would not be suitable if you were sending a message to an elderly relative. Similarly, if you were sending a business email a point size of 36 would be too large to convey your message in a concise way, as the words would take up too much room on screen.)
- Paragraph style. This contains a drop-down list of preformatted paragraph styles that can be used for formatting purpose. These include styles for addresses, headings and lists. Each style has a preset font, font size and alignment. If you select one of these styles then the selected text, or the text that comes after this point in the message, will have this style applied to it.

- Bold, italics and underline. These standard formatting options can be applied to any piece of text within the message. They should be used to emphasise certain words, phrases or sentences but they should be used sparingly, otherwise the impact will be lessened. In general, use bold and italics for emphasis and only use underlining if absolutely necessary. This is because underlined text is harder to read than normal, bold or italicised text and also because hyperlinks in HTML are, by default, denoted by underlining. A hyperlink is a piece of text or an image that, when it is activated by being clicked on, takes the user to a linked page on the Web. Hyperlinks can be inserted into email messages that are created in Rich Text (HTML) thus giving them greater versatility. For instance, if you want to tell someone about your own Web page you have just designed, you could send them an email that contains a hyperlink that goes straight to that location on the Web. This is a powerful shortcut for directing people to pages on the Web and because hyperlinks are automatically underlined when they are created, it is advisable that underlining is not used for normal formatting, if possible.

Hyperlinks are the threads which connect all of the sites and pages on the Web. Increasingly, more programs, such as word processors, have the ability to include hyperlinks.

- Text colour. Email messages that only use plain black text can be a thing of the past with HTML formatting. This option gives a drop-down menu with a selection of colours that can be applied to text. However, this is another option that should be used with care. Some colours, such as red and fluorescent greens and yellows, can be difficult to read and tiring on the eyes if they are used for large blocks of text. Use bright colours for emphasis and subtle ones, such as dark blue, for longer paragraphs. Even with a selection of colours at your disposal, black on a white background it still one of the most effective ways of producing text.

- Numbered list. This option inserts a numbered list into the selected text or any text that is entered after this is selected.
- Bulleted list. This is the same as the numbered list, except that each item in the list is denoted with a bullet point rather than a number.
- Decrease and increase the indentation. This moves the selected text forward or backwards to the next tab point. This applies to a whole paragraph and the cursor only has to be inserted at any point in the paragraph for this action to be effective. It also inserts a line space below the paragraph to which the indentation command has been applied.

If you want a message to look as informal as possible, use left or centre alignment. For a more professional look, use justify so the text is aligned at the right and left margins.

- Alignment options. These are options for aligning selected items of text or setting the default at the beginning of a message that will apply for all of the text that will be entered. The selections that can be made are: Align Left, Centre, Align Right or Justify. Align Left creates a flush left hand margin and a ragged right hand one. Align Right creates a flush right hand margin and a ragged left hand one. Centre places the text in the centre of the page, with ragged margins at both sides. Justify creates flush margins on the left hand and right hand margins. As a general rule, justified text should be used for more formal messages and align left for more informal emails to family and friends. Centred text works best as a presentational device for items such as invitations or advertisements.

- Insert Horizontal Line. This is a standard HTML command and it inserts a line under the point at which the cursor is inserted. Once the line has been inserted, it is possible to perform some basic formatting tasks on it. Click once on the line to select it. Use the alignment buttons to position it at the left, right or centre of the page. Click on one of the resizing handles to make it larger or smaller. These are small black boxes that are located at each corner of the line and also in the middle of each side of it. Click and drag on one of the boxes to resize. If the corner boxes are used, the line's height and width can be altered together. If you click and hold on the line a four-headed arrow should appear. This allows you to drag the line to a new position on the page.

- Create a Hyperlink. This is a command that is closely associated with HTML and is standard in HTML Web authoring software packages, such as Microsoft FrontPage, Adobe PageMill and Macromedia Dreamweaver. Any item of text or an image can be made into a hyperlink and this is a shortcut device that can take the user directly to the specified item on the Internet. The most common use for this is to link to a Web page or an email address, although there are also other options available. To create a hyperlink.

1. Highlight the piece of text you want to make into the hyperlink by clicking the text crosshair just before it and then holding down the mouse button and dragging over the text to be selected. If the item to be used is a single word, it can be selected by double clicking on it.

2. Click on the Create a Hyperlink button.

3. In the Hyperlink dialog box select the type of hyperlink you want to create. This will determine the prefix that is used for the hyperlink and this will differ depending on the type of hyperlink that is being created. A hyperlink to a Web page has the prefix *'http'*, which stands for HyperText Transfer Protocol. This it the protocol, or language, which allows different computers around the world to view the same Web page and in a way it is a universal translator. A hyperlink can also be created to an email address and this has the prefix *'mailto:'*. When an email hyperlink is accessed, the user is taken to their own email program where a new message will have already been launched, with the email address that was used in the hyperlink inserted in the To box. Another type of hyperlink that can be used in an email is one to a newsgroup. This begins with the prefix *'news'*.

4. The other box in the Hyperlink dialog box is for the URL of the item to which you want to create the hyperlink. This is a unique address that is used to identify every item on the Internet. The type prefix will have already been inserted, depending on what was selected in the previous step. Next, you have to add the body of the URL. For a Web page this will probably start with '*www.*' (although some Web pages just have the 'http' prefix and then the page name) followed by the domain name of the site. This will be something along the lines of 'mypage.com'. A good way to obtain Web addresses is to visit the site and then copy the whole thing from the address box line that is near the top of the browser. Then return to your email and paste it into the URL box in the Hyperlink dialog box. Similarly, email addresses can be copied from your address book and then pasted into place. If you use this method for URLs, make sure that the 'http' prefix is only included once. If the paste command causes the 'http' to be inserted again, highlight it and then delete it with the Delete or Backspace keys, as appropriate, on the keyboard.

URL stands for Uniform Resource Locator and it denotes a Web page, email or newsgroup address.

If you want to get into Web page design, take a look at Web Page Design in easy steps.

5. Select OK.
6. The selected item should now appear underlined, denoting that it is a hyperlink.
7. To test a hyperlink that you have inserted in an email, send a message to yourself and then click on the hyperlink. When you pass the cursor over it, the type of hyperlink and its target destination will appear in the Status bar at the bottom of the email window. When you click on it, you should be taken to the specified Web page or to a new message in your email program, with the recipient's name pre-inserted.

- Insert picture. This enables you to choose a picture to be inserted into the email. When you click on this button it takes you to the Picture dialog box. This contains a number of options:
  - Picture Source. This is the location from which the picture is going to be inserted. It can either be from the hard drive of your computer or an external device such as a digital camera, a scanner, a picture

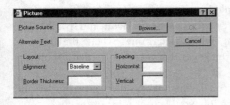

CD-ROM or a form of removable storage such as a floppy disc or a Zip disc.
  - Next to the Picture Source box is a Browse button. Click on this to locate a suitable image. This is just the same as looking for a file

within your computer's file management system. For display in an email the image has to be in either JPEG or GIF format. If you want to email an image that is created in a format other than these, it should be attached to the email rather than included in the body of it. When you have located the image you want to insert, select Open. This then inserts the file path into the Picture Source box i.e. it enters information that tells the email program where to look to locate the image.

- Underneath the Picture Source box is one entitled Alternate Text. This can be used to include a brief description about the image, which appears when the cursor is passed over it. (This only applies once the recipient has received the message and not while it is in the authoring stage.) If you want to save an image that has been sent to you in the body of an email (rather than as an attachment) right click and select 'Save Picture As' from the contextual menu. Then select a location on your hard drive where you want this image saved. This information could also be included with an email of this type if you think the recipient would be unsure about saving the image.

The other options in the Picture dialog box are for layout and spacing. The layout options include alignment, which determines where the image is located on the page, and border thickness that inserts a border around the image.

The border setting can be between 0, which means there is no border, and 999. In reality anything much over 100 would cover most of the image.

The spacing option determines how much space there is between the image and the side and top of the page. These values are also between 0 and 999.

Inserting a picture into an email is an alternative to sending it as an attachment. However, you should check that the recipient has the facility to view this type of email. Also, images sent in this way create slightly larger files than sending the image as an attachment, although the difference is not much.

Formatting the background

If you yearn for a bit more colour in the background of your email messages, rather than just plain white, then you do not have to worry since this is perfectly possible, using the stationery option (see later).

However, if you are using a coloured background make sure there is enough of a contrast between it and the text: black text on a dark grey background is not a good way to increase readability.

Background colours can be inserted for individual messages while they are being composed:

1. Open a new message.
2. Select Format>Background from the mail menu bar.
3. Select Colour and choose a colour. This will only apply to the current message.
4. Repeat the process to change the colour if it makes the text difficult to read.

Stationery

In the early days of email it was considered a considerable feat to send and receive a message that contained nothing more than black text on a white background. However, this is now considered to be the very minimum in terms of layout and design and in some quarters it is seen as being positively drab and uninspiring. Thankfully, those days are well and truly consigned to the computing history books and it is now possible to include elaborate designs with outgoing email messages. This can be done by creating your own designs in HTML format or by using the pre-designed HTML templates that are known as stationery. This can be selected to form the background and layout of email messages and they include background designs, colour, graphics and fonts. Some of the stationery templates that are available in Outlook Express are for occasions such as:

If you have selected a stationery style, make sure it is only applied to the intended messages and not included with anything that would be inappropriate.

- Birth announcements
- Birthday celebrations
- Get well soon
- Party invitations
- Congratulations
- New house
- Romantic messages
- Anniversaries
- Family gatherings

To use stationery in an email:

1. Select Tools>Options from the menu bar.
2. In the Options dialog box, click on the Compose tab.
3. Under Stationery, select Mail (the other option here is for News, which can be used if you want to use a stationery format when posting a message to a newsgroup).
4. Click on the Select button. This will take you to the Select Stationery dialog box. The available stationery templates should be listed here and they will be displayed as HTML files. Each file will have a name that describes the type of stationery that it is.

5. Select a stationery file by clicking on it once. Check on the Show preview box to see a small preview of what the stationery looks like.

6. Select OK. This returns you to the Options dialog box. Select OK.

This stationery template will be used for all new mail that you create, unless you specify otherwise.

Most templates have some text already pre-inserted into them, but it is possible to highlight this and then overtype it, to include your own individual message. It is also possible to add text as you would with a plain text email message.

If you do not want to set a default stationery for all newly created messages, it is possible to select stationery templates for individual emails:

1. Select Message>New Message Using from the main menu bar.

2. Select Stationery and then choose the appropriate stationery template as above. This will over-ride any stationery selections that have already been made in the Compose dialog box.

It is also possible to apply a stationery template once you have started composing a new message:

1. Select Format>Apply Stationery

2. Select a stationery template as above.

To turn off the stationery option, select Tools>Options>Compose and check off the Mail (or News) box under Stationery.

If you do not see any files when you access the Select Stationery dialog box, return to the Compose dialog box and select the Download More button. This will connect you to a Web site where you can download more stationery templates. This is done by clicking on the 'Get It Now' button next to the category of stationery that you require. This then downloads an executable file onto your hard drive. Make a note of the folder into which the file was downloaded and then locate it within your file management software and open it by double clicking on it (it should be identifiable by its name and an '–exe' file extension). When you return to the Select Stationery dialog box the new stationery should be available. The Web address for adding new stationery is (for some reason stationery is spelled 'stationary'):

http://home-publishing.com/outlookexpress/stationary.htm

In addition to using the pre-designed stationery templates it is also possible to create your own customised stationery:

1. Select Tools>Options>Compose as above.
2. Under the Stationery heading, click on the Create New button. This will open the Stationery Wizard, which guides you step-by-step through the process of creating your own personalised stationery.

If you include several images in your stationery, this will add considerably to the file size of your messages. Think 'Less is more' in terms of design and also downloading time.

3. The first page of the wizard contains a brief description of what is contained within a stationery template. Read this and select Next.
4. In the Background dialog box, check on the Picture box if you want to include a graphic in your stationery. Select the Browse button to choose an image from your hard drive. Once this has been chosen it can be positioned Top, Centre or Bottom and Left, Centre or Right. There is also a Tile option which means the image is repeated so that is covers the whole page. If you do not want an image to be included, check off the Picture box.
5. To insert a coloured background, check on the Colour box. Select a colour from the drop-down menu that is situated below the Colour

box. If a picture and a colour are selected, the colour will only be visible on the area that is not covered by the picture.

6. Select Next.
7. In the Font dialog box, select a Font, Size and Colour. This can be viewed in the Preview window, so try out a few to see what they look like before you settle on a final choice. There are also boxes that can be checked on for Bold or Italics.
8. Select Next.
9. In the Margins dialog box, select a size, in pixels, for the left and top margins.
10. Select Next.
11. In the Complete dialog box, give your stationery a title in the Name box. This should be something that you will be able to recognise in several months time e.g. 'Happy 21st' rather than just 'Birthday'.
12. Select Finish to complete the stationery creation process. This file should now be available when you look in the Select Stationery dialog box.

Even though stationery can add an extra dimension to your email messages there are some points that should be remembered when using it:

- If you set the stationery in the Compose dialog box, then this will be used for all new messages. This may not be appropriate in all circumstances and so you may have to turn off the stationery for certain

If you are unsure about whether someone will be able to view your stationery designs, email them first and ask them if their program is HTML compatible.

messages. If this happens regularly then it could become annoying. To overcome this, just select stationery as required for individual messages.

- Some recipients of your stationery-based messages may not share your enthusiasm for artistic HTML designs. This is particularly true if you are sending business emails, in which case stationery should be treated in the same way as humour: very cautiously.
- Some recipients may not have email programs that are capable of reading messages in HTML format. If this is the case, all of your design work will have been wasted.

Font settings

All email programs have a default font setting and Outlook Express is no different. However, this may not be to everyone's taste and so there is an option for selecting your own default font:

1. Select Tools>Options from the main menu bar.
2. Select the Compose tab.
3. Under Compose Font, select Font Setting for either Mail or News (which is for newsgroups).
4. In the Font dialog box, select a Font, Font style and Size. Under effects there are also options for Underline and Colour. Underline should be

When choosing a font size, keep in mind the age group of your recipients. Our eyesight deteriorates as we get older and younger people can read smaller font sizes. Size 10 is a good general size for most fonts, although this can depend on the individual font.

avoided if at all possible as it generally makes text harder to read and it could be confused with hyperlinks (links to Web pages) as these usually appear underlined. The default colour is black but this can be changed using the options from the colour drop-down menu. When selecting a colour, make sure that it is one that is easy to read on screen, particularly if you are already using a coloured background. Colours such as yellow , light green and light blue tend to be less clear than darker colours such as navy blue and olive.

5. View your selections in the Sample box and once you are happy with them, select OK. This takes you back to the Compose dialog box. Select OK again to confirm your new font settings.

Opening and closing conventions

One of the most contentious issues concerning the format and appearance of emails is the opening and closing conventions. In hard copy letters these are laid down in reasonably hard and fast rules:

- Begin by addressing the recipient 'Dear Mr Smith', 'Dear Mrs/Miss/ Ms Jones', 'Dear John' or 'Dear Susan' or, if you do not have a named individual to write to, 'Dear Sir or Madam'.
- End by using 'Yours sincerely' if you have opened the letter by addressing a named individual.
- End by using 'Yours faithfully' if you have opened the letter with 'Dear Sir or Madam'.

Whatever opening and closing conventions you use, someone may say that this is not the proper style. If you are happy with what you have done then ignore them.

While there are still a lot of grey areas concerning these conventions, at least it is generally accepted how letters should be begun and ended. However, with emails things are not as clear-cut.

There are generally two schools of thought about opening and closing conventions for emails. The first claims that since it is only an electronic version of what would be written on paper the same conventions should apply. The opposite argument is that since this is an evolution of a paper letter, new conventions can apply. The truth of the matter is that there are no hard and fast rules about how emails should be opened and closed. However, some points to bear in mind are:

- Unless you are sending an email to an organisation, you will always have the address of an individual person. Therefore the dreadful 'Dear Sir or Madam' can be dispensed with.
- The recipient will always see your name when receiving the message. So there is less need to include your full name at the end.
- If you are sending a formal email to someone you have not communicated with before it can be the safest option to stick with a 'Dear …' opening and a 'Yours sincerely' closing.
- Personal emails are the same as personal letters – address them in whatever way you want.
- Emails with no opening or closing can seem a bit blunt and impersonal.
- A popular compromise is to include the person's first name at the beginning and your own first name at the end.

Unlike postal letters, a degree of flexibility is required when opening and closing emails. There is no right and wrong, but some styles are more likely to make the recipient feel at ease than others. Go with what feels right and if in doubt avoid any kind of humorous introduction or ending: email has a capacity for exaggerating even a minor misjudgement in this area.

Signatures

When dealing with closing conventions in an email it is possible to include predefined elements automatically, such as your name and email address. This is known as a signature which appears at the end of a message with the sender's specified contact information. To create a signature:

It is possible to create different signatures for different uses. If you do this, make sure you select the intended signature for each recipient.

1. Select Tools>Options from the main menu bar and in the Options dialog box select the Signatures tab.
2. If you want a signature to appear on all messages by default, check on the Add signatures to all outgoing messages. This should be used with care, because you may want to use different signatures for different

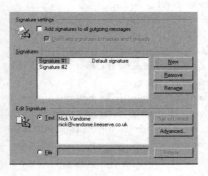

messages, depending on who you are writing to. (If you check this box on, an additional box is activated which can be used to check on or off whether signatures are included with replies and forwards.)

3. Under Signatures, select New to add a new signature.

4. In the Edit Signature box, check on the Text button and add the text you want to appear as the signature.

5. Select New again to create another signature, or OK to save the one that you have just completed. (If you want to use a text file as your signature, check on the File button and then select a file from your hard drive.)

If you have not checked on the Add signatures to all outgoing messages button, you can include signatures with emails as follows:

1. Open a new message and compose the text.

2. Select Insert>Signature from the menu bar. If you have only created one signature this will automatically be inserted. If you have created more than one, there will be a list of the available signatures that you can use.

3. Once a signature has been selected it will appear at the end of the current message (in some email programs, a signature is not visible in the outgoing message; it only appears when it is viewed by the recipient).

Creating a vCard

A vCard is similar to a signature, except that it is sent as an attachment with the sender's contact details. In many respects it serves as an electronic business card. A vCard is created from the author's details that are contained within the address book.

To create a vCard:

1. Select the Addresses button on the main toolbar.
2. Select File>New Contact from the menu bar or click on the New button on the toolbar.
3. Enter your own contact details in the Properties dialog box. This will add an entry for yourself into the address book. This will be the information that is displayed on the vCard.
4. Select your own name in the address book.
5. Select File>Export>Business Card (vCard) from the address book menu bar.
6. A dialog box will appear, asking for a location into which to save your vCard. You can save it to a location on your hard drive and it will have an '–vcf' file extension.

The option for creating a business card can be set by selecting Options>Compose from the menu bar.

In a business context, vCards are very useful.

To attach a vCard

Open a new message window and compose the text of the email.

1. Select Insert > My Business Card from the menu bar. Once a vCard has been attached, a small index card icon appears at the right-hand side of the header information for the message.

Spelling and grammar

As with opening and closing conventions, there is a school of thought that argues that since email is more informal it does not have to be checked as carefully as a document produced on paper. However, this is little more than a weak excuse for trying to excuse poorly written or checked messages. The speed at which emails can be created and sent should not be mistaken for informality, and every effort should be made to ensure they are as accurate and professional as possible. This includes the formatting and also the spelling of an email: a spelling mistake is just as noticeable in an email as it is in a hard copy letter. There are two ways to ensure that an email is as error free as possible:

- Proof read it as you would with a hard copy item. This may seem like an onerous task after you have rattled off the text in a few minutes, but it could well pay dividends, particularly with a business email. Look for spelling errors, duplicate words, plurals that have been omitted, grammatical errors, jargon or convoluted language, long sentences and items that just do not make sense.

- Use the spell checker. This goes through your text and identifies any spelling mistakes, or potential spelling mistakes. Unlike some of the more powerful word processing spell checkers it does not check the grammar as well but, of the two, the spelling is probably more important. To activate the spell checker while you are writing an email, click on the Spelling button on the New Message toolbar (it is denoted with ABC on the button) or select Tools > Spelling from the menu bar. When the spell checker comes across a word it does not recognise it will highlight it in the 'Not in Dictionary' box. Underneath this is a box that contains the word that the spell checker thinks it should be changed to. A further box below this has other possible suggested replacements, although they are not considered to be as likely choices. You then have the option of selecting various buttons: Ignore, which ignores the word and continues with the spelling check; Ignore All, which ignores all subsequent occurrences of this word; Change, which changes the word to the one in the Change To box, or the Suggestions box if one of these has been selected; Change All, which changes all occurrences of this word to the selected choice; Add, which adds the highlighted word to the user dictionary so that it will be recognised the next time it occurs. This is useful for real names that are used more than once.

Copying and pasting text

One of the great inventions in word processing programs is the ability to copy text from one location and paste it into another. Thankfully this has not been overlooked in Outlook Express and it is possible to perform the standard tasks of cut, copy and paste. This can be done while you are creating a message in the New Message window, by using the Cut, Copy and Paste buttons on the toolbar or by selecting the same options from the Edit menu. To apply any of these options, the text has to first be highlighted. For a single word this can be done by double clicking on it. For a single sentence it can be done by triple clicking on it. For any other section of text it can be done by clicking and dragging the text crosshair over the items you want to select. The tasks that these options perform are:

- Cut. This removes the highlighted text from its current location. However, it is copied onto the clipboard so that is can be pasted elsewhere.
- Copy. This places a copy of the highlighted text on the clipboard and leaves the original item in place.
- Paste. This inserts the contents of the clipboard at the point where the cursor is inserted.

Importing text

As well as using copy and paste to insert text into an email from another file, it is also possible to insert the entire contents of a file directly into an email message. This can be useful if you do not want to open up the file, copy the text, return to your email and paste the text. However, this only works with text files

 If your email program does not let you import text from another program, try copying it from the original document and then pasting it into the email message.

i.e. files with a '–txt' extension and HTML files. If an HTML file is inserted then only the text will be included and not any images. To insert text directly into an email:

1. In a new mail message, select Insert>Text from File.
2. Locate the file on your computer that you want to insert into the email.
3. Select Open.
4. The text can be edited in the normal way once it has been inserted into the email message.

Digital certificates

A digital certificate, (also known as a digital ID or digital signing) is a form of security for sending emails. They can be obtained from sites on the Web and

they allow you to prove your identity when you are sending a message. Several email programs now have the facility to include digital certificates but they will probably only have a limited appeal to those are paranoid about an unauthorised person seeing their messages, or those who like to use the latest technology just for the sake of it. It is possible to obtain a digital certificate from a Web site, such as:

Verisign at *www.verisign.com/*

or directly through your email program. In Outlook Express this is done as follows:

1. Select Tools > Options > Security from the menu bar.
2. Under the Secure Mail option, select Get Digital ID. This will then connect you to the Web and, in the case of Outlook Express, it takes you to a page on the Microsoft site that has links to various companies who offer digital certificates. Take a look at the various sites to see what they have to offer. Most companies charge for providing digital certificates,

A certificate has to have the same email address as the location from which it is sent.

but it is not exorbitant – in the case of Verisign a one year certificate costs $14.95, and you also get a 60 day free trial.
3. Follow the step-by-step instructions on the Web site for obtaining your certificate.
4. To check that your digital certificate has been installed correctly, select Tools > Options from the menu bar and select the Digital IDs button under Secure Mail. The certificate that you have just obtained should be visible here.

On the Web there are directories of digital signatures, in which it is possible to look up the owners of various digital IDs. Try entering 'digital signature directories' into a search engine.

In order for a recipient to be able to read a message that you have sent with a digital certificate, they also have to have a copy of it. This can be achieved by sending them an email with the certificate attached. They can then save the certificate, by adding it to their address book, so that the next time you send them a message, they will be able to verify that it is from you.

To attach a digital certificate to an email message:

1. Select Tools>Options>Security from the menu bar and check on the Digitally sign all outgoing messages box if you want a digital signature to be used by default. Or open a new message, compose it and select the Sign button on the new message toolbar. This will only add a digital signature to this message.

Encryption

Encryption is similar to using a digital signature, except that you need to have the recipient's digital certificate as well as giving them yours. Encryption is a form of code: it works by using a secret key to encode a message. The message is then sent with the key, for the recipient to unlock the code. Each person has to have the other's digital certificate because this is where the encryption keys are held. This type of communication is useful if you are dealing in highly sensitive material, but for the average user it is probably more trouble than it is worth. As with digital signing, encryption can be applied to all messages by default by selecting Tools>Options>Security from the main menu bar and then checking on the Encrypt contents and attachments for all outgoing messages box. Alternatively, select the Encrypt button on the new message toolbar.

Including Attachments

The technical side of attachments

One of the greatest advances in the development of email has been the ability to send additional documents with the plain email text. These are known as attachments and they have expanded the possibilities for using email considerably. For the user this appears to be an effortless process: they click a button, select a file to be attached, click OK and the email is ready to be sent, complete with the attachment, which could be anything from a digital image to a multimedia slideshow. However, the technical side behind this quick and painless operation is considerably more complex.

The benefits of attachments

Using attachments rather than just plain text email is a bit like having access to colour television after years of watching a black and white set, only better. Email attachments open up a whole new world for both the personal and the business email user:

- Family photographs can be emailed around the world in a few minutes or seconds. This way family events can be shown almost as they happen: no more having to wait several days for relatives in Australia to see the latest addition to the family or Christmas and birthday celebrations. All that is needed is a digital camera and a scanner and the images can be captured, downloaded into the computer and then attached to an email. The results are not only quick, but also highly effective.

- Animated cards and greetings can be sent as attachments for special occasions. This can be done by creating a file in a presentation program, such as Microsoft PowerPoint (*www.microsoft.com/*) or the animation program Macromedia Flash (*www.macromedia.com/*), and then sending it to the recipient. In some cases this is done as a file associated with the program in which it was created and in others a stand-alone, executable program is created which can be viewed on any computer.

If you are using a program such as Flash, make sure the recipient has the required Player to view the file. Alternatively, save the file as a program file i.e. an 'exe' file.

- Musicians can share their music even if they are hundreds, or thousands, of miles apart. Most modern computers have sound recording programs and although they are fairly basic they are still good enough to record sound files of an acceptable quality for general use. For musicians who require a higher quality of sound reproduction, there are more advanced sound recording programs available on the market. Sound files can also be used to attach a variety of other items to emails, such as sound effects.
- Video clips. For the camcorder enthusiast, video clips can also be attached to emails, providing they are recorded on a digital video or your computer has the necessary software to download video from a conventional camcorder. This adds an extra dimension to family events, but video clips can create extremely large files, which then take

a long time to send and receive. Brevity is the keyword when using video clips.

- Email attachments are ideal for people who want to send long business documents, written in a program such as Microsoft Word. Since word-processed documents take up a lot less space than image, sound or video files, it is perfectly feasible to attach a report or memo that is dozens of pages in length. This can then be emailed to an office that is situated in a completely different geographical location. This has the advantage that it is immediate, which can be a major consideration in the breakneck world of business, and the whole process can be completed without printing out a single sheet of paper.

- Businessmen such as architects and engineers can use image attachments to quickly solve on-the-job problems. For instance, if a piece of building work runs into problems because of a defect in a piece of material, a digital image of it can be captured that can then be emailed to head office to see if they can solve the problem. If necessary, the client could then be alerted to the situation using the same image. This type of instant diagnosis can also be useful for hardware problems within the computer industry when a software engineer may need to see an image of a motherboard, or a similar piece of equipment, to assess the fault. This type of use for emails and attachments has given new meaning to the phrase 'a mobile workforce'.

If you are sending attachments such as digital photographs, make sure the originals are the best picture quality possible and the smallest file size. Otherwise it could be a waste of effort and downloading time for the recipient.

Using attachments carefully

While the benefits of using attachments are clear there is a certain amount of care and attention that should go into their use. This includes issues such as file size, program compatibility and the transmission of viruses. These can apply to the person who is receiving the email and also, for some issues, the company hosting your email account.

Size issues

One of the most important issues for delivery of items over the Internet is the size of the files that are being transmitted. This affects Web pages, particularly if they are rich in multimedia content, and also emails. All data transmitted over the Internet is done so via cables, which can only carry so much information at a time. This is known as bandwidth and it is an area that telecommunications and Internet companies are constantly trying to improve, so more data can be fed through the cables at the same time. This is essential to the Internet, particularly at a time when there is an increasing array of data types that can be transmitted and the users are demanding ever more sophisticated multimedia effects. However, this comes at a cost: the more content there is in a file then the bigger it becomes. This then takes longer to transmit over the Internet (either over the Web or in an email) and so the recipient may get bored and lose interest. For Web page designers it is a constant battle to create increasingly complex pages while still maintaining an acceptable downloading time (in the high speed world of the Internet this is measured in seconds).

Virtually any computer file can be attached to an email, but this should only be done if the process is going to be of benefit to both parties involved.

The size of files being transmitted is measured in bytes, kilobytes and megabytes. (The next range is gigabytes, but anything this large would bring most Internet servers to a grinding halt.) In general, anything over a megabyte (MB) in size is regarded as being a liability on the Internet in terms of downloading time. This does not mean that files of this size cannot be used, but users should be well aware that the larger the file size, the longer it will take to download.

Size issues are just as important for emails as they are for Web pages on the Internet. In some ways they are more important because an email, and any attachments, has to be downloaded completely before it can be accessed, whereas Web pages can deploy certain technologies that allow the user to view at least part of a page before the whole thing has been downloaded. Also, when you send an email it will take a similar time to send as it will to download at the other end. So if you are worried about being online for too long then it is best not to create email with enormous attachments.

If an email consists of plain text and no attachments then the file size will only be a few kilobytes (KB) and this will only take a few seconds to send and receive, which is perfectly acceptable to all concerned. However, if attachments are added then this could increase the size of the overall message considerably.

If emails and their attachments are too large, some mail servers will 'time-out' which means they will stop sending a message if it takes too long to download.

Program compatibility issues

When creating attachments there are dozens of different programs that can be used for each item, whether it is a word-processed document, an image or a sound file. This is good news for the user who is creating the attachment file because it means they have a selection of tools at their disposal and they can use their favourite program for the relevant medium in which they are working. However, there is an important consideration to bear in mind when using programs to create attachments:

- The recipient of the file has to be able to read it i.e. they must have the program which created it, or at least a compatible one.
- The issue of compatibility is an important one because it can waste a lot of time and cause considerable frustration if someone receives an attachment and then finds that he cannot open it. One way to avoid this is to contact the recipient first and ask them if they can access files created in a particular program (such as PowerPoint).

Other issues that should be kept in mind when considering compatibility are:

- Not everyone will have the same version of the program in which an attachment is created. For instance, if you are using the latest version of a word processing program, such as Word, then people with earlier version will not be able to open these files. In most programs it is possible to select options when a document is saved that allow a file to be read by an earlier version of the program. So if a document was created in the latest version of Word and you suspect the recipient only has Word 6/95, this can be selected when the file is saved. (Double-check this when the file is saved for the final time by selecting Save As and choosing the relevant version in the Save As Type box.) The important fact to remember about program versions is that a program can convert files that have been created in an earlier version of the software. However, older versions of a program cannot open files created on a more recent version of the software. If in doubt, save the file using the earliest possible option in the Save As Type dialog box.

If you are unsure about whether someone has a compatible program to the one in which you have created an attachment, check with them first.

- Not everyone uses the same programs. Just because someone is a fan of a particular program, it does not mean everyone else is. Also, just because the majority of computer users create their documents using Microsoft software, this does not mean you can automatically presume that everyone will be able to view your Microsoft-produced documents. There is a vast diversity of software on the market, if you are prepared to look hard enough, and there are always users who are prepared to swim against the tide.
- Not everyone uses the same type of computers. While IBM compatible PCs dominate the world market there is still a sizeable population that use Apple Macintosh. This group is currently increasing in size, thanks to the popularity of the iMac and iBook ranges and a general resurgence in Apple's fortunes in the personal computer market. The significance of this is that Mac computers have their own operating system, which is not compatible with the one that runs on the vast majority of PCs i.e. Windows. Therefore if a file has been created on a Mac, there is a good chance that it will not be able to be read on a PC (unless it is converted

into a suitable format). There are a few exceptions to this, most notably for image files, but it should be kept in mind if attachments are going to be sent from a Mac to a PC.

Transmission of viruses

If there is one thing that is guaranteed to strike fear into any computer user who is involved with the Web and email it is the thought of contracting a virus. A computer virus is a small program that is designed to conduct a task of a destructive nature once it has been activated. They are typically created by male computer enthusiasts in their mid-twenties, for no better reason than to prove they can do it. However, the results can be devastating in terms of computer downtime and corrupted data. Viruses can be embedded into large pieces of software or they can be transmitted via email. The latter is becoming an increasingly popular method of distribution for cyber-vandals because of the speed at which the virus can be spread, as was demonstrated with two of the most destructive viruses to date: Melissa and the Love Bug. When these viruses were activated they then automatically sent themselves to all of the addresses in the recipient's address book and continued in this fashion until there were so many emails being sent around the world that a large number of email servers could not cope with the volume of traffic and so had to be temporarily closed down. In addition, the Love Bug also had a destructive capability in that it could erase some types of files (mainly image files and audio files) from the hard drive of the recipient's computer and, following its first incarnation, it mutated into similar, but more powerful, viruses.

If you are sent an email from an unknown source and it has an attachment, delete the whole message immediately without even opening it. Never open the attachment.

The threat of viruses being sent by email is one that is being taken very seriously by governments around the world, particularly as one virus can be distributed on a global basis and cause billions of pounds worth of damage. Despite this doom and gloom, there is some good news on the email virus front for the home user:

- If ISPs are alerted to a new virus being in operation they can sometimes put filters in place to stop them entering their email systems. However, cyber-vandals are usually at least one step ahead of the authorities and viruses have often spread before people are really aware of their existence.

- Email viruses are invariably sent contained in attachments that accompany emails; they are not in the body of the email itself. Therefore if you receive an email with no attachment, you can be reasonably sure that it will not contain a virus. This may change as the virus authors develop new techniques but, at present, an attachment-free email can be considered to be as virus free as any item on the Internet.

- Viruses in attachments are only activated if the attachment is opened. Therefore, if you are in any doubt about the source of an email with an attachment, do not open the attachment. Opening the email itself should not cause any harm but if you open the attachment, any viruses it contains will be activated and installed on your hard drive. If you do not trust an attachment, delete it by selecting the email and selecting Delete from the toolbar.

Check the Web sites of your ISP and major search engines, such as Yahoo, for the latest news about any current viruses that have been unleashed recently.

Types of attachments

Program files

Files created in common software packages such as Word, Excel and PowerPoint are frequently used as attachments, particularly in the business world. This is because it is a quick way of sharing information without having to reformat it and it offers more flexibility if it is in a digital format rather than a hard copy as would be the case if the document had been faxed. The main points to remember here are the ones mentioned earlier:

- Make sure the person receiving the file has the same program as the one in which the file was created (or at least a compatible one). If in doubt, use the Save As option to save the file in the earliest possible version of the program.
- Bear in mind the size of the file and the downloading time. Even in the business world this can be an issue if a file is unusually large. It is always a good idea to check with the IT department if you are unsure about the guidelines for sending attachments via external email.

Images files

Image files, i.e. digital photographs or graphics, are among the most popular, and the most versatile for sending as attachments via email The main reasons for this are:

- Images can be created in formats that can easily be shared and viewed via Internet browsers and they are also more compatible with different operating systems, such as Windows and the Mac. Therefore you do not have to worry so much about the recipient being able to view your priceless images. The two most common formats that are used for sending and viewing images on the Internet are JPEG (which stands for Joint Photographic Experts Group) and GIF (which stands for Graphical Interchange Format). These are not only used to display images and graphics on Web pages but they can also be used when sending images as email attachments. JPEG images can display up to 16 million colours and so they are more commonly used for photographic images. GIFs display 256 colours and they are better for graphics with solid colour such as logos. However, GIFs can also be used for photographs and the difference in quality between the two formats is not as great as the disparity in the number of colours they can display may suggest.

- Image files can be compressed so that they create relatively small file sizes that still retain good image quality.

There are dozens of different file formats for digital images. These are known as bitmap images because they are created by using millions of tiny coloured dots to make up the picture. Each dot contains important colour information relating to the overall image and this is known as the resolution of the image. The more dots in an image then the higher the resolution and the larger the file size. Image resolution is a vital consideration when dealing with digital images. Although JPEGs and GIFs are the formats used for display on the Web this does not mean you have to be restricted to these formats when you are emailing images. The format that is used may depend on what the image is going to be used for.

There are several ways to capture images in a digital format:

A digital camera

These look like conventional cameras but they are becoming increasingly popular because they do not require any film or developing and the images can be downloaded directly onto a computer and then manipulated as required.

The images are captured by the camera onto a memory card, which is inserted into the camera and is about a quarter of the size of a standard floppy disc. These are available in a variety of capacity sizes, ranging from 4 MB to 64 MB, and in some cases even higher. Images can be captured at different resolution settings and this affects the number of images that can be stored on a card at one time. At the lowest setting a 16 MB memory card can hold approximately 120 images, depending on the type of camera. Once the images have been downloaded from the memory card, it can be wiped clean and then reused a limitless number of times.

Another advantage of digital cameras is that they have a display panel (an LCD panel) at the back that allows you see the image immediately after it has been captured. If you do not like it, you can delete it and take another one. This way, you are not left with dozen of images that are unusable.

The most important element of digital cameras is the resolution at which they can capture images i.e. how many pixels (coloured dots) that make up the picture. The greater the number of pixels then the higher the resolution, resulting in a higher quality image. So while most users strive for as high a resolution as possible there is a downside to this. The cameras that capture the highest resolution images are more expensive than their lower resolution counterparts, and high-resolution images create much larger files.

For a detailed look at digital photography and associated issues, have a look at Digital Photography in easy steps.

The resolution of a digital image is measured in dots per inch (dpi) and for a good quality printed image it should be in the region of approximately 300 dpi, which will allow it to be printed at a good quality and a reasonable size (e.g. 10 inches by 8 inches). The trade-off for this level of quality is that an image at 300 dpi will create a large file. However, if you want to use images solely for distribution and viewing over the Internet then you can capture them at a resolution as low as 72 dpi and still be confident that they will be viewed at a high quality. The reason for this is that most computer monitors can only display 72 dpi and so anything higher than this makes little difference to the final output. Therefore if you are capturing an image that will be emailed and then viewed on a computer it is perfectly acceptable to use the lowest setting on your camera. This will create a file that is small enough to attach to an email and, as long as the recipient only views it on their computer, it will be of a high enough quality for the use it was intended for. However, there is always the possibility that the recipient will also want to print the image. If this is the case then a lower resolution image will not print as clearly as a high resolution one. This is particularly noticeable if the image is enlarged when it is printed: a low-resolution image may look ragged as the individual pixels become visible. This is known as a pixelated image and it can also occur if an image is enlarged on screen.

Once a digital image has been captured there are several things that can be done to it before it is attached to an email and sent into the wide blue yonder:

- Basic editing tasks can be performed on it. These include adjusting the colour, the contrast, the hue, the saturation and the colour balance. This is done with an image-editing program and some of these have a function for adjusting all of the colour attributes of an image in a single operation. Another option is to adjust each element individually. The instant fix is the quickest way to edit the colour in an image and although it can, at times, produce effective results, using the individual method can create a better end product. Getting the colour adjustments spot on is a technique that takes patience and a certain degree of trial and error. When viewing images for editing, make sure your monitor is set to view the highest number of colours possible (usually up to 16 million). This will give the best colour representation of your image. It is also worth suggesting to anyone who is going to be viewing your images to adjust their monitor to the same setting. Even if this is done, the images may still look slightly different on the recipient's computer because monitors all differ slightly in their colour reproduction, in much the same way as one television monitor differs from another.

When you start editing images, make a copy of each one first by using the Save As command. Then, if you do make a mess of things, you still have the image in its original state.

- Cropping and sizing. All image-editing packages have facilities for cropping an image, i.e. deleting areas around the edges that detract from the overall image, and sizing it to make it larger or smaller. This can have a significant effect on the framing of an image and it provides a versatility that was only previously available to professional photographers.
- Simple touch-up techniques. These include removing red-eye, covering scratches and small blemishes on an image and even removing wrinkles and bags under people's eyes.

- Major touch-up techniques. These include removing entire people and objects from an image and then filing in the space to make it appear as if they were never there, or repairing old and damaged images. This type of editing is done by cloning one area of an image over another and although it can take a bit of experimenting to perfect this technique, it can dramatically alter the way images look. Because of features like this, images that have come from a digital source should always be treated with a certain amount of circumspection – what you see is not necessarily how the scene was when the image was captured.

- Special effects. Most image editing programs have a range of special effects, or filters, that can be applied to an image. These include distorting, embossing, blurring, sharpening, charcoal effect and changing the perspective. These techniques can also be used to create collages with two or more images.

Use special effects sparingly. If you scatter them around like confetti then their impact will be lost and people will begin to find them irritating.

There are numerous image-editing programs on the market and some of them are:

- Adobe Photoshop. This is the market leader in the image editing market and it contains all of the required features for performing even the most complicated editing tasks, and more besides. It is generally used by commercial designers and photographers but it is also popular with the home user. There is a full package on the market and also a Limited Edition (LE) version that costs approximately £99 and is still a very powerful program. The one drawback with Photoshop is that it may be a bit daunting for someone who does not have any experience of image editing programs: the user interface presumes a certain amount of prior knowledge. Further information about Photoshop

can be obtained from the Adobe Web site at *www.adobe.com/* where
it can be ordered or a review copy downloaded.

- Adobe PhotoDeluxe. This is the consumer version of Photoshop and
  while it contains some of the same editing features as its more powerful
  stable-mate, it has a much easier interface in that there are icon based
  menus that guide the user through all of the processes required to edit
  and amend an image. PhotoDeluxe also concentrates on special effects
  and the uses to which digital images can be put, such as being inserted
  into cards, calendars or put onto mugs or T-shirts. In addition, the
  latest version of PhotoDeluxe comes bundled with another program,
  ActiveShare. This can also be used as an image editing program but it
  also allows for images to be stored and sorted in digital photograph
  albums. But perhaps the best use for ActiveShare is the facilities for
  placing images on a shared album on the Web. People can then be

invited to view these images by sending them an email. It is also possible to email images to people by clicking on a button within ActiveShare. PhotoDeluxe costs approximately £39 and further information about the program can be obtained from Adobe as earlier. The Web site also contains information about ActiveShare, or their Web site can be visited at *www.activeshare.com/*

- Paint Shop Pro. This is an efficient and versatile program that bridges the gap between the consumer and the commercial user. It has a similar range of features to the Adobe products and it excels at converting image files into different formats. A shareware version of Paint Shop Pro can be downloaded from the Web site at *www.jasc.com/* and the full version costs approximately £80.

Paint Shop Pro is an excellent program for converting images from one format to another. Other programs do this too but Paint Shop Pro is one of the most efficient at it.

- Ulead PhotoExpress. This is similar to PhotoDeluxe in its look and feel. There is plenty of help in guiding the user through the editing tasks and there are also numerous projects into which images can be inserted. As with ActiveShare, it also has an email link by which images can automatically be attached to an email message. The commercial version of PhotoExpress is Ulead PhotoImpact and further details of both of these can be found at the Web site at *www.ulead.com/*
- Microsoft PhotoDraw. This comes packaged with Office 2000 and is designed to be easily integrated with the other Microsoft products in

this suite. If you are a fan of Microsoft then PhotoDraw is a worthwhile choice, particularly as the user interface will look very familiar.

Digital photography is a fast growing area and one that has considerable potential for people who want to attach their images to emails. For more information about this area look at the following Web sites:

- Kodak: *www.kodak.com/* One of the market leaders in digital imaging equipment and imaging services.

- Hewlett Packard: *www.hp.com/* Heavily involved in the digital imaging market. They also specialise in colour ink jet printers for outputting images.
- Canon: *www.canon.com/* A camera-making specialist that is investing heavily in the digital market.
- Nikon: *www.nikon.com/* Another camera maker that has realised the importance of addressing the digital market.

Scanners

If you do not have the money or the inclination to invest in a digital camera then a good alternative could be to buy a scanner. This can be used to convert your existing photographs into digital images that can then be used in the same way as any that are taken with a digital camera. Scanners have plummeted in price in recent years and it is now possible to buy then from £50 upwards. Many computer retailers even include them in a package with a PC and if you have a lot of photographs that you want to convert then it is a useful option.

As with all types of technology there are a vast number of scanners on the market and the two most important things to remember are:

- Make sure the scanner comes with TWAIN compliant software. This is just a fancy way of saying that your computer, (and any image editing programs you are using) and your scanner will be able to communicate with each other. This should come with the scanner in the form of a CD-ROM that will install the necessary software (drivers).

- Decide what type of scanner you require i.e. what you want it for and how sophisticated it has to be. Once you have done this do not let any sales staff try and persuade you that you require a more advanced, and more expensive, model.

The most common type of scanner on the market is the flatbed variety. This looks and operates a bit like a photocopier: the item to be scanned is placed on a glass plate and then a light source is passed over it and the reflective image is captured on a chip called a Charge Coupled Device (CCD). As with a digital camera, the resolution of a scanned image is measured in dots per inch and this can be adjusted with the scanning software or later in an image-editing program. Flatbed scanners are cheap and robust and they produce excellent digital images.

A slightly more versatile type of scanner is the sheet feed model. This can be used in the same way as a flatbed scanner but it can also have several pages fed into it at a time, in a similar fashion to a fax machine. For the 35mm film enthusiast adapters can be attached to scanners so that transparencies can be converted into a digital format. This produces images of excellent clarity but scanners that have this facility are usually more expensive.

Once images have been captured by a scanner they can then be edited in an image editing program and then put to a variety of uses, including being attached to an email

Photo CDs

An increasingly popular option for obtaining digital images is to have them produced from traditional film at the same time as hard copy prints are being made. Therefore, when you get your pictures back you will have the regular prints and also a CD ROM containing all of the images. This additional service is not expensive and it costs approximately £3 more than just getting hard copy prints. This produces high quality images that can be attached to an email directly from the CD ROM.

Portable Document Format (pdf)

PDF is a file format that has been developed by Adobe for storing and transferring documents electronically. It is a platform independent system, which means the files can be opened on virtually any computer. The main feature of PDF files is that they retain the formatting and design of the original document, including fonts and graphics. This means that a document that has been created in a word processing or a desktop publishing program can be converted to PDF and it will still look exactly the same. This makes PDF ideal for transferring documents that have to retain their formatting, such as newsletters or brochures.

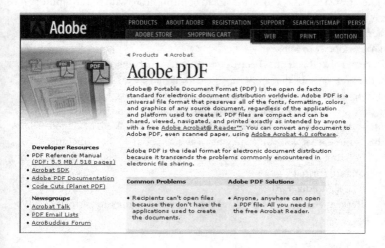

To create PDF files you require a program called Adobe Acrobat which can be used to convert files created in other programs into PDF format at the touch, or two, of a button. This is a powerful piece of software that can convert files from most popular software packages and also includes additional functionality such as hypertext links.

However, not everyone will want to buy Acrobat to create his or her own PDF files. Despite this it is still an area that is worthy of consideration when you are dealing with email and attachments. An increasing number of Web sites are now using PDF files to display documents that require to have their original formatting retained. This is done by linking directly to the PDF file rather than an HTML one. The user can then view the file, providing they have a plug-in to do so. A plug-in is a small helper program that enables a computer or a browser to view files that it could not otherwise open. In some ways a plug-in is like a translator as it allows the file to communicate with the computer on which it is situated. The plug-in to view PDF files is called Adobe Acrobat Reader. It is free of charge and can be downloaded from the Web at:

www.adobe.com/acrobat

Once Acrobat Reader has been downloaded, it can be used to view PDF files from the Web or ones that are sent via email. When a PDF file is accessed, the Reader opens it automatically and it should be a seamless operation.

As far as using PDF files as email attachments is concerned, they are an excellent device for sending items that you find on the Web, or obtain from another source, that you think may be of use to people. These include:

- Product brochures, which can be sent in their original glossy, high quality format.
- Maps and diagrams.
- Reports that require to retain their original, professional format.

Although PDF is a versatile and effective way for distributing documents as email attachments there are a couple of points that should be kept in mind:

- The recipient will have to have Acrobat Reader installed on their computer in order to be able to open the PDF file that they have been sent. If they do not have it then they may not be aware that it can be downloaded free of charge. Therefore, whenever you send a PDF file as an attachment, include a note about the Reader and how it can be downloaded from the Adobe site. Better still, include the following link to the Adobe Web site (*www.adobe.com/acrobat*). This way the recipient of the email will be able to click on the link in the email and they will be taken directly to the Adobe site, where they can download the Reader. This is an excellent way of directing people to specific Web sites by using links in an email.

- Due to their high level of formatting, PDF files can be fairly large in size. Keep this in mind if you are attaching long PDF files since downloading time could become an issue.

PDF files should be used if you want to send someone a file so that they can print out an exact copy of the original document.

If you are sending a PDF file as an attachment, include the link to the Adobe Web site so that the recipient can download Acrobat Reader if they do not already have it.

Saving attachments

As well as sending files attached to emails, most email users will receive a variety of attachments in their Inbox. The first thing to do with these is to make sure that they come from a trusted source and to try and ensure that they do not contain any viruses. This is sometimes easier said than done, since even if you know the person who has sent the email this is not to say that the attachment did not contain a virus before they attached it. With some viruses, particularly if they have not been activated, it is very hard to detect their presence before they begin their destructive work. One way to identify incoming viruses is to install a robust virus checker, such as Dr. Solomon or Norton's. Even with this form of protection, there is no guarantee that all viruses will be prevented from reaching your computer. Although the virus checkers are being updated virtually constantly, the virus authors are usually a few steps ahead so it is an ongoing battle. As a general rule: if you are unsure about an email attachment, do not open it and delete the whole email from your system.

For a full list of resources about email viruses and general email security, see the 'Security and Viruses' chapter.

If you are as confident as you can be that an attachment has come from a trusted source and does not contain a virus, then you can open it.

Files that are attached to an email do not have to remain there: they can be saved to a location on your computer or a form of removable storage such as a floppy disc or a Zip disc. Of these two, a floppy disc can be used if the attachment is something like a word processed file or a file that does not take up too much room. This is because the capacity of a floppy disc is only 1.4 MB and if you want to save a lot of large video or sound files to this, there may not be enough space.

Zip discs are like super-floppy discs. They are slightly bigger and thicker and they can hold considerably more data with the two standard sizes being 100 MB and 250 MB. (Some discs of this type are currently capable of holding a massive 1 gigabyte (GB) of data.) Zip discs have to be used in a Zip drive that is specifically designed for this purpose. These come as either internal or external devices: an external Zip drive is connected to the computer with cable and the internal one fits into the body of your hard drive. If you are experienced at fitting internal items such as CD-ROM drives or internal modems then it should be possible to fit an internal Zip drive yourself. If the inside of your CPU is all a bit of a mystery, then use an external drive or get a professional computer retailer to insert an internal one. If you are using an external Zip drive, try and get one with a USB connection, if your computer supports it. This stands for Universal Serial Bus and is a new standard for transfer of data from a cable into a computer. It is much faster than the traditional parallel port cable and it will save a lot of time if you are regularly saving data onto a Zip disc. A USB cable can be identified because one of its connections is a flat, thin rectangle.

Zip discs are also a good way to back up your old email messages, as well as attachments. This will provide you with an archive copy if you want to have a record of your messages and also free up some space on your hard drive.

When you have decided how you want to save attachments which you receive in emails, you can then do this:

1. Select the email that contains the attachment by clicking on it once in the Inbox, or open it up so the content is visible. Depending on the version of your program, the attachment will appear in a box under the addressee information or as an icon somewhere in the body of the email. The icon will denote what file type the attachment is.

Or:

2. Select File>Save Attachments from the menu bar. (This is the same command regardless of how you access the email with the attachment. However, if you select it in the Inbox there will be an option from the Save Attachments menu that shows the file that is selected. Click on this to continue.)

3. In the Save Attachment dialog box, navigate to the location on your computer, or the drive containing your removable storage.

4. Select the exact folder where you want the file saved to and select Save.

5. Check that the file has been saved into the right folder. (In Windows, use Windows Explorer or File Manager; on a Mac use Finder.)

Do not use the Save As command to try and save an attachment as this will only save the email message itself and not the attachment.

More than one attachment can be saved at a time, but all of the selected items have to be saved in the same location. To do this:

1. Select or open a message and select Save Attachments as above.
2. If there is more than one attachment with the email, they will all be listed in the Save All Attachments box. If all of the files are not selected, do so by clicking on one and then holding down Control and clicking on the others.
3. Select OK and save the attachments into the right location, as above.

It has been known for attachments to become scrambled during the send and receive process. If this happens, politely ask the sender if they can repeat the process.

Printing attachments

It is possible to print attachments once they have been saved to the hard drive, or the selected format of removable storage, in the same way as printing any other document. However, it is also possible to print them directly from the email in the Inbox. This is a quicker method but it does not allow you the opportunity to open the file and perform any editing task that may be required i.e. cropping an image or improving its colour. To print an attachment directly from the email in which it was received:

1. Select the email in the Inbox or open it so the attached file is visible.
2. Select File>Print from the menu bar. (Select Print Preview to preview how the email message itself will print, but not the attachment.)
3. In the Print dialog box, select the target printer in the Printer Name box.
4. In the Print style box select the Memo Style option.
5. In the Print options box check on the Print attached files with item(s).
6. Select the Define Styles button to access print options for the attachment. In the Define Print Styles dialog box select Edit for the options. These include: Format, which defines the format in which the attachment will be printed i.e. memo or table; Paper, which defines the paper size, the paper source, the print margins (the area on the paper that will not be printed on) and the orientation, which can be either portrait or landscape; and Header and Footer, which can be used to insert information that prints at the top and bottom of every page. Select OK once these options have been set and Close to exit from the Define Print Styles dialog box.
7. Select OK to print the email message and any attachments that are with it.

Attachments can also be printed in the same way as any other file. First save them as above and then open and print them as normal.

Organising Emails

Reasons for organising

When you get connected to the Internet and start sending and receiving emails, you may think that you will never get enough incoming messages to worry about organising them into separate folders in your program. However, it is surprising how quickly email traffic can build up and you may soon find you are receiving messages from a variety of different sources. These could include:

- Your children
- Your parents
- Friends
- Work colleagues
- Business associates
- Marketing emails from companies that you have done business with on the Web

Some of these messages may be trivial and so they can be deleted. Others may be more important, or it could be that you just do not like throwing things away. Therefore you will want to store all of these messages somewhere. Since most emails are not very large in terms of file size, this is not a problem and it is not uncommon for people to have hundreds of emails stored on their computer. However, if it gets to this stage then perhaps it is time for a little spring-cleaning. Emails can be organised through the use of folders. There are some folders that have already been created in Outlook Express, but there is plenty of scope for adding new ones and moving emails around within the program.

Folders

Folders within Outlook Express are just like electronic versions of paper or cardboard folders that most people use to store things at home or work, whether it is household bills, bank statements or old press cuttings. In an email program, folders can perform similar tasks, except they store electronic data in the form of messages and their attachments. The folders in Outlook Express are displayed in the Folder List at the left-hand side of the screen. If this is not visible:

1. Select View>Layout from the menu bar.
2. Click on the box next to Folder List so there is a black dot in it.

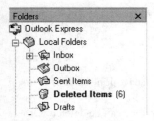

In Outlook Express, there are five folders that are pre-inserted into the folders list. These are located as sub-folders of the main Local Folders box and they are:

- Inbox. This is where incoming emails are placed.
- Outbox. This is where outgoing emails are placed before they are sent to their destination.
- Sent Items. This contains details of emails that have been sent, including a copy of the message.

- Deleted Items. This contains emails that have been deleted from the Inbox or another folder within the program. At this point the messages here have not been deleted from the system, they have only been removed from their original location. To delete a message permanently, it has to also be deleted from this folder. Therefore the Deleted Items folder acts as a safety net so you do not remove important messages by mistake.
- Drafts. This is where unfinished emails are stored or ones that you want to send at a later date.

Emails can be moved freely between these five folders but, unlike folders you add yourself, none of these can be renamed or deleted. In this respect they are one of the few things that cannot be changed in the program.

Look through all of your folders regularly and delete any items that you no longer need. This will ensure that your hard drive does not get clogged up with unneeded messages.

Folder notation

The folder system in Outlook Express is very similar to that of the structure of folders and documents in Windows Explorer. The main features of this are:

- A folder system is a hierarchical one: there can numerous levels of sub-folders coming from one main folder.
- If a folder has a plus sign in a box at the left hand side of it, this indicates that there is at least one level of sub-folders linked to it.
- Click once on a cross to view the next sub-level. This will be displayed in the Folder List, directly below the main folder.

- If you click on the folder name, rather than the plus sign, the content of the folder will be displayed in the main window rather than in the Folder List.
- Once a folder has been expanded fully, this is indicated by a minus sign in a box next to it.
- Click once on the minus sign to contract the folder so that only the selected level is visible.
- If there are unopened items in a folder, this is indicated by a blue number in brackets after the folder name.

Creating folders

It is possible to create new folders and sub-folders anywhere within the structure of your email program. Each folder can have numerous sub-folders in theory, but in practice it is best to limit the number of sub-folders to a maximum of three or four. If there are more than this, it may be difficult to remember exactly where you placed certain items within the structure.

Before you begin creating folders and sub-folders, it is worth doing a rough sketch of how you want your folder structure to look. While this is not essential, it can save a certain amount of renaming and moving once the folders have been created. So if you are creating a folder structure for family emails, you many want to create a main folder entitled something like 'General family' and then create sub-folders for each individual family member and maybe one for special occasions. Then, if required, you can create sub-folders for each person in the structure.

The first step to creating a new folder is to select the point at which you want it to appear. This is done within the Folder List window. The item at the top of this list is entitled Outlook Express and this only contains general information about the program and the current status of your Inbox and your Newsgroup messages. Double click on it to view its contents in the main window. Double click again to view the full contents of the Folder List. The first item to which new folders can be added is the Local Folders folder. Either click on this once or select another folder within the structure. To add a new folder:

1. With a folder selected, click on File>New>Folder on the menu bar. (The new folder will be connected to the selected item, and in effect become a sub-folder of it.) This can also be achieved by right clicking on the selected folder.

2. In the Create Folder dialog box, type a name for the new folder.

3. If you decide that you want to place this folder in a different location, you can change this in the Create Folder dialog box also, before the operation has been completed. Do this by choosing a new location in the bottom window of the dialog box.

4. Select OK to place the new folder into your structure.

Deleting folders

If you realise you have created a folder you do not want or if, in time, you find you are not using it, then it is possible to delete the item from your structure. This can be a good way of stopping your structure becoming a rambling collection of files and it is good email housekeeping to review your folder structure approximately every six months, to weed out unwanted items. However, before you delete a folder, make sure it does not contain any messages that may be of use. To delete a folder:

1. Select the item you want to delete by clicking on it once.
2. Select File>Folder>Delete from the menu bar, or right click and select Delete from the contextual menu.
3. A warning message will appear, asking if you want to move the selected folder to the Deleted Items folder. If you do, select Yes.
4. If a folder contains sub-folders, then all of the levels up to the top one, i.e. the one that is selected, will be moved to the Deleted Items folder.

To remove a folder permanently:

1. Select the folder in the Deleted items folder.
2. Delete the folder using one of the methods in Step 2 above.
3. Once the delete operation has been initiated a warning box will appear asking if you are sure that you want to permanently delete this item. It will also inform you that this action cannot be undone. Make sure that this is what you want to do and, if it is, select Yes.

Always double check that there is nothing you need in a folder you are deleting. If in doubt, save it to a floppy disc or a Zip disc.

Renaming folders

Apart from the five system folders (Inbox, Outbox, Sent Items, Deleted Items and Drafts) no folder name is set in stone and it possible to change them whenever you want. This could be because you have another folder with a similar name or that you find one item does not adequately describe the use to which the folder is put. To rename a folder:

1. Select the folder to be renamed.
2. Select File>Folder>Rename from the menu bar or right click and select Rename from the contextual menu.
3. In the Rename Folder dialog box, type a new name for the folder.
4. Select OK.

Or:

1. If it is the first time a folder has been given a unique name i.e. it is currently called Folder 1 or something similar, click on the folder name once and then click again about a second later. The folder name should become highlighted in blue with a black border around it. Overtype the new name.

Folders can be renamed as many times as you like, but whenever you rename a folder, make sure it is a name that is relevant to the items in it. At the time of renaming you may have a clear idea of what is in the folder, but if you do not look at it for six months you may have forgotten exactly what is in there.

Give a folder at the top of a hierarchy a general name such as 'Writing' and then create and name sub-folders to contain messages relating to specific topics.

Moving folders

Folders, and their contents, can be moved to different locations within the email structure. When this is done, all messages and sub-folders within the selected items are moved too. To move a folder:

1. Select the folder to be moved by clicking on it once.
2. Select File>Folder>Move from the menu bar (there is no contextual menu available for this operation).
3. In the Move dialog box, select the new location where you want the folder to be situated. Or, select the New Folder button to create a new folder into which to move the selected one (this cannot be a sub-folder of the selected item).
4. Select OK.

Or:

1. Select the folder to be moved.
2. Click and drag it to its new location within the Folder List window. While the folder is being dragged a circle with a line through it will appear on the screen. This indicates that the folder is not positioned over a location to which it can be moved. When it is in the correct position i.e. over another folder, the circle changes to the cursor arrow and a small square with a shaded border. Release the mouse at this point and the folder will be placed in this location.

Main folders (i.e. those at the top of the hierarchy) can be moved into other folders, thereby creating a new sub-folder.

Moving, deleting and copying messages

Individual messages can be manipulated in a similar way to folders. The main difference is that, for operations such as moving, deleting and copying, more than one message can be selected at a time. (Individual messages cannot be renamed because they do not have a name in the same way as a folder does, only a Sender and Subject name.)

Use the contextual menus (right click on a message on a PC and Ctrl click on a Mac) to view shortcuts for operations relating to moving, deleting and copying messages.

To move, copy or delete multiple messages:

1. Select the first message to be edited by clicking on it once.
2. Hold down Ctrl and select all of the other required messages. (If the messages all appear consecutively the whole group can be selected by clicking on the first one, then moving to the last one on the list and selecting it while holding down Shift. This will select the first and last item and also those in between.)
3. Select Edit>Move to Folder from the menu bar, or right click Move to Folder, to move the selected messages to a new folder. Select a destination folder in the Move dialog box.
4. Select Edit>Copy to Folder from the menu bar, or right click Copy to Folder, to copy the selected messages to a new folder. Select a destination folder in the Copy dialog box.
5. Select Edit>Delete from the menu bar, or right click Delete, to send the selected messages to the Deleted items folder. (To delete all the

messages from the Deleted items folder, select Edit>Empty Deleted Items folder. A warning message will appear, asking you to confirm that you want to delete these items. If you do, select Yes.)

All of the above commands apply equally to individual messages as well as multiple ones.

Archiving or backing up

If you have a lot of email messages stored in folders within Outlook Express, you may want to store these somewhere other than on your hard disc, for safekeeping. This can be done by archiving, or backing up, your messages. These two terms are interchangeable in Outlook Express and they have the same meaning: copying your data to another location where it can be stored for safekeeping and retrieval at a later date if required. Another phrase that is sometimes used in connection with this action is compacting, since the message is compressed for storage purposes. The contents of an entire folder are compacted when the folder is backed up and it can then be copied onto a form of removable storage such as a floppy disc or a Zip disc.

To back up a folder:

1. Select the folder that you want to back up by clicking on it once in the Folders List.
2. Select File>Folders>Compact from the menu bar. This compacts the contents of the selected folder.
3. Once the folder has been compacted it can now be copied onto a removable disc.
4. To see where the backed up folder is stored on the hard drive, right click on it and select Properties from the contextual menu.
5. Make a note of the path name for the folder. This is the directory in which the folder is stored. It will probably be something along the lines of 'C:\Programs Files\Outlook Express\My Folders\Inbox.
6. Open your file management program (Windows Explorer or File Manager in Windows or Finder on a Mac) and navigate to the file location that you wrote down in the previous step.
7. Select the compacted email folder and save it to disc. (The folder will have a file extension of '–.dbx' and can be saved by clicking on it and selecting Edit>Copy from the menu bar.) Then, navigate to the removable disc, click on it and select Edit>Paste from the menu bar.

The above procedure of finding where folders are actually located on the hard drive is a good way to find out how much space your email messages are taking up. If you have been using email for several months, you may find that there are literally hundreds of items that are unnecessarily taking up valuable

When you have backed up items from your email program, keep them in a safe place, preferably away from your computer. If necessary, keep the disc in a fireproof box.

space on your hard drive. Look in the directory where your email folders are stored and check the size of each folder. Pay particular attention to the Sent Items folder. This is one that has a message added each time you send an email and it is easy to forget about the items that are stored here. Delete each unwanted item individually or delete a group by clicking on the first one and then clicking on the last one while holding down Shift. Then right click on the selected items and select Delete to remove them.

Rules for incoming email

Most people like receiving email, most of the time. However, junk email, or spam as it is known on the Internet, can be a major irritation if it is received in large quantities. It is therefore important to be able to have the option for determining which emails you allow to be downloaded into your Inbox and which ones you do not. Outlook Express has such an option and it is known as setting email rules. This allows you to set certain criteria for blocking unwanted messages and you can also specify what happens to them once they have been blocked. This is a very useful device for regulating your Inbox and deciding what you want to appear rather than giving the Internet advertisers free rein. This can also be used to block messages from specific individuals and the same types of rules can be applied to newsgroup messages.

To apply rules to incoming emails:

1. Select Tools>Message Rules>Mail from the menu bar.
2. In the Mail Rules dialog box, select New.
3. Conditions and Actions for the new rule can be specified in the New Mail Rule dialog box.
4. Select the Conditions for your rule. This allows you to specify the conditions that have to be met for the rule to be applied. Several conditions can be applied to a single rule and each rule must have at least one condition. The available conditions are:

   - Where the From line contains people. This can be used to set a condition for a specific individual if they appear in the From box in the email.
   - Where the Subject line contains specific words. This allows you to use individual words or phrases that are part of the email's subject line as the condition for the action.

ISP use their own filters to try and stop unwanted messages reaching their subscribers' mailboxes. These can be particularly useful if there is a new virus on the loose.

   - Where the message body contains specific words. This is the same as above, except the chosen words must appear in the body of the email
   - Where the To line contains people. This is the same as the first condition, except the named person has to appear in the To box in the email.

- Where the Cc line contains people. This is the same as above, except the named person has to appear in the Cc box.
- Where the message is marked as priority. This applies if the message has a red exclamation mark next to it, indicating that the sender considers his message to be especially important. Some people block these messages, on the grounds that it is not up to the sender to decide what is important to the recipient. Some email marketing companies use this technique to try and catch the user's attention, but it can be counterproductive.

Junk emailers are adept at covering their tracks and they very rarely include the actual location from where a message originates. This can make them hard to filter.

- Where the message is from the specified account. This sets conditions for all emails that come from one account. This can be used if there is more than one registered user for an account and you want to block all communication from this location.
- Where the message size is more than size. This allows you to block a message if its file size is over a certain amount. This could be because you do not want to spend a long time online, download long messages that you might not need. (For this reason, it is always a good idea, if you are sending a long email, to send a short message first, telling the recipient what you are sending, how big it is and if this is okay. This will then give then the chance to change any conditions such as this that they may have in place.)

- Where the message has an attachment. Since email viruses are frequently spread by viruses, it can a useful security measure to set a condition for all messages that contain attachments. However, this could also mean that you block items that you actually want to receive such as family photographs or electronic holiday brochures.
- Where the message is secure. This allows for actions to be set for signed or encrypted messages. Since not all conditions and actions involve blocking or deleting messages, this could involve storing all of these types of messages in a specific folder.
- For all messages. This allows you to set actions for all the messages you receive.

5. Select the Actions for your rule. This gives you a number of options for what you want to happen to an incoming message that matches one or more of the criteria in the Conditions box. Each rule can have several actions and it must have at least one. The available actions are:
   - Move it to a specified folder. This places the email in a folder within your structure that you specify, rather than automatically placing it in the Inbox.
   - Copy it to a specified folder. This is similar to the above action, except that it leaves the message in its original folder as well as placing a copy in the specified one.
   - Delete it. This deletes the message from your system.

Actions can be used to organise your messages as they are downloaded, rather than having to do this manually once they are in your Inbox.

- Forward it to people. This automatically sends it onto the specified people in your address book.

Do not use too many different colours to identify messages. This could become confusing, particularly if you do not use your email for a week or so.

- Highlight it with colour. This colours the message, to alert you to the fact that it is affected by one or more conditions. It is possible to specify the colour that is used. (See later)
- Flag it. This places a small coloured flag next to a message, to indicate it is affected by one or more conditions.
- Mark it as read. This places the message in the relevant folder, with an open envelope next to it.
- Mark the message as watched or ignored. This can be used if it is an email that links several different users. You can either choose to look at a message or ignore it.
- Stop processing more rules. This action can be used if the condition is successful in processing the incoming emails in the correct way. This stops the email program looking for any more rules following the current one. This can be used in conjunction with one or more of the above actions.
- Do not Download it from the server. This is a useful action for items that you definitely do not want anywhere near your computer, such as those that might contain viruses, or marketing material from persistent, and unwanted, companies. If you use this action, be sure that you have set the conditions so that only unwanted

email will not be downloaded and you do not inadvertently block any items that you actually want.
- Delete it from the server. This not only does not download an email, but it actively deletes it from the server. This can be used as the ultimate sanction for unwanted items.

If you want to have a general rule to deal with junk email, use the condition for the Subject line to contain specific words such as 'money' and 'free'.

6. Rule description. This is where descriptions of the selected rules and conditions are displayed. For some of these the specific criteria also have to be set. For instance, for the conditions that involve named individuals, these names have to be entered within the rule description box. So if the 'Where the From line contains people' condition has been selected, this will appear in the description box, and the words 'contain people' will be underlined. Click on the underlined words to move to the Select People dialog box. Enter the name of the people who you want to be affected by this rule, or select them using the Address book button. The actions and conditions that require values assigned to them are (including the selectable variables, all accessed by clicking on the underlined words in the rule description box):
- Where the From line contains people – enter a name or select one from the address book.
- Where the Subject line contains specific words – enter specific words or phrases.

- Where the message body contains specific words – enter specific words or phrases.
- Where the To line contains people – enter a name or select one from the address book.
- Where the Cc line contains people – enter a name or select one from the address book.
- Where the message is marked as priority – select either high priority or low priority messages.
- Where the message is from the specified account – select an email account.
- Where the message size is more than size – enter a size over which messages will not be downloaded, in kilobytes (KB).

If children are going to be accessing your email account, create a filter to try and block any messages with an adult content.

- Where the message is secure – select from signed messages or encrypted ones.
- Move it to a specified folder – select a folder in the Move dialog box.
- Copy it to a specified folder – select a folder in the Copy dialog box.
- Forward it to people – select the people that it should be forwarded to by entering their email address in the Select People dialog box, or select them by accessing their details using the Address Book button.

- Highlight it with colour – select a colour to highlight the incoming message with. The available options can be selected from a drop-down menu in the Select Colour dialog box.
- Mark the message as watched or ignored – set the state of the threaded message as Watch Message or Ignore Message in the Watch or Ignore dialog box.
- Stop processing more rules
- Do not Download it from the server. This does not have any variables, but if it is selected all of the other actions are greyed out (which means they cannot be selected). However, conditions can still be set for this action.

7. Name of the rule. This is the individual name for the set of conditions and actions that have been specified. By default the name will be something like 'New Mail Rule #1'. Highlight this by clicking and dragging over the text and then overtype it with a unique name, such as 'Unwanted offers'. Select OK.

8. Check the details in the New Mail Rule dialog box and if everything is as you want it, select OK. This set of conditions and actions should now be applied to all incoming mail.

Blocking senders

As well as setting up rules to filter your messages, it is also possible to block an individual sender. This can be done by setting conditions and actions as above but, if you know the actual sender of a message (since you have received something from them before), you can block their messages in a few steps:

1. Select the message whose sender you want to block (by clicking on it once or opening it by double clicking).

2. Select Message>Block Sender from the menu bar.

3. A warning message will appear, telling you the email address that has been added to the blocked senders list and asking if you want all of their messages that you have already to be removed from their present location. If you do, select Yes. (Senders can be blocked from both email locations and newsgroups: check on the appropriate boxes in the Blocked Sender list by selecting Tools>Message Rules>Blocked Senders List from the menu bar.)

Adding someone to the blocked senders list does not permanently prevent you from receiving email from this address, it just adds them to a list that can then be modified. To reinstate someone from the blocked senders list:

1. Select Tools>Message Rules from the menu bar.
2. Select Blocked Senders List.
3. Select the email address that you want to reinstate and select Remove. This will remove it from the Blocked Senders List and allow you to receive email and newsgroups messages from this destination.

Organising messages

When messages arrive in your Inbox they are, by default, organised in date order, with the most recently received message appearing at the bottom of the list. However, there are several other ways in which messages can be organised in any folder within Outlook Express. This can be useful if you have a lot of items in a folder and you want to look for specific items, such as emails with attachments or with priority flags. The options for organising emails that show by default are (these appear at the head of the relevant column):

- Priority
- Attachment
- Flag
- From

- Subject
- Received

In addition to these, the following column can be used by selecting View>Columns from the menu bar (or right clicking on the column bar and selecting Columns) and checking on any of the following options:

- Size
- Account
- Sent
- To
- Watch
- Ignore

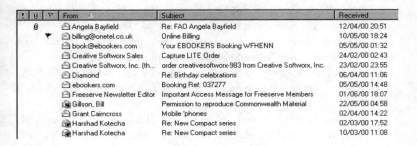

To sort messages according to these categories, click on the relevant heading at the top of the column. This will then sort your messages into alphabetical order, if the heading is one such as From or Subject, or group any of the selected objects together, such as priority tags or attachments. If you want them sorted in the opposite order i.e. descending instead of ascending, click on the column heading again. Columns can also be ordered by right clicking on the heading and selecting Sort Ascending or Sort Descending from the contextual menu.

Mailboxes

With Outlook Express it is possible for more than one person to have an email account within the same program. This is known as creating different identities, and each new one has its own mailbox, complete with password for security. This does not create a new email address; it just allows other people (or the same person under a different identity) to use the current email address. To create a new identity:

1. Select File>Identities>Add New Identity from the menu bar.
2. In the New Identity dialog box, enter the name of the person who will be using the new mailbox.
3. If you want to include a password with the new identity, select the 'Tell me more' button in the Password section. Select OK.
4. In the Enter Password dialog box, type in a password in the New Password Box and then enter it again in the Confirm New Password box. Select OK.
5. You will be returned to the New Identity dialog box again. Select OK.
6. The Identity Added dialog box will appear and ask if you want to switch to the identity that has just been created. Select Yes.
7. The Internet Connection Wizard will appear. Select 'Use an existing Internet mail account' to use the new identity with the existing email account. Select Next.
8. In the Confirm Setting dialog box, check on Change settings and select Next.

9. In the Your Name dialog box, enter the name of the person using the new mailbox. Otherwise it will retain the name of the account holder and this is what will appear as the name of the sender in any emails from this mailbox. Each identity can enter their own name and this does not alter the name of the main identity i.e. the account holder, although this is the actual email address that will be included with the new identities messages.

10. Leave the rest of the settings as they are, as they affect the connections to the email account.

11. In the final dialog box, select Finish.

12. If you are using another email program in addition to Outlook Express, a dialog box will appear asking you if you want to import messages and address book details from this program. Select 'Import from' or 'Do not import at this time' as required.

13. Select Finish. The new identity is now installed and can send and receive emails in the same way as the account holder.

To switch between identities:

1. Select File>Switch Identity from the menu bar.

2. In the Switch Identities dialog box, select the identity that you want to switch to and select OK.

3. If the selected identity has a password, this will need to be entered before it can be accessed.

4. The name of the new identity will be shown at the top right hand corner of the program.

5. When a different identity connects to the Internet and the account holder email server, they may be asked for a password to access the account. This will have been entered when the account was first set up and you will have to obtain it from the person who organised this.

Using a different email account with a new identity

Different identities give people a certain amount of freedom when working with email, but if they follow the earlier procedure they are still using someone else's account, even though they can send messages under their own name. One way around this is to use a different email account with the new identity. This gives the user considerably more flexibility and also their own email address to give out, instead of having to give out one that bears no resemblance to their actual name.

Email Services

Web-based email

What is a Web-based email account?

One of the drawbacks about having your own email with an Internet Service Provider (ISP) is that it is not mobile. Your account is, usually, linked to a single phone number, and it has to be accessed through this phone line. In addition, you have to register with your ISP and so you are tied to them for your email service. (It is possible to use different email programs to access your messages, but the service still comes from your ISP.) This type of email service is fine if you only ever want to access email messages from your home or work computer. However, as more users come to rely on email in their personal and working lives, they are finding that they want to be able to have access to email wherever they are, next door to where their own account is located or at the other side of the world. This is where Web-based email accounts come into play.

A Web-based email account is one that is not run by an ISP and it does not even have to have a specific email program. Instead of using a dedicated email program, the sending and receiving of messages is done through an Internet browser, such as Microsoft Explorer or Netscape Navigator. Essentially, each Web-based email provider gives its users their own page on their Web site. This is then used for the sending and receiving of messages. Each user has their own password, so they are only ones that can access the area of the site that contains their emails. This means that anyone who has a Web-based email account can access their messages from any computer that can be linked to the Internet. This has numerous advantages, the most obvious being that people can travel freely and still feel confident that their emails are within reach.

Web-based email is accessed through a Web browser rather than an email program.

Most Web-based email accounts are available free of charge and they usually contain similar functions to regular email accounts. These include:

- An address book, which enables you to store email addresses and contacts.
- Sending and receiving attachments. Web-based accounts usually allow for attachments to be sent and received, although you may need to delete some, or save them to your hard drive, if you are receiving a lot of attachments, because there could be a limit on the amount of space that your account can take up.
- Including URLs. It is possible to insert the address of a Web page into a Web-based email message. Simply type in the Web address and this should automatically be converted into a URL, i.e. a link that will take the user directly to that page once they click on it.

There are usually a few minor restrictions that are attached to Web-based email accounts. The first is the amount of information that is stored in your account. This is usually approximately 2 MB, which still leaves plenty of scope for storing messages. However, if you receive a lot of attachments it is a good idea to save these to disc periodically and then delete them from your account.

This is good practice anyway, because if you exceed your storage capacity then your account may not accept any new messages, or some may be deleted automatically by the company hosting your Web-based account.

The second restriction is if your account is inactive i.e. not used, for a period of time. This can vary, but the average is about 60 days. If this happens then your account could be marked 'inactive' which means that it will not accept any new messages and stored messages may be deleted. (This can also happen if you do not sign in to your account within approximately 2 weeks of it being set up.) Inactive accounts can be reactivated by accessing the home page of the company providing the service and signing in again using your original password. This will still function and you should be able to carry on using your account as before. With some companies, if an account is inactive for a year, it is deleted permanently.

Finding Web-based email providers

There are dozens of Web-based email providers and the place to find them, logically enough, is on the Web itself. Go to your favourite search engine on the Web and type in 'Web-based email'. You should be presented with dozens of hits, offering everything from information about what Web-based email is, to the companies themselves that offer this service. There are also sites that offer reviews of Web-based email providers and two of these to look at are:

- *www.web-email-addresses.com/*
- *www.free-email-address.com/*

You can set up as many Web-based email accounts as you like and try each one to see which you prefer.

Web-based email options

The market leader in Web-based email is Hotmail, which not only offers an email service, but also a number of additional services as well, most of which are designed to get you to buy something. This is fairly common with Web-based email sites, since the way the companies make their money is from advertisements on their site.

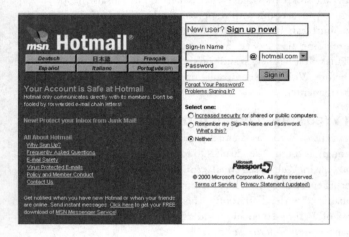

If you use Outlook Express 5 and above, you can go directly to the Hotmail Web site by selecting Tools>New Account Signup> Hotmail from the main menu bar.

However, there are numerous other providers that provide an excellent product and some of them are (in no particular order):

- *www.aol.com*
- *www.intouch-software.com*
- *www.friendlyemail.com*
- *www.mypad.com*
- *www.microsoft.com*
- *www.hotmail.com*
- *www.msn.com*
- *www.iname.com*
- *www.geocities.com*
- *www.infospace.com*
- *www.lycos.com*
- *www.netscape.com*
- *www.pathfinder.com*
- *www.switchboard.com*
- *www.juno.com*
- *www.whowhere.com*
- *www.email.com*
- *www.netaddress.com*
- *www.apexmail.com*
- *www.eudora.com*
- *www.excite.com*
- *www.ivillage.com*
- *www.mailcity.com*
- *www.usa.net*
- *www.yahoo.com*
- *www.rocketmail.com*

When you are looking for a Web-based email service visit a few of the sites to see what they have to offer and to see if you like the look and feel of the site. Several Web-based email services are provided through established search engines such as Yahoo or Excite and these are very popular and you will not have to look far to find them. At the end of the day there is nothing to stop users having numerous Web-based email accounts. However, if you decide to do this, do so on an experimental basis, with a view to choosing the best one at the end of a set period. Otherwise you will end up tying yourself in knots trying to remember all of your accounts, and working out which address to give out to people. At most, have three Web-based accounts: one for social messages; one for work; and one when you have to include an email address when you are filling in an online form.

If you do not want to give out your personal email address when filling in online forms, use a Web-based address instead. This will cut down your personal junk email.

Creating an account

The process of creating a Web-based email account is quick, logical and straightforward. If at any point you feel it is getting too complicated, or there are questions you are not happy answering, exit from the site and find another provider for this service. As shown with the list in the previous section, there is no shortage of sites from which to choose.

Creating an account can be done by following a few logical steps:

1. Access the Web site of the company who you want to host your Web-based email account. This can be done by opening a Web browser (such

as Internet Explorer or Netscape Navigator) and typing in the name in the Address box near the top of the screen. Alternatively, select your favourite search engine and, in the Search box, type in the name of the site you wish to go to e.g. Hotmail, Yahoo Mail, Eudora etc.

2. The first page you will see will be the company's home page. This will contain details of what they offer, how to access it, and how to register.

3. There should be a button visible on the home page that says something along the lines of 'Register' or 'Register Now'. Click on this to take you to the first page of the registration process for a Web-based email account.

4. On some sites there will be a brief introduction to the service that is provided, while on others it just goes straight to the registration form.

5. All Web-based email providers require new users to fill in a registration form. This can be done by filling in the relevant boxes on screen. In some cases there are items that have to be filled in, such as name, while others are optional, such as occupation. Either way, a warning message appears if you try to complete the form before all of the required boxes have been filled in. Although the information sought does not usually go into a lot of detail, some people are still reluctant to enter personal details into an online form. In reality, with Web-based email registrations, you could enter a set of completely incorrect information and nobody would be any the wiser, and they would probably not care too much either.

Web-based email companies make their money from advertising. This is usually on the Web site itself and you should not receive a lot of unsolicited marketing email from them in your Inbox, either Web-based or personal.

6. At the end of the form you are asked to enter your username for the email account that will be created on the site. This is usually some combination of your name, followed by '@thecompanyname.com'. The final part of the address is frequently pre-inserted so you only have to enter the first part. You will also be asked to enter a password and then re-enter it to make sure you have not mis-typed it. This will be the password that you enter when you access your account. For security reasons, you may also be asked to include a question and answer that only you could know. This can be used if there is a problem with your account and you have to contact the company that is hosting the site.

7. Once the registration form has been completed, a terms and conditions notice should appear. This is a form of contract that sets out the rules and regulations for using your Web-based email account. It also usually exempts the company from various forms of liability. This notice has to be accepted for your account to become active.

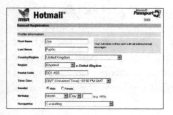

8. After the terms and conditions have been accepted, you will receive a message that you have successfully created a Web-based email account, and you will be shown your new email address. At this point, you can start sending and receiving emails to and from your new account.

Accessing an account

The first thing to do with a new Web-based email account is to test it to make sure it works properly. If you have created the Web-based service from your own computer (and it already has its own dedicated email account) you can test it immediately, from your desktop:

1. Disconnect from the Internet and close down all open sites. This will be like accessing the Web-based service from a completely new machine and you will be able to go through each of the steps, as required.

2. Open your browser and enter the name of the provider of your Web-based account. (At this point it would be a good idea to enter this site on your list of favourite sites. These are sites that you visit most frequently and they can be added to a pick-list so that you do not have to enter the whole URL every time you want to access the site. To add a site to your Favorites list, select Favorites > Add to Favorites (Netscape uses the terminology 'Bookmarks', but it refers to the same thing) from the menu bar of your browser. When you want to access this site, select Favorites (Bookmarks in Netscape) from the menu bar and select the required name from the list.)

3. On the email provider's home page, there will be a box for your user name. This is the first part of your Web-based email address i.e. your own name in some format. There will also be a box for your password. Both of these items will have been entered into the registration form but if you have forgotten your password there will probably be a button or a hyperlink that takes you to an option to select another one. You may also be able to ask the Web-based provider to remember these details automatically, to make it easier and quicker for you to log-on.

4. Once you have entered your user name and password, select a button titled Sign In (or similar) to access your account.

5. When you first view your account you will probably have at least one message already waiting for you. This will be from the account host, telling you about the service that you have registered with. Read this and then delete it, unless it has any information you think you may need to refer back to.

6. To send a test message, select the New/New Message button (or equivalent) and enter your dedicated email account name in the To box. In the subject line, enter a short message such as 'Test' and then add a few words of text in the message body area. Then click on the Send button.

7. Open up your dedicated email program and download any new messages. If every thing is working properly, the message from your Web-based account should appear in your Inbox.

8. Once the initial message has arrived, select Reply and send another test message, this time back to the Web-based account.

9. If necessary, return to the Web-based account and sign in again.

10. In the Inbox should be the message that has been sent from your dedicated email account. If it does not appear, select Refresh from the browser's toolbar. If it is still not visible, close down the browser and disconnect from the Internet. When you reconnect the message should appear. If this does not work, try sending another message from your own computer or another one.

With some Web-based email accounts, if you do not access them at least once within a period of time after it has been set up (usually about 60 days) then the account will expire.

Information misuse

One of the biggest fears of people submitting their personal details over the Internet is that they are going to be misused in some way, or sold to a marketing organisation that will then bombard them with junk email. This is a valid concern and one that should be addressed by all reputable providers of Web-based email.

Look for a statement regarding what they do regarding your personal details, including some of the following:

- An assurance that your email address will not be sold onto a third party for marketing purposes.
- An assurance that the company hosting your account will only contact you with items that you have specifically requested.
- An assurance that none of your personal details will be divulged.
- A statement along the lines that any unnecessary information will be discarded once the registration process has been completed.
- A commitment to use scanning software to detect viruses that may be present in your account or the whole site. This is important not only

for your own files but also to see how highly the company rates protecting themselves from virus attacks. This could affect individual users since some Web-based providers have had to shut down for a period of time in the past because of attacks on their sites. This is not only a problem for the company but also its clients who hold email accounts with them.

However, a word of warning: just because a company has what seems like an impressive statement about protecting your privacy, not bombarding you with junk email, and striving for world peace, it does not necessarily mean it will follow this through. By its very nature, the Internet is an unregulated creation where fraud and misinformation can easily be perpetrated. There is very little to stop a company setting up on the Web, promising all sorts of laudable things and then doing exactly the opposite. If you have any doubts about any Web-based email site, move on to another one. In general, there is a greater degree of security with the larger, more established operators in this field.

Email good practice

It always pays to try and be as efficient and as safety conscious with your email accounts, whether they are Web-based or dedicated to a single ISP. However, since Web-based accounts rely heavily on the use of passwords there are more potential risks for misuse. Therefore some common sense steps should be taken to try and ensure that your account remains safe and secure:

- Never give out your password verbally. If you tell someone your password they could then go to the site of your Web-based email account and access your personal account. Once someone has your password this is relatively easy to do, since your username appears in your email address whenever you send a message.

- Never give out your password online. In some ways this is more dangerous than giving it out verbally, since anyone who asks for it online probably wants it specifically for malicious purposes. There should be no reason for anyone to ask you for your password and you should always be very wary if anyone does. Even if someone contacts your online claiming to be something like a system administrator, do not give out your password. Due to the anonymity that the Internet gives people, it can be impossible to ascertain a person's real identity from an email or an online message. A large dose of scepticism is a good thing when dealing with individuals in cyberspace.

- Never give out personal details such as your home address over the Internet. There have been cases where people's whole identities have been stolen from information that has been taken from the Web. While this is rare, it does illustrate the type of thing that can happen from disclosing information online. The only reason for entering your home address in an online form is if you have ordered something that will be delivered to your home. However, if anyone asks for any personal details for no good reason, ignore the request completely.

- Change your password at regular intervals (this could vary, depending on how paranoid you are, but it is worth changing it every three or four months). Changing a password can usually be done using a button on the home page and it is sometime the same one that is used if you have forgotten your password. When changing a password, try and use a new one that is equally easy for you to remember as the original and equally difficult for anyone else to guess.

- Be careful when dealing with attachments. This is one of the most popular ways of transmitting viruses and you will not be popular if you let one loose within your account provider's site. You may also corrupt your own files, if you are using your own computer. Some providers have software that automatically scans all attachments for viruses but this may not be available on all sites and it is not an exact science because the virus creators are usually a step or two ahead of the people trying to locate them. If you do not recognise the name of the sender of an attachment, do not open it. Delete it from your Inbox and, if you are really suspicious of something, alert the system administrator.

- Treat junk email (spam) with the disdain it deserves and, if you receive any, delete it immediately. Do not bother opening it and under no circumstances reply to it. If you do it will only serve to heighten the spammer's interest and you will be bombarded with further messages. If they think you are concerned enough to reply to the original message they may therefore conclude that they will be able to grind you down into buying something if they send you enough messages. Unfortunately, in some cases, this is true.

- Use a Web-based email provider that has filters for automatically deleting messages from unwanted sources. These can be set up to recognise messages from a specific email address or ones that contain certain words or phrases in the subject header (such as 'Money' or 'Sex'). If your account cannot be set up with filters then it may be a good idea to look for a different provider. Whatever filters you have in place there will probably be times when unwanted or offensive email slips through into your Inbox. If it is only a minor annoyance, then delete it and forget about it. However, if it is of an overtly offensive nature, contact the system administrator. For more on dealing with junk email, see the chapter entitled 'Junk Email'.

Forwarding services

Although Web-based email is a convenient way to be able to access messages from any computer around the world, it does have one drawback in that you have to create another email address, you cannot simply transfer your desktop email address to a Web-based provider. This means that you have to either give different email addresses to different people, or tell them to send messages to different addresses at different times. Understandably, this can get confusing for all involved.

One way around this problem is to use an email forwarding service. These are companies who let you view your ISP-based email account through their own Web page. This means that you can view your account from any computer that has an Internet connection. Although forwarding services do not offer such a selection of options as a dedicated email program, it is still possible to send messages, set up an address book and, in most cases, receive attachments. There are dozen of companies that offer this service on the Web and the main one in the UK is called Twigger, which can be found at:

- *www.twigger.co.uk*

Once you have accessed the Web site you do the following to access your ISP email account:

1. Enter your username. This is the name that your account is registered under with your ISP. (If you have an account with Freeserve, your user name will be the part that appears after the @ in your email address.)

2. Enter your password. This is the password that was given when you first set up an account with your ISP. If your connection to your account is set up to remember your password automatically, you may have forgotten your password, in which case you will have to contact your ISP.

3. Select your ISP from the drop-down list provided. This is an extremely extensive list, but if your ISP is not on it then you can email Twigger at 'provider@twigger.com' and they will add it to their list.

4. Select Go.

5. If you have entered your details correctly, you will be able to see your ISP email account.

The email forwarding service provided by Twigger is free and it has a basic interface for sending and receiving messages while you are away from your own computer. You can also view attachments, add names to an address book and check the spelling in your messages. Once you have accessed your account, any new messages will be displayed in your Twigger Inbox. Click on the name of the sender to view the text of the message. Even if you view your messages through Twigger, they will still be available when you check your mail on your own computer through your normal email program.

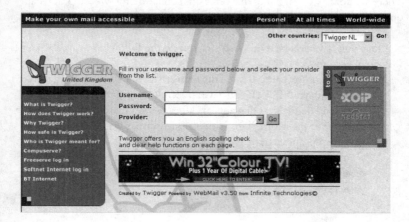

Other email forwarding services

There are hundreds of email forwarding services (if you are using a forwarding service, do not pay for it: there are so many free ones that this is completely unnecessary) on the Web and some to try are:

- Army.Net at *www.army.net/* Forwarding service for army members.
- Bigfoot at *www.bigfoot.com/* Global e-mail directory including forwarding services.
- ElvisMail.com at *www.elvismail.com/* Free email forwarding.
- Email Planet at *www.emailplanet.com/* Allows travellers to download email from any computer, at any time, anywhere in the world.
- Find mE-Mail at *www.findmemail.com/*
- Groovy.nu at *http://groovy.nu/* Free redirection/email forwarding.
- iName at *www.iname.com/* Free Web-based or forwarded email accounts.
- MailZone at *www.mailzone.com/* Free internet e-mail service.
- Navy.Org at *www.navy.org/* Forwarding service for navy members.
- NetForward at *www.netwforward.com/*
- NetSpace1 at *www.netspace.com/* Forwarding, and auto responders.
- RelayMail at *www.relaymail.net/* Email forwarding for those in need of a permanent address.
- Student Network at *www.student.org.uk/* Built by students for students. Offers email forwarding, advice, penpals and more.
- Travellers' Email at *www.backpackers.net/* Allows travellers to download email from any computer, at any time.
- Vanity E-Mail at *www.vanityemail.com/* E-mail forwarding service with a variety of domain names to choose from.
- WorldPost at *www.worldpost.com/* Forwarding, auto responding and web page redirecting.

Electronic cards

Everyone likes to get a card on their birthday or at Christmas and this concept has been embraced on the Internet, with the result that there are hundreds of Web sites that offer to send electronic greeting cards on your behalf. These cover almost every event and occasion imaginable and it is not only quick and straightforward, it is also cheap.

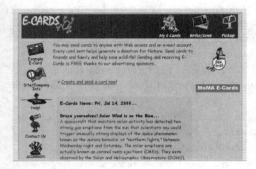

Some Web sites that offer this service are:

- *www.ecards.com*
- *www.ecards.org*
- *www.orangepie.com*
- *www.linkopedia.com/postoffice.html*
- *www.animatedgreetings.com*
- *www.superecards.com*
- *www.greeting-cards.com*
- *www.happypost.com/card.html*

- *www.care2.com/send/catflags1.html*
- *www.laughspot.com*
- *www.egreetings.com/sports*
- *www.eyefordesign.com/main/main.html*
- *www.tehabi.com/postcards/*
- *www.aruba-ecards.com*
- *www.casema.net/~nwitlox/cards*
- *www.chatmix.com/postcard.html*
- *www.pacprod.com/card.htm*
- *www.city-net.com/~bmfpro*
- *www.lovecards.com*
- *www.lionshouse.org/greetings.htm*
- *www.dronezone.com/kw/valentn.htm*
- *www.salesearcher.com/greetingcards.htm*

When an electronic card is sent, the recipient receives an email message directing them to the Web site where the card is held, rather than the card as an attachment.

Some sites ask you to register with them before you can create e-cards and others just let you get to work straightaway. Have a good look at the sites to see the types of cards they offer and the types of designs they use. Some of the areas covered are:
- Anniversaries
- Announcements
- Birthdays

- Blank greeting cards
- Bon Voyage
- Congratulations
- Cyber Hugs
- Engagement
- Friendships
- Full Moon cards
- Flowers
- Farewell
- Good Luck

- Get Well Soon
- Invitations
- New Baby
- Romantic
- Sympathy
- Thank You
- I'm Sorry

- Halloween
- Christmas
- Boxing Day
- Mother's Day
- Father's Day
- Valentine's Day
- Easter
- Graduation
- First Day of Spring
- First Day of Summer

If you cannot find something to suit your needs on one of these sites then it probably does not exist, and you may have to resort to creating your own card from scratch.

Once you have found an e-card site that you like you can start creating your masterpiece. All of these sites guide you through the process and it is usually along similar lines to these:

1. Select the type of card that you want to create.
2. Select an image.
3. Select background music.
4. Enter the message that you want to include.
5. Indicate that you have finished designing your card.
6. Enter information for sending the card. This will include your email address, the recipient's email address and sometimes some additional details that are not necessarily required.
7. Select Send to email the card to the recipient.
8. Most sites will send you an email notifying you that you have successfully completed the card and that the recipient has been notified of its existence.

If you receive an e-card it will not come as an email attachment. Instead there will be a link to the site where the card is stored and waiting for you. In some cases you can click on the link and this will take you directly to your card. Other sites operate by including an authorisation number which should be copied by clicking and dragging the mouse over it and then selecting Edit>Copy from the menu bar. Then, go to the relevant site, where you will find a box into which the authorisation number should be inserted, by clicking in the box and selecting Edit>Paste from the toolbar. This will then allow you access to your e-card.

E-cards are an entertaining and fun way to keep in touch and, because of the pre-designed images, eye-catching cards can be sent in a matter of a few minutes.

Don't use e-cards as your sole method of communication for someone's birthday or suchlike. If they do not check their email regularly they may miss it and think you have forgotten.

Email to fax

For those people who do not think the fax machine is a communications dinosaur (and there has been some research carried out that suggests the fax machine is being used more than ever, despite its predicted demise at the hands of email) there are various online companies who offer email to fax services. This involves sending an email from your computer that is then printed out on someone else's fax machine. This can be useful if the person you wish to contact does not have a computer or the facility to print email messages.

An email can be sent to a fax machine as follows:

1. Compose an email in the normal way.
2. In the To box of the message header, enter the fax number and then the number that will be given to you by the company providing the service.
3. The email will be sent to the destination fax number. In some cases this service is even free. If this is the case, it is achieved by a site that relies heavily on advertisements.

Some email to fax companies do not support attachments or HTML files. If you want something a bit more than plain text, you may have to look at other alternatives.

Some companies which offer email to fax services include:

- Faxaway at *www.fax-away.com/*
- Home Page at *www.ufax.com/*
- Worldwide Free Faxing at *www.zipfax.com/*
- eFax at *www.efax.com/*
- Exstream Data at *www.efaxinc.com/*
- OfficeDomain at *http://messagesaap.com/*
- Advantexcel Corp at *www.fnmail.com/*
- FaxPC.com at *www.faxpc.com/*

Most computers can also send faxes of their own, using standard communications software that is bundled with most machines these days. Check your system help files for details.

Electronic invitations

If you have ever despaired at the thought of organising a dinner party or a corporate event, then electronic invitations could be the solution to your problems. These are run through a Web site and they work as follows:

1. You specify the email addresses of the people you want to invite to your event.
2. Messages are sent automatically to all of the prospective participants.
3. When the email arrives the recipients have the choice of accepting the invitation, declining it, or accepting tentatively. Each person can also see how the other people have responded, in case this has a bearing on their decision.
4. If no response is forthcoming, an electronic reminder is sent after a few days.
5. Once an invitation has been accepted, it is possible to place it in the calendar in Microsoft Outlook, if this program is installed.

One of the companies most involved with electronic invitations is:

- Evite at *www.evite.com/*

Outlook

Attributes of Outlook

While Outlook Express is more than adequate for everyday email tasks it does not contain the personal organisation features of its big brother Outlook 2000. This is not only an email program but it also serves as a form of electronic personal assistant and it can be used to create contact information, schedule meetings, insert calendar information and list daily, weekly, monthly and yearly tasks. In general it is more of a business-orientated program but it can also be useful for home users, particularly if they work from home, or have a hectic existence that requires some electronic organisational assistance.

Latest features

Outlook began life with Outlook 97 and since then it has been developed using feedback from the users into its current incarnation of Outlook 2000, which is packaged with the Microsoft Office 2000 suite of programs. Some of the improvements that have been made to the latest version of the program are:

- Greater integration with other Office 2000 programs such as Word, Excel, PowerPoint and Access. This includes being able to create documents in these programs and then being able to email them via Outlook.
- Greater integration with the Internet.
- Outlook Startup Wizard. This can be used to customise the Outlook installation process. It can also import items such as your address book and previous email program settings into Outlook. This can be done not only for previous versions of Outlook or Outlook Express, but also for other email programs such as Messenger and Eudora.
- Rules Wizard. This is a wizard that applies rules to incoming emails. Depending on the rules, an action is then performed on the message.
- Switch Formats on the Fly. This allows users to switch formats between HTML, RTF and plain text at any time while composing an email.
- Enhanced Preview Pane. This is now capable of displaying attachments and hyperlinks, in addition to the text of an email message.

Preview Pane allows you to view the contents of an email message in a window below where it is listed in the Inbox; there is no need to open the message separately.

- iCalendar. This can be used to publish details from your Outlook calendar over the Internet for others to view. It can also be used to request meetings and respond to similar requests.
- Message Disposition Notifications. This is a useful feature that can be used to discover whether a recipient has opened an email message.
- Improved integration with Microsoft Internet Explorer.
- QuickFind Contact. Information that has been entered into the Contacts folder can be accessed from other elements of Outlook. Users can easily find and open a Contact from anywhere in Outlook.
- Save as Web Page. This enables you to publish calendars over the Internet in HTML.

Outlook is closely integrated with the Web and it is a good choice if you want to make a lot of your work available in this format.

- Calendar Screen tips. This provides details of items within the calendar when the cursor is pointed over them.
- Calendar Background Colour. Different colours are used to show which periods are free on the calendar and which ones have appointments entered.
- Enhanced Calendar Printing. This gives users greater flexibility when printing out calendar information and each month can be printed exactly onto a single page.
- Adding and Removing Attendees. This makes it easier to add or remove individuals from a meeting that has already been scheduled.

- Enhanced Open Other Users' Calendars. This offers a list of the calendars that have been accessed most recently.
- Hide Private Appointments. If there are calendar appointments that you do not want anyone else to see, these can be hidden from view.
- Enhanced Mail Merge. This can be used to send a mail merge document to some, or all, of the names on the Contacts list.
- Outlook Shortcuts Bar . This enables users to put shortcuts in an easily accessible bar that can be permanently displayed in Outlook. Shortcuts can be made to files, folders and even your favourite Web pages. If a Web page is placed in the shortcuts bar, it will be displayed within Outlook if it is selected.

System requirements

Outlook comes packaged with Microsoft Office 2000. This is not a small program to install and the whole of disc 1 (there are four discs altogether) including Word, Excel, PowerPoint, Access and Outlook has to be installed as an all-inclusive package. The minimum requirements for Outlook 2000 are:

- PC with Pentium 75 MHz or higher processor.
- For Windows 95 or Windows 98: 16 MB of RAM for the operating system, plus 8 Mb RAM for Outlook.
- For Windows NT Workstation 4.0 or later: 32 MB of RAM for the operating system, plus 8 Mb RAM for Outlook.
- 178 MB for Disc 1 of Office 2000 (Word, Excel, PowerPoint, Access and Outlook).
- CD-ROM drive.
- VGA or higher resolution monitor. Super VGA recommended.
- Microsoft Windows 95 or later, or Microsoft Windows NT Workstation 4.0 or later.

Outlook Bar

On the Outlook Bar, which appears down the left-hand side of the screen and is accessed by selecting View > Outlook Bar from the menu bar, there are icons which act as shortcuts to the various elements of the program.

These are:

- Outlook Today. A very useful feature of the progrm. This lists the relevant items that are available within Outlook. These items can include such things as forthcoming calendar appointments, unopened emails and any tasks that you have set.
- Calendar. This is a regular (standard) calendar which offers the user space under the entry or each day to enter appointments and meeting times.
- Contacts. This section of the program acts, in effect, like an address book where you can enter comprehensive details for business and social contacts.
- Tasks. This is where you can write down tasks that you have to perform. This serves as a reminder as much as anything.
- Notes. These can be used as electronic versions of Post-It notes. They are intended for short reminders to yourself, about anything that you think you might forget. In general, they

are used for items that are not too important – these can be placed in the calendar.

- Deleted Items. This is where items are sent when they are deleted from other areas of Outlook. If they are then deleted from here they will be permanently removed.

The Deleted Items folder is like a safety net for items that you have removed from other parts of Outlook. However, if they are removed from here you cannot retrieve them.

Menu bars

The bar at the top of Outlook contains the various menus that pertain to each of the elements in the program. Some of them have different options, depending on the element that has been selected. For instance, there could be slightly different options for the Calendar menu bar and the Tasks menu bar, although generally all of the commands are the same or similar.

If an option is greyed out, it means it is not available for the option you have selected. The menu options are:

Click on an element in the Outlook Bar and then click on the menus on the menu bar to see the options that are available for that item.

File

- New. This creates a new item of the selected element. So if the Inbox is selected, there will be options for creating a new email message. If the Calendar is selected, there will be options for a new appointment and so on.
- Open. This can be used to open items within Outlook, including calendar appointments for other people if you are working on a network.
- Close All Items. This closes everything that is being worked on, such as emails. If you select this, make sure that everything to be saved has been.
- Save As. This enables you to save an item such as an email under another name.
- Save Attachments. This is used to save attachments that are sent with email messages. Once this option has been selected you can save a single attachment, or a group of attachments, onto your own hard drive or a shared folder on a network.
- Folder. This has various options for creating new folders within Outlook.

- Import and Export. This allows you to import and export files between programs and, if you are linked to a network, between different computers.
- Archive. This can be used to tidy up your folders and store old items in an archive folder. If this is selected, a dialog box appears, asking which folders you want to archive and the date from which you want the archiving to take place. Make the relevant selections and then select OK. Files can also be archived automatically, using the AutoArchive function. To do this, select Tools>Options>Other>AutoArchive and then select the setting that you want to apply for AutoArchiving. This can be a useful feature if you feel you are getting swamped with messages.
- Page Setup. This defines how your page is setup, primarily for printing purposes.
- Print Preview. This allows you to see how items such as email messages, or calendars, will look when they are printed. A very useful feature.
- Print. This prints out the current active document.
- Exit. This closes your current Outlook session.
- Exit and Log Off. This closes your current Outlook session and logs you off the network, if you are working on one.

Due to its powerful organisational tools, Outlook is ideal for use on an internal network such as an intranet.

Edit

- Undo. This undoes editing actions that have been previously performed.
- Cut. This removes an item from the active document and stores it on the clipboard.
- Copy. This copies an item and stores it on the clipboard. This is similar to Cut, except that the original item is not removed.
- Paste. This places an item on the clipboard into a new location. This does not have to be something that was cut or copied from Outlook: it is possible to copy text or images from another program and paste them into a file in Outlook. Only the most recent item that is placed on the clipboard can be pasted into a document.
- Clear. This deletes a selected object without placing it on the clipboard.
- Select All. This selects all of the items in the active application i.e. all of the messages in a folder or all of the text in an email message.
- Delete. This removes an item permanently.

- Move to Folder. This allows one item, such as an email, to be moved to another folder within Outlook 2000 itself. Select a message then select Move to Folder and select a location in the Move Items dialog box.
- Copy to Folder. This is similar to above, except that the original file stays in its original location.
- Mark as Read. This indicates an email message has been read, by placing an open white envelope next to it. This can be done even if the message has not actually been opened.
- Mark as Unread. This indicates an email message has not been read, by placing a closed yellow envelope next to it.
- Mark All as Read. This indicates that all email messages have been read.
- Categories. This allows you to assign keywords to similar items so that you can organise them easily. Items within different elements of Outlook can be assigned the same category.

The Mark as Read option can also be applied to newsgroup headers that you have downloaded. This way, you can ignore them in future.

Outlook has its own built-in newsreader for accessing newsgroups. For more on newsgroups, see the 'Mailing Lists and Newsgroups' chapter.

View

The options here can be used to customise the way that elements of Outlook are displayed.

- Current view. This has options for displaying the items in the active element. The options are different for each item i.e. the options for the Inbox current view are different from those for the Calendar current view. They all have at least half a dozen options and it is worth experimenting with various ones to see which suit your needs the best. Work with each option for a day or two to get the feel of them.
- Outlook Bar. If this is checked on, the bar at the left hand side of the program is visible at all times. This contains shortcuts to all of the elements of Outlook and it is best to leave it checked on unless there is a good reason not to.
- Folder List. If this is checked on, it displays the folder hierarchy within Outlook. As with the Outlook Bar, it is best to keep this checked on.
- Preview Pane. This provides a separate window to preview the currently selected item. It is used most frequently for email messages, so that at

least some of the content can be viewed by selecting the message header rather than having to open the message itself. However, the preview pane can also be used with the other elements of Outlook. (Each item can have the Preview Pane checked on or off, independently of the other items.)

- AutoPreview. This is only available for the Inbox and the Tasks elements of Outlook. This displays a limited amount of text for all emails and tasks. It is similar to the preview pane, except that it offers a preview for all items, not just the selected one.
- Toolbars. This gives access to the various Outlook toolbars, for accessing functions.
- Status bar. This appears at the bottom of the screen and displays various items of information, such as the number of items in a folder.

Go To (sub menu of View)

This is used for navigating between Outlook folders and elements.

The options in the Go menu take you directly to the other elements of Outlook and can also connect you to the Web.

Tools

This contains numerous options for performing operations with Outlook and also customising its appearance.

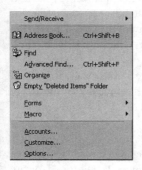

- Send and Receive. This sends messages that are waiting and downloads your incoming messages from your mail server.
- Address Book. Select this to access your email address book.
- Find. This can be used to look for specific items, according to names or keywords. Select this option and then enter the item you want to find in the Look for box. Any items that match the search criteria will be displayed in the window below.
- Advanced Find. This contains options for refining your search criteria.
- Organize. This contains options for organising your folders and messages. It can be used to move email messages or to colour code messages from specific senders.
- Rules Wizard. This can be used to create conditions that apply to messages and then subsequent actions that are performed when these conditions are

met. This can include sending certain types of email straight to the Wastebasket or giving them colour coding.

- Out of Office Assistant. This is an option for letting other users know that you are away from your computer – for example, while you are at a conference, on a training course or on holiday. If you select this option you can check the 'I am currently Out of the Office' box in the Out of Office Assistant dialog box and enter a message that you want to appear as an AutoReply to the sender.

It is also possible to have a sender's message automatically forwarded to one of your colleagues. (If you do this, tell people in the AutoReply box where their message is being forwarded to.) To forward a message from the Out of Office Assistant dialog box:

1. Select Add Rule
2. In the Edit Rule dialog box, check on the 'Sent directly to me' box.
3. Under the 'Perform these actions' heading, select Forward (or any other action you want performed on incoming messages).
4. Select the To button to choose a recipient for the message to be forwarded to.
5. Select OK.

If you are using Outlook on a network, make use of the Out of Office Assistant. It will keep your colleagues informed about your whereabouts, rather than displaying an empty calendar.

- Empty Deleted Items Folder. This permanently removes (erases) any items that have been placed in the Wastebasket (via the Deleted Items folder, accessible from the Outlook Bar).

- Forms. This has options for selecting pre-designed forms or creating your own. These can be used to standardise the way information is distributed within Outlook.
- Options. This contains preferences for the individual elements of Outlook and also some general ones. These will be looked at for the individual elements later.

Actions

This has different instructions for each element of Outlook and these are looked at for the individual elements later.

Help

This contains the Outlook Contents and Index help and also a link to online help facilities.

The online help takes you to a page on the Web that has tips, upgrades and patches.

Email/Inbox

This is the first element of Outlook and almost certainly the most frequently used one. It operates in a similar way to Outlook Express and it also integrates closely with the other elements of Outlook. It is identified by the Inbox title and icon on the Outlook Bar and this is an email function.

When the Inbox icon is selected in the Folder list, the Standard toolbar is visible underneath the standard menu bar (this toolbar is specific to the functions within the email element):

- New Mail Message. This is depicted by an icon with a sheet of paper and an open envelope.
- Print. This is depicted by an icon of a printer.
- Move to Folder. This is depicted by an icon of a sheet of paper and a small yellow folder.
- Delete. This is depicted by a black cross.
- Reply. This is depicted by an icon of a single head, with a left pointing arrow pointing towards it.
- Reply to All. This is depicted by an icon of two heads, with a left pointing arrow pointing towards them.
- Forward. This is depicted by an icon of a single head, with a right pointing arrow pointing towards it.
- Address book. This is depicted by an icon of an open book.
- Send and Receive. This is depicted by an icon of two envelopes.

- Find. This is depicted by an icon of an envelope with a magnifying glass over it.
- Organize. Note that this is depicted by an icon of a broken apart mosaic.

Composing

To compose an email message in Outlook:

1. Select the New Mail Message icon from the toolbar.
2. In the To box, enter the name of the recipient, or click on the To button and select a name from the Address book (to add entries into the Address book, see later).

If you have entered a recipient's name before, Outlook will remember this and complete it from just the first two or three letters the next time.

3. In the Cc box, enter the names of anyone who you want to copy the message to.
4. In the Subject box, enter a subject title for the message.
5. Click in the main window and compose your message.
6. Use the Formatting toolbar to format the text in your message. This appears underneath the Standard toolbar and the options are (from left to right as they appear on the toolbar):
   - Style. This allows you to apply a pre-defined style to a paragraph.
   - Font
   - Font size
   - Font colour

- Bold
- Italic
- Underline
- Align left
- Align centre
- Align right
- Bulleted list
- Numbered list
- Decrease indent
- Increase indent
- Insert horizontal line.

7. Select the Send button to send your message.

Sending and receiving

There are a number of choices that can be made when you send and receive messages:

- Select the Send and Receive button on the Standard toolbar to send messages and download those that are waiting on your email server (if you are connected to a network, this may be done automatically).
- Select the Reply button to compose a message to the person who sent you the original email. With this option you do not have to add the recipient's address and the Reply button is available on the Standard toolbar or when you are composing a message.
- Select the Reply to All button to send a reply to all of the people who were included in an original message to you.
- Forward. Send an original message on to another recipient. This involves entering the recipient's name in the To box.

There are also a variety of options that can be applied when sending and receiving messages. These are accessed by opening a new mail message and then selecting View > Options or by selecting the Options icon on the Compose Message toolbar. The options available are:

- Message settings. These can be used to specify settings for Importance and Sensitivity.
- Use voting buttons. This can be used to add voting buttons to an email. These are buttons that respondents can select to indicate a certain response. The default buttons are Approve and Reject but you can add your own – type the name into the box and separate each entry by a semi colon. This can be a useful way to quickly get the views of a group of people.

Voting buttons are best used for simple options, such as the time of a meeting, rather than for items such as major policy decisions.

- Tell me when this message has been delivered. This generates a reply when a message has been successfully delivered.
- Tell me when this message has been read. This generates a reply when a recipient has opened a message.
- Have replies sent to xx. This can be used to specify a folder for replies to an original message.
- Save sent messages to xx This can be used to specify a folder for placing copies of all messages that you send. The default is Sent Items.
- Do not deliver before xx. This can be used to set a specific delivery date for a message.

- Expires after xx. This can be used to automatically remove items after a specified period of time.

Once you have selected your settings for sending and receiving messages, enter the recipient by clicking on the To button. This will take you to the Select Names dialog box in the address book. Select a recipient from the list and select the To or Cc buttons, depending on whether you want to send it directly to this person or copy it to them. Once you have selected all of the recipients, click OK. Then, enter a subject for your email and compose the message. Attachments can be added by selecting the paperclip icon on the toolbar and choosing a file to attach.

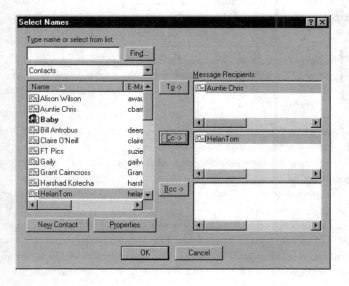

Address book entries

To add a contact to an address book:

1. Select the Address Book button on the main toolbar. (This is depicted by an open book and can also be opened when you are composing an email message.)
2. Select the New Entry icon (which is depicted by a white index card) or the New button if you are composing a message.
3. Select the type of entry you want to make and into which address book you wish to place it.
4. Enter the recipient's contact details.
5. Select OK. This contact should be available the next time you access your address book.

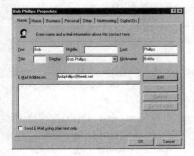

Keep your address book details up-to-date as it could have important consequences when dealing with business contacts. Inaccurate information in an electronic format is just as damaging as if it is in a diary or a notebook.

Adding a signature

A signature in an email is a predefined piece of text that can be inserted automatically at the end of a message. This can consist of anything, but usually it is your name and contact details. To add an existing signature when you are composing a message, select the Signature button on the compose message toolbar or select Insert>Signature from the menu bar. This will display the current signatures that are available. Select one and this will appear in the recipient's message. To create a new signature:

1. Access the signature dialog box as above. Select More to create a new signature.

2. If a message is displayed saying that you do not have any signatures and asking if you would like to create one, select Yes.

3. In the Create New Signature dialog box, enter a name for your signature and then check on the Start with a blank Signature box to create a new, blank signature. There is another box that can be checked on and that uses an existing signature as a template for a new one. Select Next.

4. In the Edit Signature dialog box, enter the text that you want to serve as your signature. This can be formatted and be as long or as short as you like.

5. Select Finish to add the new signature. You can create several different signatures for use when sending emails to different people.

Be careful with amusing signatures. Not everyone will share your sense of humour and it is possible to attach the wrong signature to a message. If in doubt, leave it off.

Calendar

The calendar element of Outlook can be used to create and view appointments on a daily, weekly, monthly or even yearly basis.

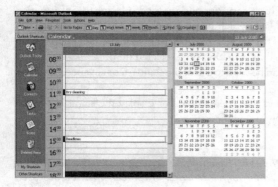

Viewing options

There are a number of ways in which the information within the calendar can be viewed and these are accessed through the View menu:

- Current View. This offers various ways for displaying the information held within the calendar. This includes by day/week/month, appointments or events.
- Outlook Bar. This displays the standard Outlook Bar.
- Folder List. This displays the standard view of the folders within Outlook.
- Day. This displays calendar information for the current day.

- Work Week. This displays calendar information for the five-day working week.
- Week. The displays information for a seven-day calendar week.
- Month. This displays information for the current month.
- TaskPad View. This has various options for displaying the information held on the TaskPad, which is another element of Outlook.
- Preview Pane. This creates a window below the calendar, which displays additional information on a selected item.
- Toolbars. This can be used to select the standard or advanced Outlook toolbars.
- Status Bar. This can be used to hide or display the status bar at the bottom of the Outlook window.

Hotmail, the Web-based email service, also has a facility for adding calendar appointments. These can then be accessed from any computer.

Creating appointments

To create an appointment on the calendar:

1. Select the date and time where you want to insert an appointment and double click on this on the calendar, or select Actions > New Appointment from the menu bar.
2. In the appointment dialog box, enter details of the appointment. These include subject, location and start and finish time of the appointment.

3.   Select the Recurrence tab to enter details for a recurring appointment i.e. one that you want to appear at the same time every day, week, month or year.
4.   Select the Invite Attendees tab to invite other people to a meeting or a specific event. They are then sent an email inviting them to attend.

Viewing other users' calendars

If you are using Outlook on a network, it is possible to view appointments on other people's calendars as well as your own:
1.   Select File>Open>Other User's Folder from the menu bar.
2.   Select the name of the person whose appointments you want to view and select OK.

To give other users access to your own calendar and appointments:
1.   Right click on the calendar icon in the Outlook Bar.
2.   Select Properties.
3.   In the Calendar Properties dialog box, select the Permissions tab.
4.   Under Permissions, check on the Read Items box.
5.   Select OK.

If you cannot see someone else's calendar appointments, let them know. It could be because they have blocked permission for people to view them, or it could just be that they do not know how to set the properties so that other people can view their calendar. If this is the case, let them know the procedure above.

Contacts

The contacts element of Outlook is like an extended address book. It can be used to enter contact information about people and also communicate with them, and others within the same contact group, over the Internet.

To create a new contact:

1. Select the Contacts button on the Outlook Bar.
2. Select the New Contact button at the left hand side of the Contact toolbar.
3. Select the General tab and enter the contact information.
4. Select the Details tab to add additional information about the contact.

The entries in the Contacts window show basic contact information. However, if you double click on one of these you will be able to view, or edit, several items of business and social contact information.

Tasks

The tasks element of Outlook can be used as a reminder for jobs you have to do. This can be used for entries similar to those in the calendar, but they can be covered in greater detail.

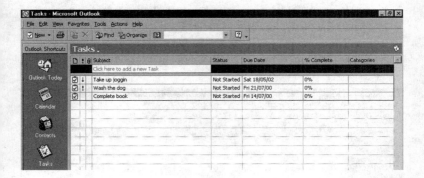

To add a new task.

1. Select the Tasks button on the Outlook Bar.
2. Select the New Task button at the left hand side of the task toolbar.
3. Select the Task tab and enter details for the new task. This can include:
   - subject
   - due date
   - start date
   - priority
   - status
4. Select the Recurrence button to add a recurring task.

Notes

The notes element of Outlook is like an electronic version of Post-It notes. These can be used to avoid having dozens of small pieces of paper lying around your desk or stuck to the side of your computer.

To create a new note:

1. Select the Notes button on the Outlook Bar.
2. Select the New Note button situated at the left hand side of the Task toolbar.
3. Type your message on the yellow note that appears.

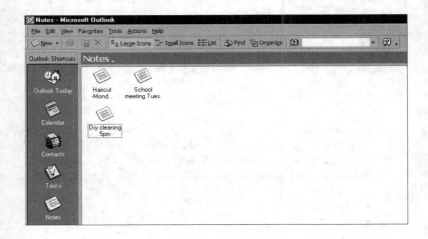

Eudora

Eudora modes

As shown in the Email Programs chapter, one of the most popular email programs, Eudora, is available in three different modes:

Sponsored mode

This is the mode that is installed when the program is downloaded from the Eudora Web site, at *www.eudora.com/* This is a full-featured version of the program and it is free. The only minor drawback is, because of this, small advertisements appear at the bottom left hand corner of the program. These do not interfere with the user interface and they are as unobtrusive as it is possible to be with elements of this nature.

Paid mode

This is the same as the Sponsored mode, except that the advertisements do not appear. Because of this the program is not free and can be bought online for $49.95. The purchase process is straightforward and the program is automatically downloaded onto the purchaser's hard drive.

Light mode

This is a throwback to the days when Eudora only had a paid for version and a free version. The free version was named Eudora Light and this has been retained for supporters of what many consider an email program classic. In its present form, the Light mode has fewer features and tools than the other two versions.

Eudora has fiercely loyal users who have followed the program since its early days of development in the late 1980s and early 1990s. It has also picked up a large number of converts along the way and it is a program that is worth giving a try to, particularly if you thought you had to make do with whatever email program appears on your computer.

Features

Eudora has enough features to match even the most sophisticated of its competitors and the following is a description of the ones that can be found in the Sponsored mode of the program:

Since Eudora is a stand alone email client and is not linked with the development of any form of Web browser, the programmers can concentrate solely on improving its functions and messaging services.

Menu bar

The menu bar is located at the top of the program and it contains menus under key heading words:

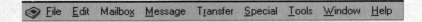

File menu

This is the menu that contains commands for creating and sending messages.

- New File: This creates a new text file. This is not the same as a new email message but it can be useful if you are writing a long email because there is more space on screen and when the new file is created there are several useful formatting tools available. When the message is completed it can be saved (see later) and then attached to an email.

By default, files in this format are saved as text files with the '–txt' extension.

- **Open File.** This allows you to open a file in Eudora, that has either been created using the New File command as earlier, or in another program. This can either be in the text file format, HTML ('–htm'), stationery format ('–sta') or Rich Text Format ('–rtf').
- **Open Attachment.** This can be used to open an attachment that has been sent with an incoming email.
- **Close.** This closes the current file that is open, whether it is one that has been created as earlier or an email that has been received from an external source.
- **Save.** This saves the currently active file. This should be done at regular intervals if you are composing a long message, in case the computer crashes.
- **Save As.** This can be used to save the currently active file under a different name. This can be a useful way to make a copy of a file or to save it into a different format.
- **Save As Stationery.** This allows you to save a unique design as a template that can then be used for further messages. Items such as the text colour, background colour and inserted images can be set as part of a Stationery design and then reused to create a consistent look for some, or all, of your emails.

Do not get too carried away with stationery designs. Use graphics sparingly, do not use overly bright colours and make sure there is a good contrast between your text and your background colour.

- Send Queued Messages. This automatically sends messages that you have been storing up until you connect to the Internet. It connects you and then sends the messages.
- Check Mail. This connects you to the Internet and your mail server and checks to see if there are any messages. If there are, they will be downloaded into your Inbox.
- Print. This prints the current file or email message.
- Print Preview. This gives an onscreen representation of what the printed document will look like on paper.
- Print Setup. This allows you to specify various settings for the printer. This will vary according to the printer that is being used, but the types of options are paper size, orientation and monochrome or colour.
- Import. This is a valuable command that allows you to import messages and address book information from other email programs, such as Outlook Express. Use this if you want to copy items into Eudora. If you do this, they will remain in their original location too.
- Exit. This closes down the Eudora program. If you have any items that require to be saved a warning dialog box will appear alerting you to this fact.

If you use the Import command, Eudora will set up a new folder containing all of the imported items. If you then download new messages in another program, you will have to use import again if you want these ones to appear in Eudora.

Edit menu

This menu contains formatting commands that can be used to simplify the process of creating an email.

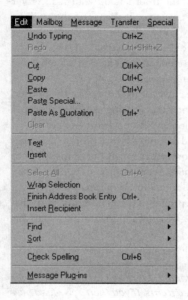

- Undo. This reverses the last action performed on an item of text. However, it operates on multiple levels, which means it can reverse numerous actions, not just the most recent one.
- Redo. This is the opposite of the undo command in that it reinstates operations that have been undone.

- Cut. This removes a selected item and places it on the clipboard so that it can be used elsewhere.
- Copy. This copies a selected item and leaves the original in place.
- Paste. This inserts an item that has been cut or copied at the point where the cursor has been inserted.
- Paste Special. This can be used to insert text that has been cut or copied in a format other than plain text. This could include Rich Text Format or HTML. When this command is used there is a sub-menu that can be used to specify the format in which you would like the text to be pasted.
- Paste As Quotation. This inserts the cut or copied piece of text with quotation marks at the beginning and the end.
- Clear. This removes selected text completely and it is not copied to the clipboard.
- Text. This contains a sub-menu that has a range of options for formatting text in a file or an email message. This includes: Plain, Bold, Italic, Underline, Typewriter, Add Quote Level, Remove Quote Level, Size, Color, Font, Margins, Left, Right, Center, Bulleted List, Make Hyperlink and Clear Formatting.
- Insert. This contains a sub-menu that has options for inserting Pictures or Horizontal Lines.
- Select All. This selects all of the text in a file or an email message. This is useful if you want to apply the same command to the whole file.
- Wrap Selection. This inserts a carriage return at the end of each line in a selection. Eudora also does this when it sends an email message.
- Finish Address Book Entry. This is a command that automatically inserts the name of a contact in your address book by recognising the first few letters of their name. By default this is the nickname, or name

they are known as, that is entered in the address book. Enter the first two or three letters of the nickname as it appears in the address book and then select this command. As long as there is not another name starting with the letters you have typed, the nickname will be inserted and the email will be sent to that person. To insert the recipient's actual email address, hold down Shift when you select this command.

- Insert Recipient. Places the name of the selected recipient at the point in a file or an email where the cursor has been inserted.

- Find. This can be used to locate words, phrases or real names within a message. There is a sub-menu, which has commands for Find Text (which can be used to find words with a message), Find Text Again (which can be used to find the next occurrence of the word or phrase specified in Find Text) and Find Messages (which can be used to find emails within system folders). You can specify certain criteria for finding messages including what headings to look under and specific elements that the message contains.

- Sort. This is used to reorder messages in specified folders. There are several ways in which messages can be sorted and these are by: Status, Priority, Attachment, Label, Sender, Date, Size, Server Status and Subject. When one of these options is chosen, the items within the active folder will be reorganised accordingly.

- Check Spelling. This checks the spelling in the active document.

- Message Plug-ins. This contains a number of formatting options that can be applied to the whole of the active document. These include: Upper Case, Lower Case, Toggle Case, Word Case, Sentence Case, Sort and Unwrap Text.

Mailbox menu

This can be used to navigate around the various folders within Eudora and also to move to other email programs:

- In. This takes you to the Inbox, which is where incoming messages appear.
- Out. This takes you to the Outbox, which is where copies of items sent are stored.
- Trash. This takes you to the Trash, which is where items are placed when they are deleted. To delete them permanently, they have to also be deleted from the Trash folder.
- New. This allows you to create a new mailbox, or folder. Select this option, then enter a name in the New Mailbox dialog box. Check on Make it a folder, if this is what you want to do.
- Imported Mailboxes. If you have imported items from another email program, they will be listed here and you will be able to access them in the original program as well as in Eudora.

Message menu

This allows you to download and organise the message you receive:

- New Message. This opens the window for a new email message. The information for the recipient, the subject and anyone who it is being copied to have to be entered, as does the text for the message.
- Reply. This is used when you have received a message and you want to reply to the person who sent it originally. With this option the sender's email address is automatically inserted in the To box of the new message. This also includes the content of the original message.
- Reply To All. This is used if you receive a message as part of a group of people. Select this option if you want to reply to everyone in the group, not just the person who sent the original message.
- Forward. This is used if you want to send a message you have received on to someone else. In this instance the name of the intended recipient would have to be inserted into the To box.

- Redirect. This is similar to forwarding, except that the From box contains the name of the person who sent the message originally, with the person redirecting it named after them, in brackets and with the words 'by way of' before their email address.
- Send Again. This is used if an email has been returned by your mail server. The reason for this is usually an incorrect email address, although it could also be because of a fault with the server. Use Send Again once you have made all the possible checks to find out whether it is going to the right place or not.
- New Message To. This opens a new message to the selected recipient.
- Forward To. This opens a forwarded message to the selected recipient.
- Redirect To. This redirects a message to the selected recipient.
- New Message With. This opens a new message with the selected stationery.
- Reply With. Opens a reply message with the selected stationery.
- Reply To All With. Opens a reply message with the selected stationery, to all the people in a group which you are part of.

If you are replying to a group, make sure that you want everyone to see your reply. If there is someone you want to leave out, select recipients individually.

- Send File. This is similar to attaching a file to an email.
- Attach. This attaches a file to be sent with the email. It can be any type of file, but make sure the recipient has the relevant software to be able to open it.

- Send Immediately. This sends the active message. If you are not online the message will be queued.
- Change. This has a sub-menu that has several options for altering how messages are displayed within a folder.
- Delete. This sends the selected message, or messages, to the Trash folder. To delete them permanently, select this folder and then delete them again.
- Undelete. This reverses the delete command.
- Purge Messages. This permanently removes all selected messages from both your computer and the mail server. If you are not online, this option is greyed out, which means it is not available.

Transfer menu

This menu can be used to transfer items from one folder to another. To do this, first open a folder and select a message, or messages, that you want to move.

- In. This moves the selected item(s) to the Inbox.
- Out. This moves the selected item(s) to the Outbox.
- Trash. This moves the selected item(s) to the Trash folder.

- **New.** This allows you to create a new folder and move the selected item(s) into it immediately. If this option is chosen, type in a name for the new folder in the New Mailbox dialog box.
- Messages can also be moved to folders within other email programs that are on your system, such as Microsoft Outlook Express or Netscape Messenger. If this is chosen, you also have to specify which folder in the other folder you want the item(s) transferred to. This is similar to importing messages, except the item is removed from Eudora if you transfer it to another program.

Special menu

This menu has options for filtering messages, removing items and setting passwords. Filters can be used to stop emails, or types of emails, from reaching your Inbox. They are created by specifying certain criteria and then actions that are taken if these criteria are met.

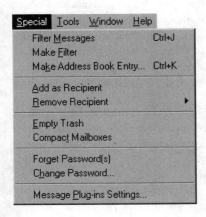

- Filter Messages. This activates filters that have been set up manually.
- Make Filter. This allows you to create filters that apply to specific email messages. This is usually used to block junk mail that you are receiving. To create a filter, select the Make Filter option. In the Make Filter dialog box, select the conditions that have to be matched for the following filter actions to apply. The choices are Incoming, Outgoing or Manual. (The default has both Incoming and Manual checked on.) Then, in the next section, specify what the message has to contain. This can be From, which allows you to create a filter that applies to the sender of the active message; Any Recipient, which allows you to select any address from your address book; and Subject, which allows you to put in criteria for the subject of incoming messages. The third section is where you insert the action that will be performed on the message if it meets one of the specified criteria. The choices here are: Transfer to New Mailbox (in which case you have to insert a name for the new mailbox that will be created); Transfer to Existing Mailbox (in which case you have to specify which mailbox on your system it is to be moved to); and Delete Message (Transfer to Trash), which moves the message to the Trash folder. Once all of this information has been entered, select Create Filter to make this set of conditions and actions active. Select Add Details if you want to include further conditions and actions with the filter.
- Make Address Book Entry. This allows you to insert the email address and related details of a selected message directly into your address book. This is an excellent shortcut for creating address book entries as

it means you do not have to type in the email address manually. This also has the advantage that there is no chance of you entering an address incorrectly.

- Add as Recipient. This allows you to add an email address to the Quick Recipient list. Do this by selecting an address in an email and then selecting this option. This is similar to the Make Address Book Entry command, except it only inserts the email address and not the related information too.
- Remove Recipient. This removes the selected email address from the Quick Recipient list.
- Empty Trash. This removes all of the items that have been placed in the Trash folder. This action deletes them permanently from your computer and a warning message appears to double check that this is what you want to do.
- Compact Mailboxes. This clears out any wasted space that has been created in your mailboxes by transferring or deleting messages. It is a good idea to select this option periodically, to ensure your system is working as efficiently as possible.
- Forget Password. If you have entered any passwords for accessing your message, this command ensures they will be forgotten for the current session. However, if you close down Eudora and then open it again, the passwords will be required.
- Change Password. This allows you to change the current password.
- Message Plug-ins Settings. This allows you to view any plug-in settings that are currently installed.

Tools menu

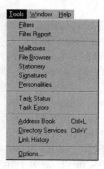

- Filters. This gives access to the more advanced dialog box for creating filters. This is the one that is accessed by selecting Make Filter>Add Details from the Special menu.
- Filter Report. This gives a report on any messages that have been affected by a filter.
- Mailboxes. This displays the list of mailboxes that are contained within your system. They are situated at the top left-hand side of the screen, underneath the toolbar. This allows you to create, edit and delete items within the mailboxes. Click on each mailbox within the mailbox window to access the items that it contains.
- File Browser. This acts as a basic file management system. It allows you to quickly navigate through the files on your computer. They can then be selected and attached to emails. When the file browser is selected it

opens over the mailboxes window. Use the scroll bars to search through the files on your computer.

- Stationery. This allows you to access the stationery window, which appears in the same place as the file browser window or the mailboxes window. Stationery is used as a template if you want to save a particular style, or message, for use on other occasions. If you want to create a new item of stationery, right click in the stationery window. From the contextual menu, select New. A standard mail window appears. Insert the information that you want to include, such as the recipient, the subject, the background colour, the font size and style, and any images. Select File > Save As Stationery from the menu bar. Save the file into the Stationery folder (which is the default option). The file will have an extension of '–.sta'. When you want to use a stationery file, as a completed document or as a template for a new item, select it from the stationery window, or select File > Open from the menu bar and open the file from the Stationery folder.

- Signatures. This allows you to access the signature window, which appears in the same place as the three previous items. This can be used to create files that can be inserted at the end of an email, if you want to include a preformatted ending. To access the editing options for this, right click in the signatures window. The available options are: New, Edit, Delete and Rename.

Give your signatures clearly identifiable names, rather than 'Signature 1' etc. This way you will not get confused when you are adding them to messages.

- Personalities. This allows you to access the personalities window, which appears in the same place as the four previous items. This can be used to access different email accounts, if you have more than one.

- Task Status. This allows you to access the task status window, which appears at the bottom of the screen. This shows you how various background operations are progressing, such as sending and receiving messages. In Eudora you can perform several tasks at once, so you can send messages, receive message and compose messages all at the same time. The task status window lets you see how each task is progressing, which is particularly useful if you are waiting for an item to be downloaded or sent.

- Task Errors. This displays any errors that have occurred with sending or receiving messages. The error messages appear in the task status window and they can be for a variety of reasons, such as an incorrectly addressed email, or a problem with your or the recipient's email server.

- Address Book. This opens your address book. New contacts can then be added by selecting the New button, or removed by clicking on them and selecting the Del button.

- Directory Services. This can give you access to various servers to find out information about other people who are linked to the network.

- Link History. This gives a list of the hyperlinks that are available from your program. In Eudora's Sponsored mode, most of these are related to the advertisements that appear at the bottom left hand corner of the program. The link history window lists whether you have visited these links and when. In addition to the advertisements, there are also links to the Eudora online tutorial and for registration.

- Options. This contains numerous options relating to the way your version of Eudora works. These are looked at in greater detail in the next section.

Options

Although the Options command is part of the Tools menu, there are so many elements that it needs to be covered in its own right. Most of the options relate to the way the program operates and most aspects of it can be customised.

The elements of the Options menu are:

Getting Started

This contains your basic personal information, which was obtained when you first downloaded Eudora. This includes:

- Real Name. This is your actual name, as you entered it during the downloading process.

- Return Address. This is the email address that you want to be associated with the program.
- Mail Server (Incoming). This lists the mail server that will be delivering your email messages.
- Login Name. This is the name that you originally logged in to the mail server with.
- SMTP (Simple Mail Transfer Protocol) Server (Outgoing). This lists the mailer server that will be sending your email messages.

Simple Mail Transfer Protocol is a programming language that is generally accepted for the transfer of outgoing mail messages on the Internet. It is commonly used by most ISPs.

Checking Mail

This contains options for specifying how Eudora checks for new messages. These are:

- Check for mail every xx minutes. Enter a limit for how long the program has to wait before it checks for new messages from the server. Do not make it too low (under 15 minutes) or else a lot of unnecessary checks will be performed.
- Don't check without a network connection. If this button is checked on, you have to be connected to the Internet for the check to be performed.
- Don't check when using battery. This is a power saving device, if you are using a laptop.

- Send on check. If this option is checked on, any messages that are queued i.e. in the Outbox waiting to be sent, will be delivered at the same time as new messages are checked.
- Save password. If this option is checked on, your Eudora password is saved and it remains so even if you close down your computer and then reboot. If this option is selected, make sure that no one has unauthorised access to your computer. If they do, they will be able to go directly into your email program, without having to know your password. They would then have access to the messages you have received and, perhaps more dangerously, they would also be able to send email messages that would appear as if they had come from you. The results could be embarrassing or worse.

If possible, use the same password for all programs that require it. This way there is less chance of forgetting one. However, make sure that you do not give it out to anyone else.

Incoming Mail

This allows you to choose various settings that govern how your incoming emails are dealt with. The options available are:

- Server configuration. This can be either POP (Post Office Protocol) or IMAP (Internet Message Access Protocol). This is the method that your mail server uses to send and receive messages. If you do not know which protocol your server uses, check with your ISP. The options for incoming mail vary depending on the server configuration of your ISP. For POP servers the following options are available:

- Leave mail on server. If this box is checked on, any messages that are downloaded to your computer are also kept on your ISP's mail server. By default, this is checked off, which means the messages are deleted from the mail server once they are downloaded. Most system administrators do not like keeping messages on the server once they have been downloaded, since they take up valuable space and can slow down system performance. In some cases, even if this option is checked on it will be overridden by the system administrator and your messages will in fact be deleted once they have been downloaded.

Some ISPs do not allow you to leave mail on the server arguing, justifiably, that it would cause unnecessary strain on the storage capacity of their server.

- Delete from server after xx days. This gives you the option of selecting how long you want items kept on the server before they are deleted.
- Delete from server when emptied from Trash. This automatically deletes an item from the server if it is removed from the Trash folder. This means that the message has been well and truly deleted, for good.
- Skip messages over xx in size. This gives you the option of specifying the maximum size of file you are willing to accept as an email. Do not set this too low (below 50K) as it may mean you miss out on items such as digital images or video clips.
- Offline. Check this option on if you do not want to be connected to the Internet, unless you specify otherwise.

- Authentication style. This allows you to select how you want to be authenticated by the server. The default is with your password.

For IMAP servers the following options are available:

- For new mail, download:
  - Minimal headers only. If this is checked on, only the most basic information about the message is downloaded, not including the body text and any attachments.
  - Full message except attachments over xx K. This can be used to specify the maximum size of attachments that can be included with a message.
- When I delete a message:
  - Mark it as deleted. This identifies the message as being deleted so that you can quickly see which messages have been removed from certain folders.
  - Move it to. This allows you to specify where messages will be placed once they have been deleted. The default for this is the Trash folder.
- Authentication style. This determines how user authentication will be achieved with the server. The default is to use the user's password.

Messages will only be permanently deleted once they have been removed from the Trash folder. Deleting a message from another part of the program is only really a semi-delete.

Sending Mail

This is used to specify options for outgoing messages from your primary email account (which is your main one if you have more than one) and they are:

- Return Address. This is your own email address and the one to which any messages will be returned, or sent, to you. This should already contain your normal email address.

- Domain to add to unqualified addresses. This is a domain name that is added if an email address is not in the standard format of '@' followed by the domain name of the recipient.

- SMTP server. This is the name of your ISP's mail server that deals with your email account. This information should already be inserted here, using the prefix 'smtp' which stands for Simple Mail Transfer Protocol.

- Allow authentication. This enables Eudora to login to your ISP's email server and authenticate your account. This is not always possible but this option is checked on by default.

- Immediate send. If this is checked on, as it is by default, there will be a Send button on the toolbar when you are creating a new message. If this is clicked then the current message will be. If this option is checked off, the message will be stored in a queue of outgoing messages in the Outbox until they are ready to be sent.

- Send on check. If this option is checked on, any mail messages waiting to be sent i.e. queued, will be done so at the same time as new messages are checked for on the server. Check this option off if you want to have precise control over when you send messages, otherwise it is a useful option for making sure you do not forget about messages waiting to be sent.

- Default Stationery. This allows you to select a Stationery file that will be used as a template for all new messages you create. Whenever you start a new message, the elements of the stationery file will be used as the starting point for the new message. New stationery files can be created by selecting Tools>Stationery from the menu bar. Then right click in the Stationery window, select New, create your stationery file and then save it. This option for setting default stationery is only available in the Sponsored or Paid modes of Eudora. If a default stationery is selected, it overrides all of the following options.

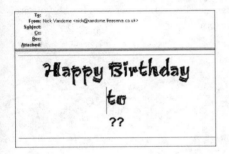

- Default Signature. This can be used to select a signature file that is automatically inserted at the end of an email message. This option is only active if the default stationery, above, is set to none. If you are using a default signature this will not appear in the message as you are creating it but it will appear on the recipient's version of the message. Signature files are created by selecting Tools>Signature from the menu bar. Then right click in the Signature window, select New, create your signature file and then save it. When you create a new message there will be a box on the new message toolbar that displays the name of the signature file that is being used, if any. If you do not want to have a signature at the end of a message, make sure the Default Signature box is set to default. One use for a signature file is to use your own hand-written signature. To do this scan your signature and, when you are creating a new signature file, select Edit > Insert > Picture from the menu bar and select the file which contains your scanned signature. This creates a larger file size but it is a good way to add a personal touch to an email. It is possible to create different signature files for both personal and business messages, but remember which one you are using for each type of correspondence.

- Word wrap. If this is checked on, carriage returns are automatically inserted into lines that Eudora considers to be too long. This is intended to ensure that they are more easily viewed on the recipient's computer. When creating emails it is worth remembering that they will be viewed on monitors that are probably different sizes to the one on which they are being created. If a default stationery file has been selected, this overrides word wrap.
- Keep copies. If this is checked on, copies of sent messages are automatically placed in the Outbox. If not they are placed in the Trash

folder. If a default stationery file has been selected, this overrides Keep copies.

- May use quoted-printable. If this is checked on, special encoding is used if special characters are included in a message. This means the recipient should be able to see the characters as they were intended. If a default stationery file has been selected, this overrides May use quoted-printable.
- Tabs in body of message. If this is checked on, pressing the tab key inserts tabs within the text. If it is checked off, the tab key moves the cursor to the To box in the message header. If a default stationery file has been selected, this overrides Tabs in body of message.

Internet Dial-Up

This contains options for how the connections to your email server are managed. They include:

- Have Eudora connect using Dial-up networking. This is an option for using Eudora over a network.
- Hang-up after sending and receiving. If this is checked on, your Internet connection will be terminated after any messages have been sent or downloaded. This is a useful device to ensure you do not remain connected to the Internet when you do not want to be, therefore running up unnecessary telephone charges.

If you select the Hang-up after sending and receiving option, check to make sure that your Internet connection has been terminated. If not, you will have to disconnect manually to avoid incurring unnecessary call charges and tying up the telephone line.

- Close connection on exit. If this is checked on, your Internet connection will be terminated if you close down Eudora. As earlier, this can help reduce the amount of time that you are connected to the Internet.
- Entry/New/Edit. These options can be used to specify new dial-up network settings.
- Only do automatic mail checks when a network connection is already established. If this is checked on mail will be checked for automatically, but only if you are connected to a network.

Replying

This contains options for how you reply to messages you have received. They include:

- Map Ctrl+R to 'Reply to All'. If this option is checked on you can press the Ctrl key and the R key at the same time to create a reply to all of the recipients of a grouped message and also the original sender.
- Copy original's priority to reply. If this option is checked on, your reply to a message will be sent with the same level of priority as the original message.
- Automatically Fcc to original mailbox. If this option is checked on, replies to a message are automatically copied to the mailbox that contains the original message, except if it is in the Inbox, in which case it is copied to the Outbox.
- Include signature on reply. If this option is checked on, your default signature will be included with all of the replies that you send.
- Quote on the selected text. If this option is checked on, you can highlight text in a message by clicking and dragging over it. Then when you reply to a message, only the selected section will be included in the reply. This is a useful option if you receive a long message but you only

want to comment on a specific part of it. The same result can be achieved by copying the relevant passage and then pasting it into your reply, but this can be a quicker and more professional looking approach.

- When reply to all. This has two options that can be selected when you are replying to a group of recipients to a message:
  - Include yourself. If this option is checked on, you will receive a copy of your own reply.
  - Put original To: recipients in Cc: field. If this option is checked on, the original sender will be placed in the To box of your reply and the other recipients will be placed in the Cc box.

Attachments

This contains options for managing how your attachments are sent. They include:

- Encoding method. This specifies how the attachment is encoded for sending to the recipient's computer. There are three options, that can be selected according to the type of computer that the recipient is using:
  - MIME. This stands for Multipurpose Internet Mail Extensions and it is one of the most common standards for email readers. The majority of PC users will have MIME email readers and this is the default option for encoding.

MIME is currently the most commonly accepted standard for sending attachments.

- BinHex. This is used by some Mac users and also users of older versions of Eudora.
- Uuencode. This is a form of encoding that should be used if you are sending attachments to users with UNIX systems or, in some cases, older PCs.

- Put text attachments in body of message. If this option is checked on, the attachment is inserted into the main part of a message, in the same way as if it were typed there directly. This only works with plain text attachments.
- Attachment directory. This gives you the option of specifying a single folder into which all attachments will be placed. To do this, double click on the bar underneath Attachment directory, and select a location from the Select a directory dialog box. The default directory is Eudora>Attach. Open this directory if you want to access attachments after the original message has been deleted.
- Delete attachments when emptying Trash. If this option is checked on, a message and its attachment are deleted if the message is removed from the Trash folder. It is possible to still save the attachment, but only if it is first moved into a different folder from that selected as the attachment directory.
- Delete automatic attachments. This gives you three options for managing attachments that are generated automatically by certain messages. These options are: Never, After sending message and When message emptied from Trash.

Fonts

This contains options for the fonts that you use in your messages and how they are displayed. They include:

- Message. This allows you to specify whether to use a proportional or a fixed-width font. There are two boxes from which to make selections:
  - Proportional. Select a proportional font by clicking on the arrow at the end of the box. Proportional fonts have the space between each character adjusted so as to give a more even look to words, phrases and sentences. Proportional fonts are excellent for online use and the most commonly used are Arial and Helvetica.
  - Fixed-width fonts. These are fonts that have the same size of space between each character.

```
This is a fixed width font
```

- Underneath these two boxes is an option for checking on proportional fonts as the default. This is recommended, as they are generally easier to read on screen.
- Size. This has options for specifying the size of font to be used in creating and viewing messages. The options are: Smallest, Small, Medium, Large, Largest. The default is Small and this provides a good compromise between readability and space. However, keep the age group of the intended recipient in mind: the older we get the more our eyesight deteriorates or if the message if going to someone, or a group,

in the over 60s age bracket then it would be advisable to select a font size of Medium at the very minimum.

- Printer. This can be used to specify the font and size of any text that is printed from Eudora. The options are for Font and Size and the defaults for these are Arial and Medium, respectively.
- Screen. This offers options for how text other than that used in actual email messages is displayed. This includes text files, signature files and summaries. The options are for Font and Size and the defaults are Arial and Small, respectively.

Display

This determines certain aspects of the appearance of your Eudora program. It is possible to customise this to a certain extent. By default all of the Display options are checked on and they are:

- Show toolbar. If this is checked on, the main toolbar is visible. If it is checked off, it disappears. Unless you have a good reason not to, such as the need for more on-screen space when composing a message, the toolbar should always be visible.
- Show toolbar tips. If this is checked on, a short description appears when the cursor is moved over a button on the toolbar.

The toolbar tips are like a mini version of the Help files. They give you a quick, and brief, look at the functions of a particular item. If no tips appear for an item, look it up in Help instead.

- Show cool tips. If this is checked on, the buttons on the toolbar become raised if the cursor is moved over them.
- Show large buttons. If this is checked on, the buttons on the toolbar are displayed at their largest size. If it is checked off, the buttons are displayed in a minimised form. This can be useful if you need to free up more space on screen.
- Show status bar. If this is checked on, the status bar at the bottom of the screen is visible. This is a grey bar that contains a brief description of a menu bar or toolbar item, when the cursor is placed over it. It also indicated whether Caps Lock or Num Lock has been selected.
- Show category icons. If this is checked on, the icons in the Display window are visible. If it is checked off, there is only a textual description of each category.
- Show MDI task bar. If this is checked on, a task bar is displayed at the bottom of the active folder window. This gives information about available mailboxes, folders and messages that have either been opened or are in the process of being created.

Viewing Mail

This determines the way in which you can view incoming messages and the options are:

- Message Window. This has three options:
  - Use Microsoft's viewer. If you have Microsoft's Internet Explorer 4 browser or above installed, check this box on to use its capabilities for displaying Web content in incoming messages and also to link to the Web, if applicable. If you do not have this browser, Eudora will use its own viewer to display items such as advanced formatting, graphics and multimedia.

- Message width window. This can be used to enter a value for the width, in characters, for displaying incoming messages. The default is 80, but this can be altered if you have a wider or narrower monitor.
- Message height window. This is the same as above, but for the height at which incoming messages are displayed.

- Preview Pane. This can be used to view a message in a window directly below the main folder window. This way you can see what is in a message just by clicking on it, rather than having to open it up. The main drawback with this is that it limits the amount of available viewing space. There are two main options for the Preview Pane:
  - Show message Preview Pane. Check this box on to activate the Preview Pane. Experiment with this to see if you like this function or not, since it is easy to turn on and off. Once the Preview Pane has been activated it can be resized by clicking on its top border and dragging it up or down the screen. The Preview Pane displays the To and Subject header information and the body of the message. If there is not enough space for the whole message, scroll bars appear to move down the text.

- Mark previewed messages as read after seconds. If this is checked on, a message that is being viewed in the Preview Pane will appear as being read in the main window after the designated length of time, which is entered into a separate text box. This means that the circle next to the message (which denotes it has not been read) will disappear.
- Automatically open next message. If this is checked on, the next message after the selected one will be opened if the selected one is deleted or moved to another folder. However, this will only apply if the next message has not already been opened.
- Zoom windows when opening. If this is checked on, a new message will be opened in a window that is designed to be the optimum size for viewing that message.
- Allow executables in HTML content. This is an option that allows Eudora to run executables (usually mini-programs written in a computer language such as JavaScript or ActiveX) if they are contained within an email that has been created in an HTML format. This gives more functionality to your email program but it is worth remembering that a lot of viruses are contained in executable programs. As a security measure, it is best to keep this option checked off, unless you have an executable that you simply must open.

If you receive an executable file from a source that you do not know, do not open it. Even if it is from a trusted source, it is worth running it through a virus checker before you open it.

Mailboxes

This contains options for the way information is displayed within the Eudora mailboxes. These options include:

- Show Mailbox Columns. This determines what type of information is displayed in relation to items in a mailbox. The options to select from are (by default, they are all selected):
  - Status
  - Priority
  - Attachment
  - Label
  - Sender
  - Date
  - Size
  - Server status
  - Subject

The more options that are selected, then the more information will be displayed for the message in a mailbox. Whichever options are selected apply to all mailboxes.

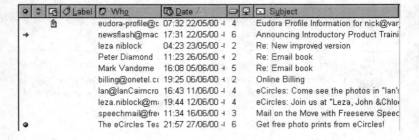

- Show mailbox lines. If this is checked on, a grid is placed over messages in a mailbox. This can help to separate them from each other.
- Close messages with mailbox. If this is checked on, any open messages will be closed if the mailbox in which they are located is closed. If it is checked off, the messages will still be open when the mailbox is next opened.
- Select newly inserted messages. If this is checked on, the most recently downloaded message is highlighted.
- When dragging in a mailbox. This refers to techniques for moving and selecting messages and the options are:
  - Allow drag and drop transfers. If this is checked on, messages can be moved between folder by clicking on them and then dragging them to their new location and releasing. This is a common method of moving files.
  - Allow drag-select of messages. If this is checked on, several messages can be selected at once by clicking on the first one and then dragging over the others, as long as they appear sequentially. By default, this is checked off, in which case, multiple messages can be selected by holding down Ctrl and clicking on each item.

Drag-select can be used if you want to move a batch of files from one folder to another, perhaps for archiving purposes.

Styled Text

This contains options for the way text looks when it is sent in an email. The options are:

- Show formatting toolbar. If this is checked on, the toolbar for formatting an email message is available whenever a new message is started.
- When sending mail with styled text (HTML). This offers various options for when an email contains text that has been formatted with HTML. If a message is created in HTML, the user will only be able to see this formatting if their email program supports this format. The options are:
  - Send both plain and styled. If this is checked on, Eudora will send messages with plain and HTML text formatted as they are in the original message.

If you send a plain and a styled message you will at least be sure that the recipient will be able to read one of them. However, this involves a slightly longer overall message.

  - Send styled text only. If this is checked on, Eudora will retain any HTML formatting, regardless of the recipient's capability to read this format.
  - Send plain text only. If this is checked on, Eudora will send messages as plain text regardless of the format in which they were created. This is useful for users who do not have the capability to read messages in HTML format.

- Ask me each time. If this is checked on, a message will appear each time you send a message that contains HTML formatting.
- When the body of a message has no styles, but the signature does have styles. This applies if a signature used with a message has been created using HTML style while the message itself has been created in plain text. There is an option box for *Send the signature with styles* and if it is checked on then the formatting of the signature will be retained.

Spell checking

This contains options for Eudora's inbuilt spell checker. The options are:

- Ignore capitalized words
- Ignore words with all capitals
- Ignore words with numbers
- Ignore words with mixed case
- Report doubled words
- Suggest words
- Phonetic words
- Split words
- Typographic words
- Check spelling automatically as you type. If this is checked on, the spell checker operates continuously. When a misspelt word is identified it is flagged up with two red lines underneath it.

At first it can be disconcerting to see the red lines underneath words if the spelling is checked automatically. If this is too distracting, check this option off. But remember to check the whole document once you have finished.

- Check spelling only when requested. If this is checked on, the spell checker will only be activated by selecting Edit>Check Spelling from the menu bar.
- Outgoing messages. This has two options for checking spelling when sending messages:
  - Ignore original text. If this is checked on, the message will be sent regardless of how accurate the text is.
  - Warn me when sending/queuing message with misspellings. If this is checked on, a warning message will appear when you try and send a message that contains spelling mistakes.

Auto-Completion

This offers various options for automatically completing entries for the To and Cc boxes when creating a new message. The options are:

- Auto-complete items in recipient field with data from:
  - Address Book. If this is checked on, names are automatically entered from the address book, once the first letter of two is entered into the recipient field.
  - History File. This displays names that have been used previously. When one or two letters are entered, the suggested name is automatically placed in the recipient box.
- Use drop-down list for completion choices. If this is checked on, entry choices are displayed in a drop-down list. There are usually a number of choices, depending on the original letters that were entered.
- Names should appear alphabetically. If this is checked on, the names in drop-down lists are displayed alphabetically.
- Add the from lines of replied-to messages. If this is checked on, the sender's name from incoming messages is added to the history file.

- Time to wait before popping up Auto-Completion box (Milliseconds). This is the time, in milliseconds, that Eudora waits until it displays the drop-down list for auto-completion. If it is set at 0, the list appears immediately.
- Maximum entries to keep history. This is the number of items that are contained in the history file. The default is 100 entries.

Date Display

This contains options for how the date is displayed in the date column of Eudora folders for messages that are contained there. The options are:
- Display date using Sender's timezone. If this is checked on, messages are displayed according to the date of the sender's timezone. Therefore, if the sender is located in Australia, this is the timezone that will be displayed.

- Display date using Local timezone. If this is checked on, messages are displayed according to your own timezone.
- Date formats. This has options for how the date next to incoming messages is displayed. There are fixed options and also those for old messages:

- Fixed. If this is checked on, the date will be displayed according to a fixed format of: time received; date received; and the message timezone, if it is different from your own.
- Age-sensitive. If this is checked on, messages are labelled according to Recent, Old and Ancient. Settings can be applied to determine timescales for what qualifies as an Old or an Ancient message and the defaults are 24 hours and 168 hours respectively. This is a useful option when viewing messages because it allows you to identify your most recent messages more quickly.

Labels

This offers a range of colours to select when labelling messages.

Getting Attention

This has settings that affect the way Eudora alerts you to the existence of new messages. The options are:

- Use dialog box. If this is checked on, a dialog box appears saying You have New Mail if you have new messages to read.
- Open mailbox. If this is checked on, the mailbox in which a new message is contained is opened automatically.
- Play a sound. If this is checked on, a sound plays to alert you to new messages. Click on the bar below this option to access more sound files from you hard drive, which have to have a '–wav' extension.
- Create filter report. If this is checked on, a report is created about any filters that are in use. This is only done if the filter report window is active, which is done by selecting Tools > Filter Report from the menu bar.

Background Tasks

This determines what background tasks are undertaken by Eudora and how they are displayed in the Task Status window, which is accessed by selecting Tools>Task Status from the menu bar. The main tasks that Eudora performs in the background are sending and receiving mail. The options are:

- Task Status Columns. This determines the columns that are displayed in the Task Status window.
- Task. This is the current task being undertaken.
- Persona. This is only active if there is more than one user set up for the account.
- Status. This displays the current action that is being undertaken.
- Details. Contains more detailed information about the current task.
- Progress. This displays how the current task is progressing.
- Wait for xx seconds of user inactivity before processing/filtering downloaded messages. This is the amount of time that Eudora will wait to perform a sending or downloading task, if you are engaged in another activity. So if you are typing a message, Eudora will not try to perform any tasks until you have stopped for the amount of time specified in this box. The shorter the time, the quicker Eudora starts performing the task.
- Bring error window to front. If this is checked on, the error window appears if an error is located while a task is being performed.
- Bring task status window to front. If this is checked on, the task status window appears when a task is being performed.

Automation

This has an option that allows Eudora to be automated, which means that you can control items in Eudora from other programs, as long as they support the Windows Automation Interface.

Extra Warnings

This contains several options for conditions under which a warning message will appear, as long as they are checked on. These conditions are if you try and do any of the following:

- Delete unread mail
- Delete queued mail
- Delete unsent mail
- Queue a message with no subject
- Queue a message bigger than xx K (default of 500K)
- Quit with messages queued to be sent
- Empty the Trash mailbox
- Start Eudora and it's not the default mailer
- Switch views of Find
- Launch a program from a message

Check off any of these options to let you perform this task without having a warning message appear.

MAPI (Messaging Application Program Interface)

This is an option that can streamline the sending of attachments. If this is checked on, attachments can be emailed directly from the program in which they were created. So instead of having to create a word-processed document, then open Eudora and attach it to an email, it can be attached directly from the source file. Select Send, or Send to, from the source program and then Mail

Recipient and a new message window will open in Eudora with the file already attached to it. There are three main options for MAPI

- Never
- When Eudora is running
- Always

Advanced Network

This contains settings for how Eudora operates when connecting with your email server. If you want to change these then it is best to contact your email administrator or ISP to ask them about the optimum settings for their server.

Auto Configure

This can be used when sending and receiving messages but there should be little reason to use it.

Kerberos

This is a security setting and does not need to be altered unless you are informed you require to do so by your ISP.

Miscellaneous

This contains the few items that do not fall into any of the previous options. They are:

- Switch messages with. This allows you to move selected messages using either the arrow keys or a combination of Alt and Ctrl and the arrow keys.
- Empty Trash when exiting. If this is checked on, the Trash folder is emptied every time you close down Eudora.

- Say OK to alerts after xx seconds. This automatically accepts an alert message after a specified amount of time, if no selection has been made. The default is 120 seconds.
- Turbo redirect by default. This is a quick method for redirecting messages.
- Include outdated Return-Receipt-To. This can be checked on to specify how messages that have been given a return-receipt tag are dealt with (i.e. messages that contain a request for the recipient to notify you once your email has been received). This does not always work and can be a hit or miss process.
- Automatically expand nicknames. If this is checked on, then nicknames, i.e. the names under which people are known in the address book, are expanded to show the full email address of the recipient. This can be a reassuring function, because you can see exactly where the message is going to be sent.
- Auto-save messages every xx minutes. This allows you to set the time at which the auto-save function is activated. This is a valuable option because it automatically ensures your messages are saved even if the program crashes. The default setting is 10 minutes.

Computers crash, it's a fact of life. If you are worried about losing your work use the auto-save function. However, it is not necessary to set it to save every couple of minutes or so as this would just become irritating.

Window

This menu contains options for how the items within your Eudora program are displayed. It also has a list of the currently open items.

- Cascade. If this is selected, all of the open items are displayed one on top of each other, with only the top bar of the window showing. The active window has a blue bar, the rest have grey bars. Click on the top bar of any window to access it – its bar will turn blue.
- Tile Horizontally. If this is selected, all of the open windows are displayed in a horizontal format. Each window is minimised so that all of the items can be displayed at once.
- Tile Vertically. This is the same as above, except that the windows are displayed vertically.
- Arrange icons. This places windows that have been changed into icons along the bottom of the main window.
- Send to back. This sends the active window to the back of the stacking order of the open items. This can be used if there a lot of windows open and you need to view a particular one at that moment.

Help

This contains various options for finding out more about Eudora and how to use it.

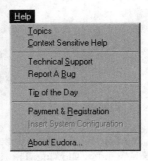

- Topics. This contains an index of all of the help topics that are available. There are three tabs: Contents, Index and Find, which can be used to locate specific items or general help topics.
- Context Sensitive Help. If this is selected, an arrow with a question mark next to it appears as the on-screen cursor. When this is positioned over an element of the program and clicked, a help box will appear explaining what that element does. The question mark disappears after each enquiry and if you want to see the help box for other items, this option has to be selected from the Help menu again.
- Technical support. This offers a range of help options, including step-by-step instructions about using Eudora, a list of Frequently Asked Questions (FAQs), the Eudora newsgroup address and a technical helpline. For some of these items you will need to be connected to the

Web: if you are not, a dialog box will appear asking if you would like to go online.

- Report a Bug. This provides a direct email link to Eudora so that you can report any bugs that you discover in the program. You will be asked a few questions, such as the exact type of browser that you are using and the version and mode of Eudora.

- Tip of the Day. If this is selected, a window opens with a tip about using Eudora. Initially this may be useful but as you become more experienced with the program you will probably not use this feature a lot.

- Payment and Registration. This enables you to upgrade to the paid version of Eudora and to register your copy, whatever mode it is. Eudora like users to register with them since it gives them information about how the program is being used. It is free to register any mode of Eudora and the company will be grateful that you have taken the time and effort to do so.

- Insert System Configuration. This can be selected when you are emailing Eudora with information about a bug. This will automatically insert information about the system you are using into the email. This way you do not have to try and find a lot of technical details.

- About Eudora. This tells you the version of the program that you are using and also its mode. There is also a link to the Eudora Web site.

A message will appear periodically to ask if you want to register your copy of Eudora. It is very friendly and gives you the choice of registering at a later date. It is worth doing this at some point, so you can be updated about the latest Eudora-related products.

Creating a new message

Sending a new message involves opening a new message window, entering a recipient's name and subject and then adding text and attachments, if required:

1. Select the New Message button on the toolbar (this is depicted by a large and a small envelope, with a star above the small one).
2. In the To box, type the first letter of the recipient's name. A drop down list will appear with everyone in your address book whose name starts with that letter. Select the one you want, or enter a new address manually.
3. Enter details for anyone who you want to copy the message to, as above, and the subject.
4. Add the text for the message in the window below the To and Subject fields.
5. To add an attachment, select the Attach File button from the main toolbar (this is depicted by an envelope with a sheet of paper paper-clipped to the front of it.) Then locate the file you want to attach and select Open. The file that has been attached will be named in the header of the message and included with the email when it is sent.
6. Select Send on the new message toolbar (see later).

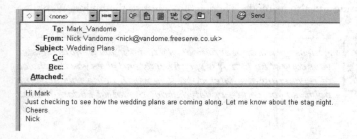

New message toolbar

When you are creating a new message, the following toolbar is available:

- Priority. This can be used to assign priority settings to an outgoing message. These range from Lowest to Highest. However, use these with care, since everyone thinks their messages are important and do not always look favourably on messages that are labelled as highest priority.
- Signature. This can be used to insert an item of predefined text at the end of an email (see later).
- Encoding. This can be used to determine how a message is encoded, if at all.
- Quoted-printable encoding. This can be used to encode long lines of text or special characters.
- Text as Attachment. If this is checked on, plain text files are treated in the same way as other attachments. If it is checked off, they are inserted into the body of the message.
- Word Wrap. If this is checked on, carriage returns are inserted automatically into long lines of text, so that the recipient should not have to scroll along the screen to view the whole message.
- Tab in Body. If this is checked on the tab key can be used to move to the next indent within a message. If it is checked off, the tab key can be used to move directly to the To box in the message header.

- Keep Copies. If this is checked on a copy of the sent message is saved into the Outbox.
- Return Receipt. If this is checked on the recipient will be asked to let you know that a message has arrived. This does not always work, through a combination of technical variations and human nature.
- Invisible Characters. If this is checked on it displays non-printing marks such as spaces between letters and paragraph marks.
- Send. Select this to send a message immediately, or queue it for delivery later, depending on your setting within Tools > Options > Sending Mail. If the Immediate Send box is checked off, the message will be queued. To send queued messages, select File > Send Queued Messages from the menu bar.

If you are writing a lot of messages, it is quicker to queue them as you go along and then send them in a batch when you have finished.

Queuing multiple messages and sending them later has one further advantage: it saves money!

Receiving messages

To download messages from your mail server, select the Check Mail button on the main toolbar. (This is depicted by a tray with an envelope and a blue arrow pointing into it.) Depending on your incoming mail settings, which are determined by selecting Tools>Options>Incoming Mail from the menu bar, this should connect you to your mail server and download your latest messages. When a new message has been received it will have a blue bullet next to it, which indicates that it has not been read. Double click on the message to open it. When a message has been opened the following toolbar is available:

- Drag to another folder. This is depicted by a tow truck and can be used to move the current message directly into another mail folder. To do this, click on the mail truck button and drag it into the required folder. This is a good way for quickly organising messages when you receive them.
- View with a fixed width font. This is depicted by a pair of sunglasses superimposed over the letters TT and if this is selected the font of the current message is converted into a fixed width one, which looks a bit like it has been created on a typewriter.
- Show all headers. This is depicted by the words Blah, blah, blah and can be used to include all of the available information in the header of the

current message. By default, only certain items are included, but if you want every last detail then click on this button.

- Edit the message. This is depicted by a pencil and allows you to edit the original message and the header information. You may want to do this if you are forwarding the message on to someone else. However, if you do edit a message make sure that any other recipients know what you have done – do not try and pass it off as the work of the original author. If this option is selected, a formatting toolbar is also available.
- Priority. This has various options in a drop down list, ranging from Highest to Lowest and can be used if you are forwarding a message.

Adding Priority tags sometimes has the opposite effect from the intended one, as the recipient can take offence at being told one message is more important than another.

Working with folders and mailboxes

Folders and mailboxes can be used to store and organise messages. A folder can contain several mailboxes, but mailboxes cannot be created inside one another. To create a new folder or mailbox:

1. Make sure the mailboxes window is visible. Select Tools>Mailboxes if it is not.
2. To create a new main folder, click on the Eudora folder, which is at the top of the structural hierarchy.
3. Select Mailbox>New from the menu bar, or right click on the folder and select New.

4. In the New Mailbox dialog box, enter a name for the new mailbox and check on the Make it a folder box.

To create a mailbox from a folder, which is like a sub-folder, click on the relevant folder and continue from Step 3, except do not check on the Make it a folder box.

Once folders and mailboxes have been created, messages can be dragged and dropped from one location to another.

Eudora is a great advocate of using drag and drop techniques, and tries to employ them wherever possible.

Signatures

Signatures are predefined pieces of text that can be automatically inserted at the end of email messages. To create these in Eudora:

1. Select Tools>Signatures from the menu bar.
2. In the signature windowpane, right click and select New.
3. In the Create New Signature dialog, enter a name for the signature and select OK.
4. Select the new signature and then add text in the right hand windowpane.
5. To insert the signature into an email message, open a new message and select the name of the signature from the drop down list which appears on the Compose Message toolbar.

Overall, Eudora is a neat, powerful and efficient email program and it is well worth having a look at.

Netscape Messenger

Creating a profile

As shown in the 'Email Programs' chapter, Messenger is the email component of Netscape's Communicator, which is built around the popular Navigator browser. Once you have downloaded and installed the program (or installed it from a CD-ROM) you will need to set up a user profile so that Messenger can identify you and your email account. First, open Messenger by selecting Communicator>Messenger from the Communicator menu bar. Initially, the program will open in the browser element, but this will take you to the email part. The dialog boxes for creating a profile should appear automatically when you first start Messenger and you can complete them at this time or wait until you are ready to send and receive messages. The profile dialog boxes can be accessed at any time by clicking on the Start button in Windows and selecting Programs>Netscape Communicator>Utilities>User Profile Manager. The items that need to be completed for a user profile are:

- Full Name and Email Address. If you already have an account with an Internet Service Provider (ISP) include the email address that you have been allocated. If you do not have an account with an ISP, get one before you begin filling in your user profile. Select Next.
- Create a Name and Directory for your Profile. This allows you to give a name to your profile, such as 'My Profile', and specify where on your computer you want this information held. The default location is usually sufficient and can be left untouched. Select Next.

- Set up your Outgoing Mail Server. This is required so that Messenger can communicate with your mail server to send messages. It will probably begin with SMTP and have the suffix of your ISP e.g. 'smtp.internetprovider.net' If you do not know your outgoing mail server address, contact your ISP and they will be able to provide it. (If you already have an email account and you are using an email program such as Outlook Express, the server information can be found by looking under Tools>Accounts>Mail>Properties>Servers.) Select Next.

- Set your Incoming Mail Server. This is similar to the outgoing mail server, except that it will probably have a POP prefix. This dialog box will also require your mail server user name, which may be a combination of your email address (sometimes the part after the @ symbol). Check with your ISP if you are unsure about either of these items. Select Next.

- Set your Newsgroup Server. This is required if you want to communicate with newsgroups over the Internet. Again, ask your ISP if you do not know this information.
- Select Finish to store the information of your new profile.
- If you want to change any of the profile settings in Messenger, select Edit>Preferences>Mail and Newsgroups>Mail Servers or Identity. Select the Edit button to make changes to your current settings.

Menu bar

Messenger is very similar in appearance to the Navigator browser and its interface works in much the same way with its use of menus and toolbars. The standard Messenger menu bar consists of:

File

The File menu contains the following options:

- New. This lets you access various elements within Messenger, including a new message window.
- New Folder. This enables you to create a new folder for storing your messages. Enter its name in the New Folder dialog box and then specify where you want it to appear within your current folder structure.
- Open Attachment. This enables you to open any attachments that you receive with incoming mail.
- Save As. This enables you to save a message under another name i.e. make a copy of it.
- Get New Messages. This option will connect you to your mail server and download any messages that are waiting for you.
- Send Unsent Messages. This will connect you to your mail server and send any messages that have been composed but not sent.

Using the Send Unsent Messages button is a good way to ensure you do not forget to send messages which you intended to. It can be used just before you finish a session.

- Update Message Count. This updates the number of unread messages.
- Subscribe. This enables you to access newsgroups and subscribe to those in which you are interested.
- Rename Folder. This can be used to give folders new names.
- Empty Trash on Local Mail. This deletes any items that have been placed in the Trash Can (Wastebasket). This removes them permanently.
- Compact Folders. This compacts the information held in your mail folders.

- Import. This allows you to import information such as messages and addresses from other email programs.

The Import function is particularly effective at importing messages and contact details from Outlook Express.

- Offline. This allows you to work offline i.e. while not connected to the Internet. This is the mode that you should be in when you are composing messages.
- Page Setup. This can be used to determine the way in which messages are printed.
- Print Preview. This enables you to see how a message will look when it is printed.
- Print. This prints the active document.
- Close. This closes the active document.
- Exit. This closes down Messenger.

Messenger can also be closed down in the same way as you would close any other program on your PC or Mac.

Edit

The Edit menu contains the following options:

- Undo. This undoes the previous action.
- Redo. This reinstates the previously undone action.
- Cut. This removes a highlighted item and places it on the clipboard.
- Copy. This copies a highlighted item and places it on the clipboard.
- Paste. This places the current contents of the clipboard into the current insertion point.
- Delete Message. This places the selected message into the Trash Can.
- Select. This has options for selecting messages within Messenger.
- Find. This allows you to look for specific words or phrases within messages.
- Find Again. This repeats the most recently specified find action.
- Search Messages. This allows you to look for messages using certain search criteria, such as the author's name or when a message was received.

- Message Filters. This can be used to set rules for incoming messages and then apply actions if the rules are met. This can include sending items from a specified sender directly into the trash folder, or sorting messages into certain folders. Filters are an excellent way to avoid having to look at large quantities of junk email and they are looked at in the relevant chapter.

If you are receiving a lot of junk email the best option is to set a rule so that it is not even downloaded from the server. To do this, you will need to know the sender or the subject.

- Folder Properties. This displays the properties of the folder in which you are currently working, such as name, location and the number of messages.

Preferences

This acts like a menu within a menu and contains a variety of settings that can be used to specify the way in which Messenger looks and operates. If an item in the Preferences window has a plus sign next to it, this means that there are other items linked to it. Click on the plus sign to see the rest of the options for that heading. These include:

Appearance

This can be used to determine which element of Communicator opens when the program is launched. This is very useful if you want to use Messenger as your email program, but you do not want to use Navigator as your browser. You can also elect to have Communicator open in Composer or Calendar. The

Appearance preferences also allow you to specify how the toolbars are displayed and the choices are:

- Pictures and Text
- Pictures Only
- Text Only

The Appearance preferences also have options for specifying the font used in your Messenger windows and also the colours for text, background and hyperlinks.

Navigator

These are settings for the Netscape browser. They include:

- Navigator starts with:
  - Blank page
  - Home page
  - Last page visited
- Location for home page. If you do not want the Netscape default to be your home page, select Use Current Page to make the page you are viewing your home page, or select Browse to specify a page on your hard drive as a home page.
  - History. This can be used to specify the number of days that pages you have visited are kept in the history folder for quick access.

Navigator is a viable browser alternative to the more ubiquitous Internet Explorer. Navigator has similar features, but it is not always as fast as Internet Explorer.

Mail and Newsgroups

This includes a number of settings that determine the way you connect to your email server and also how elements of the program are displayed:

- Identity. This contains your name and email address. Additional information, such as where you work, can also be added. This information is used if you want to add a vCard to an email, which is like an electronic business card.

- Mail Servers. This contains details of how you connect to your mail server for sending and receiving mail. If this is not completed then you will have to do so manually and you may have to ask your ISP for details about the various server settings. See the relevant section for details about specifying server settings.

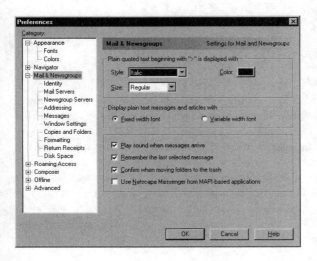

- Newsgroup Servers. This is the same as for mail servers, except it configures Messenger for accessing newsgroups.

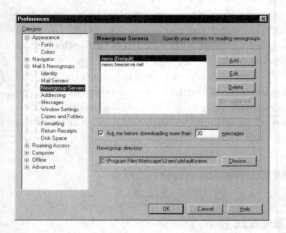

- Addressing. This contains various options for how Messenger enters addresses when you are composing a message. The options available are:
  - Look for address in the address book, or the directory server.
  - Show a list of choices for multiple possibilities.
  - Accept what I have typed.
  - Show names using display names (from address book card).
  - Show names using last name, first name.
- Messages. This contains options for dealing with outgoing and incoming messages:

- By default forward messages: As Attachment/Inline/Quoted. One of the three options can be selected to determine the format in which messages are forwarded.
- Spell check messages before sending. This can be checked on or off.
- Wrap incoming, plain text messages to window width. This can be checked on and means that incoming messages will have carriage returns inserted so that they do not exceed the width of the on-screen window. This means that you will not have to scroll along to see the whole of the message.
- Wrap outgoing, plain text messages at 72 characters. This figure can be changed and it specifies the point at which carriage returns are inserted automatically.

Text wrapping options can be used to ensure that the recipient does not have to scroll across their screen to read a message. Wrapping ensures it goes down the screen, rather than across.

- The final option is for encoding messages with 8-bit characters but this does not function properly with all email programs and servers.
- Window settings. This can be used to determine the layout of your Messenger windows. It contains the following options:
    - Choose which layout you prefer for the Messenger window. This contains options for viewing the folder list down the whole of the left hand side of the Messenger window, or the Preview Pane occupying the whole of the bottom half of the window. If you

change this setting you will have to close down a window and then open it up again to apply the new setting.

- Double clicking a folder or a newsgroup opens it in a new window. This can be checked on or off, depending on your preference for how these items are opened.
- Double clicking a message opens it in a new window. This is the same as above, except it applies to email messages. Both of these options can be deselected which means you will have fewer active windows to worry about when you are dealing with folders and messages.
- The final option in the window settings is for whether you want newsgroups opened in Messenger or a Message Center.

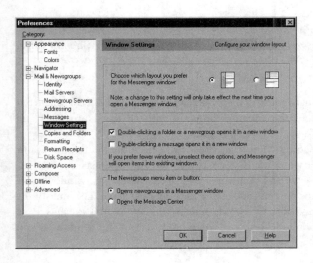

- Copies and Folders. This contains options for what happens to messages once they have been sent. These are for email messages and newsgroup items but the options are the same for both and include:
  - Place a copy in 'Sent' on 'Local Mail'. If this is checked on it saves copies of all sent messages and puts them in the Sent folder. This is a good way to create an archive of what you have sent. However, it is a good idea to periodically clear out your Sent folder, particularly if there are a lot of items there with attachments. If you do not do a bit of spring cleaning from time to time, you may find you have hundreds of messages in your Sent folder and these could be taking up a fair amount of disc space.
  - Send a blind copy (Bcc) to your own email address. This will send a copy to yourself, without the recipient knowing about it. (Although why you would want to do this when you can have a copy automatically saved into the Sent folder is a mystery.)
  - Send a blind copy to another address. This sends a copy to someone else without the recipient knowing. This should be used carefully and it is best not to set it as a default.
  - The final two options for Copies and Folders are for storing drafts and templates. By default, they are stored in the folders with the same names, but it is possible to specify a different location where you want them kept.
- Formatting. This contains options for specifying how you want your messages to look. Messenger is a strong HTML email program which means that there are a wide range of formatting techniques that can be applied. However, it is not essential that the program is used in HTML mode. The options for formatting are:

- Use the HTML editor to compose message. This is checked on by default and it enables you to create much more attractive and varied email messages. However, make sure that the recipient has the capability to read HTML-formatted messages (it is becoming increasingly common for computer users to have HTML facilities and it is widely accepted as being a standard for email messages).

The HTML editor that comes with Communicator is called Composer. This is adequate for basic Web pages but for anything more advanced you should try a dedicated program.

- Use the plain text editor to compose message. This can be checked on if you only want to send a plain text message, with a minimum of formatting.
- There are also options for prompts if the recipient of a message cannot read HTML format. These include an option for asking the sender what to do, sending it in plain text, sending it in HTML anyway or sending it as both. It is possible to override any of these settings once you are composing a message. Select the Options button on the toolbar or select View>Options from the composition menu bar. Then, in the format box underneath the toolbar, select one of the options from the drop-down list.
- Return Receipts. This contains options that can be used to notify you when a message has been delivered or read: return receipts can be requested either for when a message has been delivered, when it has been read, or both. When a receipt is received, it can be placed in your

Inbox or your Sent Mail box. You can also specify whether you send a return receipt for some messages you receive or none.

If you use a return receipt on a network, you should get a reply when a message is delivered or read. However, on the Internet it is not always so clear cut and it can depend on the recipient.

- Disk Space. This acts as a management system for the amount of space email messages are allowed to take up on your hard drive. There are options for specifying that messages over a certain size are not stored locally and also for compacting folders once they contain a certain amount of data. Use the first of these options carefully, because you may find you want to keep messages over a certain size, particularly if they contain attachments that you want to keep.

Roaming Access
This can be used to retrieve your user profile when working on another computer. This can be a slightly complicated process so contact your ISP or system administrator if you are unsure about it.

Composer
This has options for Communicator's built-in HTML editor for creating Web pages.

Offline
This contains options for specifying whether Messenger is opened in offline or online mode.

Advanced

This contains various settings for dealing with items such as JavaScript and cookies. This will apply more when using Navigator to browse the Web. This is the last of the Preferences options.

View

The View menu contains the following options:

- Show. This can be used to display the toolbars and also the folder list and the message windows.
- Sort. This can be used to sort messages in a folder according to a variety of criteria, such as date, subject or size.
- Messages. This can be used to determine how messages that are downloaded from newsgroups are displayed.
- Headers. This determines how header information is displayed in an email message.

- View Attachment Inline. This allows for attachments to be viewed within an email message, rather than having to open them separately.
- Wrap Long Lines. This ensures that carriage returns are automatically inserted into long lines of text, so that they fit more easily onto the screen.
- Increase Font. This increases the font size for viewing the current window.
- Decrease Font. This decreases the font size for viewing the current window.
- Reload. This reloads the current page.

Reload is used for Web pages when the content has changed. This could apply to an email if it contains an active Web page or a link to one.

- Show Images. This displays any images that are included with the active document.
- Refresh. This redraws the active document. (This is more commonly used with Web pages.)
- Stop. This halts the current transfer. This can be used if you are downloading an email that seems to be taking an unusually long time.
- Page Source. This is usually used on the Web to view the source HTML code of a page.
- Page Info. This can be used to display information about the current page.

- Character Set. This can be used to determine specific character sets for use when composing or reading messages.

Go

The Go menu contains the following options:

- First Unread Message. This takes you automatically to the first unread message in your Inbox.
- First Flagged Message. This takes you automatically to the first flagged message in your inbox.
- Next. This can be used to move to the next message or folder, depending on which option is selected.
- Previous. This can be used to move to the previous message, unread message or flagged message.
- Back. This takes you back to the previous message in a folder.
- Forward. This moves you to the next message in a folder.

Message

The Message menu contains the following options:

- New Message. This opens a new message window, ready for you to start composing a new email.
- Reply. This enables you to reply directly to someone who has sent you a message.
- Reply to All. This enables you to reply to a group of people in which you have been included i.e. if someone has sent a message to a group of 10 people the Reply to All function can be used to reply to the person who sent the message and also the rest of the group.
- Forward. This enables you to send a message directly on to a new recipient.
- Forward As. This allows you to forward a message in different formats, such as an attachment.
- Edit Message as New. This allows you to edit a message you have received and send it without the original header information. This way it will look like the original message came from you.

- Move Message. This enables you to move a message into another folder.
- Copy Message. This enables you to keep a message in its original folder and put a copy of it into another one.
- Add Sender to Address Book. This is a very useful option, which enables you to automatically put a sender's email address into your address book. This saves you having to enter it manually.
- Add All to Address Book. This adds the email addresses of all members of a group into your address book.
- Mark. This enables you to mark messages that have been read, or up to a certain date.
- Ignore Thread. This is used when viewing messages from newsgroups and it enables you to ignore a threaded conversation i.e. one where several messages are linked to one another.
- Watch Thread. This is similar to Ignore Thread, except it enables you to view a threaded conversation. For a more detailed look at newsgroups, see the 'Mailing Lists and Newsgroups' chapter.

Communicator

The Communicator menu contains shortcuts to the various elements of the Communicator program. Each one can be accessed at any time by selecting the relevant option from this menu, which is available in all elements of Communicator. These include:

- Navigator. This is the Web browser.
- Messenger. This is the email program.
- Composer. This is the Web page authoring tool.
- AOL Instant Messenger Service. This is a service for sending short, quick messages.

- Bookmarks. This contains Web sites that you visit regularly and have bookmarked for quick access.
- Newsgroups. This contains a list of the newsgroups to which you have subscribed.
- Address Book. This contains your email names and addresses.
- Tools. This contains a variety of options for using the Internet.
- Server Tools. This contains information about your server connections and email account.
- Window. This displays the items that you currently have open in Communicator.
- Help. The Help menu contains an index of help topics for all of the Communicator elements and also links to online help facilities.

Toolbars

Messenger displays different toolbars, depending on whether you are composing or viewing messages, and the standard one appears underneath the menu bar at the top of the program window. The items on the toolbar are depicted by small buttons with icons on them and they are (from left to right):

- Get Messages. This is depicted by a sheet of paper with a blue arrow pointing down towards it and is used to connect to your mail server and download new messages.

- New Message. This is depicted by a sheet of paper with a pen on it and is used to open up a new email message.
- Reply. This is depicted by an envelope with an arrow pointing towards it and is used to reply directly to a message you have sent.
- Reply All. This is depicted by an envelope with two arrows pointing towards it and is used to reply to all of the members of a group that you have been included in.
- Forward. This is depicted by an envelope with an arrow pointing away from it and is used to send a message you have received on to another recipient.
- File. This is depicted by an open file and is used to move directly to a file within your Messenger structure.
- Next. This is depicted by a blue down-pointing arrow and a green bullet point and is used to move to the next unread message.
- Print. This is depicted by a printer and is used to print out the current page.
- Delete. This is depicted by a wastepaper bin with a sheet of paper in it and is used to move a selected item into the trash folder.
- Stop. This is depicted by a set of traffic lights and is used to stop the current operation, such as downloading a long email message.

If you are sending someone a long email, let them know first, so that they are expecting it and not surprised by a new message taking a long time to download.

Viewing options

Messenger works on the principle of using different panes to view its various elements. By default, the Folder list, folder contents and Preview Pane are visible when you first open the program. Each element has a grey box along its top or side border, containing two small arrows. If you click here this element will be minimised and will disappear. However, the grey bar and two arrows will still be visible and the pane can be maximised by clicking on them again. Wherever you see a grey bar with two arrows on it, this means it is an element that can be minimised and maximised. Also, the borders of each pane can be expanded by clicking and dragging on them.

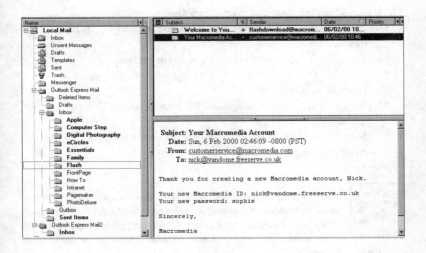

Composing messages

When you select the New Message button on the toolbar or by selecting Message > New Message from the menu bar, the composition window opens. This is where you create a new email message and it contains its own menu bar and toolbar. The main components of the composition menu bar are:

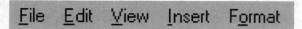

File

The composition File menu contains the following options:

- New. An essential feature. This gives you options for creating a new message.
- Save. This enables you to save the current message.
- Save As. This enables you to save the current message as a draft, a template or a file.
- Attach. This gives you options for adding an attachment to your message.
- Send Now. This connects you to your email server and sends the current message.

Always check a message thoroughly before selecting the Send Now button. Just because you can compose email quickly does not mean that you have to send it hastily. Check that you have said what you really want to and that the spelling and grammar are correct.

- Send Later. This gives the message draft status so that it can be sent later when you connect to your mail server.
- Quote Original Message. This is used when you are replying to a message and you want to include text from it. This option pastes the text into the new message and puts it in quotation marks.
- Select Addresses. This opens up the Messenger address book and enables you to select the recipient's name.
- Page Setup. This is the same as on the standard menu bar.
- Print Preview. This is the same as on the standard menu bar.
- Print. This is the same as on the standard menu bar.
- Close. This is the same as on the standard menu bar.
- Exit. This is the same as on the standard menu bar.

Edit

The composition Edit menu contains the following options:
- Undo. This is the same as on the standard menu bar.
- Cut. This is the same as on the standard menu bar.
- Copy. This is the same as on the standard menu bar.
- Paste. This is the same as on the standard menu bar.
- Paste as Quotation. This is the same as the standard paste function, except that it inserts the pasted items in quotation marks.
- Delete. This removes the highlighted item.
- Select All. This selects all of the text in the message window. This is useful if you want to apply the same formatting function to the whole message.
- Select Table. This selects a complete table, if one is being used.
- Delete Table. This deletes a complete table or any elements of it that have been selected, such as cells, rows or columns.

- Remove Link. This removes a hyperlink from a message. This is a piece of text or an image that is formatted so that it takes the user to a page of the Web or another email address. Hyperlinks are usually underlined and appear blue.
- Find. This is the same as on the standard menu bar.
- Find Again. This is the same as on the standard menu bar.
- Do Not Complete Address. This accepts email addresses just as they are typed into the To box or the body of the message, even if Messenger does not think this is a valid format.
- Show Matching Addresses. This displays a list of any matching email addresses in your address book.
- Preferences. This is the same as on the standard menu bar.

You can change the Messenger preference settings at any time, either from the main menu or from the composition menu.

View

The composition view menu contains the following options:
- Show. This enables you to display or hide the message area and composition toolbars.
- Address. This displays the addresses of the message recipients.
- Attachments. This displays any attachments that are included with the email.

- Options. This displays options for the message such as encryption and adding a return receipt. (Only one of the Address, Attachments and Options features can be displayed at one time.)
- Page Source. This displays the source code for the current page.
- Page Info. This displays general information about the current page.
- Character Set. This is the same as on the standard menu bar.

Insert

The composition Insert menu contains the following options (this can be used if you are creating a message in HTML format):

- Link. This enables you to include a hyperlink in your email, which the user can click on to take them to a Web page or an email link.
- Target. This can be used to determine whether a linked item opens up in the same window as the link or a new one.
- Image. This enables you to insert images into an email.
- Horizontal Line. This enables you to insert a horizontal line into an email.
- Table. This enables you to insert a table into an email. Once you select this option you can then specify the table's size and the number of rows and columns.
- HTML Tag. This inserts a tag that indicates there is an item of HTML in the message.
- New Line Break. This inserts a line break so you can add content on a new line. This is smaller than a carriage return.
- Break Below Image(s). This inserts a line break below any images in a message.

Format

The composition format menu contains the following options:

- Font
- Size
- Style
- Color
- Remove All Styles
- Heading
- Paragraph
- List
- Align
- Increase Indent
- Decrease Indent
- Character Properties
- Table Properties
- Page Colors and Properties

If you are used to using Netscape products then you will feel very at home with Messenger. It is also a good choice for users who are new to Netscape as it has a very pleasing interface and is straightforward to use.

Pegasus

As shown in the 'Email Programs' chapter, Pegasus is an independently produced program that is free and compact to install. It also contains enough features to compare favourably with some of its commercial counterparts.

Menu bar

File

The File menu contains the following options:

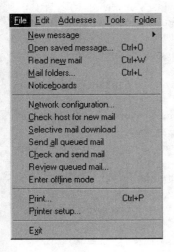

- New message. This takes you to a sub-menu with options for creating a new email message.
- Open saved message. This allows you to open messages that you have saved in draft format but not sent.
- Read new mail. This allows you to read messages that have been downloaded from the server.
- Mail folders. This takes you to the folder you have created within Pegasus.
- Noticeboards. These can be used to let other people view your messages, primarily on a network.
- Network configuration. This allows you to change, or set, configurations for connecting to your email provider.
- Check host for new mail. This connects you to the Internet and checks for new messages on your email provider's server.
- Selective mail download. This is a very useful function, which connects you to your mail server and lets you view the messages that are stored there. You can then mark them so that they are downloaded onto your computer or deleted from the server.
- Send all queued mail. This connects you to the Internet and sends any messages that are waiting.
- Check and send mail. This connects you to the Internet and downloads new messages as well as sending ones as above.
- Review queued mail. This shows details of messages that are waiting to be sent.
- Enter offline mode. This disconnects you from the Internet.
- Print. This prints the selected message.
- Printer setup. This controls the way your printer prints messages.
- Exit. This closes down Pegasus.

Edit

The Edit menu contains the following options.

- Undo. Undoes the most recently performed action.
- Redo. Reinstates an action that has been undone.
- Cut. Removes a selected item and saves it on the clipboard.
- Copy. Copies a selected item onto the clipboard.
- Paste. Inserts the current contents of the clipboard.
- Clear. Removes the selected item.
- Find text. Looks for a specified word or phrase.
- Find and replace. Looks for a specified word or phrase and replaces it with an alternative.
- Find/replace again. Performs the above action again.
- Select all. Selects all of the text in a message, which can then be edited as a block.

Addresses

The Addresses menu contains the following options for finding the email addresses of other users and creating groups:

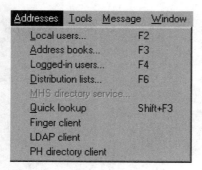

- Local users. This can be used to look up the email address of any people who are connected to the same email network.
- Address books. This can be used to select users from your own address books of contacts you have created.
- Logged-in users. This can be used to locate the email addresses of people who are currently logged on to the same network as you.
- Distribution lists. This can be used to create groups of recipients. These can then be used if you want to send the same message to all of the people in the group. You select the group name and all of the users within that group will receive the message. Press F6 to begin a new distribution list.

- MHS directory service. This is an option that is used with Novell NetWare network software. If you are working on a network with Pegasus, contact your IT administrator to see if this option is available.
- Quick lookup. This automatically inserts the most recently used email address into a new message.
- Finger client. This is used for specialised searches on a network. Consult your IT administrator to see if this is available.
- LDAP client. This is used for specialised searches on a network. Consult your IT administrator to see if this is available.
- PH directory client. This is used for specialised searches on a network. Consult your IT administrator to see if this is available.

Pegasus was designed initially for use on a network and many of its features can still be used for this.

Tools

The Tools menu contains the following options:

- Internet options. These are options for configuring your setup for sending and receiving mail. These are usually set when you first use the program.
- IMAP profiles. This stands for Internet Message Access Protocol and it is the means for accessing messages on other networks. However, it has a chequered history and is not the most stable protocol around.
- Identities. This allows for different people to create their own identities using the same email address and send and receive messages using this identity.
- Extensions. This is a group of plug-ins (small helper programs) that are included to help enhance the main Pegasus program.
- Mail filtering rules. This can be used to create rules that apply to incoming messages and then actions that are to be performed if the criteria for one of these rules are met. These can be used to automatically move specific messages (or messages from a specific sender) to a certain folder, or to delete unwanted messages.
- Glossary. This can be used to create shortcut keystrokes for frequently used words or phrases. To do this, select the Add button in the Glossary dialog box and insert the abbreviation that you want to use. Then insert the full text and select Save. When you want to use the shortcut, type the abbreviation and then press Ctrl+E to expand it.
- Notepads. This can be used to write yourself notes and reminders.
- Check spelling. This checks the spelling in the active document.

Options

Although these are part of the Tools menu, there are so many options for customising the way Pegasus looks that they can be looked at in their own right. There are dozens of them, giving the user a great deal of flexibility for customising the appearance of the program. These options include:

General

- Automatically open the new mail folder at startup. If this is checked on you are taken directly to your Inbox when you open the program.
- Preserve deleted messages until end of session. If this is checked on, messages that you delete will be kept until you next close down the program. However, once you have done this they will be removed permanently.
- Ask for confirmation before deleting objects. If this is checked on, a warning box appears when you try and delete anything.
- Allow messages to stay in the new mail folder. If this is checked on, you can keep messages in your Inbox, even after they have been read.
- Offer advanced options when preparing replies. If this is checked on, you have a wider variety of options when you are replying to a message you have received.
- Save WinPMail's desktop state between sessions. If this is checked on, the program will open up again at the same point as where it was last closed down.

WinPMail is how Pegasus refers to itself at various points in the program and Help files.

- Use system-defined colours in list windows. If this is checked on you can use the colour palettes that are provided with Pegasus.
- Autosave messages in progress every xx minutes. This can be used to specify how frequently Pegasus automatically saves the email message on which you are currently working. This can be useful if your computer crashes because it means you will not have lost all of your work.
- Name for folder for copies to self. You can specify the name of a folder for storing messages that have been sent and also copied to yourself.

Reader settings

- Select a colour for showing text that appears in quotation marks.
- Select a width (in characters) for the point at which text will automatically wrap i.e. move down to the next line.
- Always save the last window size used.
- Open the next message in the original folder if the current one is moved or deleted.
- Open the previous message in the original folder.
- Close the window and do not load another message if the current one is moved or deleted.
- Where a choice exists between HTML and Rich Text Formatting, show the fancy one. If this is checked on, you will be able to see HTML messages in all their glory.

Hyperlinks

- Enable display of clickable links (URLs) in reader. If this is checked on you will be able to access any hypertext links that are included in incoming messages. These could be links to Web pages or other email addresses. (There are also options for how you would like to access the Web through a hyperlink in an email.)
- Encryption. This has options for how Pegasus encrypts messages, if you elect to do this. Unless you have loaded another form of encryption, with a digital certificate, Pegasus will use its own built-in encryption method. This will also give you the choice of using a password and a digital signature.

If you have your own Web site, include a clickable link to this in your email messages. This will allow recipients to go directly to your page.

Signatures

This enables you to set signatures to be included automatically at the end of messages.

Reporting

This contains options for how Pegasus alerts you to the fact that you have new mail messages. The options are:

- Notify of new mail using a floating 'Telltale' window. If this is checked on, a window will appear on top of any other open windows you have active, alerting you to the fact that you have new mail.

- Place an icon in the Windows system tray. If this is checked on, a small Pegasus icon is placed in the bottom right-hand corner of the screen, alerting you to new mail. It can be made to flap its wings or you can see the exact status of any new mail by right clicking on it.

- Play a new mail alert sound. You can select various sounds that play to indicate new mail. If you have your own sound files on your hard drive, you could select one of these by clicking on the Select sound button. You can also elect to play a sound only if the program is minimised.

Sending mail

This contains options for outgoing messages and they include:

- Default 'reply to' address. This contains a text box, that can be used to specify a default address for messages to go to, if it is different from your own.

- Permanent Bcc (Blind carbon copy). This contain a text box that can be used to specify an address that is always sent a blind copy i.e. one that the recipient does not know is being sent.

- Always remove formatting. If this is checked on, any formatting such as Rich Text or HTML will be removed before the message is sent. This can be used if you are sending messages to users who do not have the facilities to read these types of messages.
- Send rich text as required. If this is checked on, messages are sent in the format in which they are composed. Rich text can also be set as a default.

Message settings

These cover a variety of options for formatting and sending messages and they include:

- Use MIME features. If this is checked on, you can use the Internet standard for sending and receiving attachments. MIME stands for Multi Purpose Internet Mail Extensions and it is a language that determines the way email messages and attachments are formatted and sent. By default, this option is checked on, and it should be left this way, unless you have a good reason to turn it off, such as you know the recipient's email program does not support MIME.

Use attachments thoughtfully and only when they are needed, not just because you have the capability to include them.

- Confirm reading/Confirm delivery. These can be checked on so that you are notified when messages have been read and/or delivered. These options work best over an internal network – over the Internet, there is no guarantee that you will be sent a return receipt to say that a message has been read.

- Copy to self. If this is checked on, you will receive a copy of each message you send.
- Message width. This can be used to specify the average width, in characters, of a line of text. The program will adjust the window size accordingly.
- Average Tab width. This can be used to set the amount by which a tab setting indents the text.
- Automatically check spelling before sending message. If this is checked on, every message will be spell checked by default before it is sent. This is a useful option if you know your spelling is a bit weak and you do not want any mistakes to slip through as a result of not using the spell checker.

Just because you are writing an email, it is no excuse to get sloppy with spelling. Take as much care as you would with a hard copy document, particularly if it is for business.

- Ask whether or not to make a copy to self. If this is checked on, it will override the Copy to self option above and prompt you as to whether you want to save a copy to your own folders and if so, which one.
- Hide the editor styles toolbar. If this is checked on, the formatting toolbar in the composition window is hidden, giving more room to enter and view the text. This only applies to the next message window opened, not the current one.

- Add extra white space around the message editor. If this is checked on it places larger margins around the text in the message editor window. This only applies to the next message window opened, not the current one.
- For replies, place the cursor on an initial blank line. If this is checked on, an extra line will be inserted at the top of any messages where you are replying to the original author. The cursor will be inserted at the beginning of this, so you can start composing your message immediately.
- Use exact character measurement for right margin. If this is checked on, the width of a message will be measured exactly in characters, rather than the actual amount of space there.
- Address completion. This gives you options for completing addresses automatically – you just have to type in the first two or three letters and Pegasus will do the rest. There are options to specify where address are auto-completed from the address book, or recently used addresses.

Toolbars

This contains options for the way you want the toolbars displayed in Pegasus:

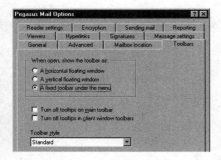

- A horizontal floating toolbar. This applies to the main toolbar when the program is opened. If it is checked on, the toolbar will be positioned horizontally and it will be possible to drag it around the window.
- A vertical floating toolbar. This is the same as above, except the toolbar is positioned vertically in the window.
- A fixed toolbar under the menu. This is the default setting and it places the toolbar directly under the menu bar at the top of the window.
- There are also options for turning off the tooltips for the main toolbar and also the toolbars that appear in subsequent windows. You can also specify the toolbar style and the options are: Standard, Business User, POP3 User or users of earlier versions of Pegasus.

There are other various selections that can be made within the Options menu, but the ones listed here are probably the most commonly used.

Message

The Message menu is only active once a new message has been started. It contains the following options:

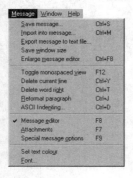

- Save message. This saves the contents of the current message.
- Import into message. This allows you to import text into the current message, from another file. Select this and then select a text file to include in your message. This is not the same as attaching a file.
- Export message to text file. This is similar to the Import command, except that it allows you to place text from an email into another file on your computer.
- Save window size. This saves the size of the active window and opens it at the same size the next time the program is opened.
- Enlarge message editor. This makes the message area as large as possible.
- Toggle monospaced view. This changes the font to monospaced i.e. a font with the same amount of space between each character.

Monospaced fonts can be used to create the effect of a typewritten letter, which can be useful if you want to convey a less hi-tech image.

- Delete current line. This removes the line in which the cursor is currently inserted. The text does not have to be highlighted.
- Delete word right. This removes the word to the right of the cursor.
- Reformat paragraph. This can be used to shorten the length of line in a paragraph.
- ASCII Indenting. This can be used to format text that is in ASCII format, as opposed to Rich Text Format.

- Message editor. This takes you to the message editor area, which is where text is added when you are composing a message.
- Attachments. This takes you to the attachment area, which is where attachments are added to a message.
- Special message options. This takes you to the area for specific settings, relating to advanced addressing and formatting functions.
- Set text colour. This allows you to change the colour of a highlighted piece of text, or for any new text after the selection has been made.
- Font. This allows you to select a font style for a highlighted piece of text, or for any new text after the selection has been made.

Folder

This menu contains options for formatting your folder structure and is not available if you are in the compose message part of the program. It contains the following options:

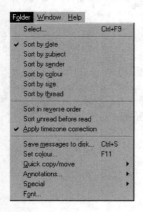

- Select. This allows you to look for messages within a folder according to certain criteria, such as sender's name or file size. Once the criteria have been set, the messages that meet this are highlighted.
- Sort by date.
- Sort by subject.
- Sort by sender.
- Sort by colour. This applies if settings have been applied so that certain messages are displayed in different colours when they are received.
- Sort by size.
- Sort by thread. This applies to newsgroup messages. A thread is a collection of email messages within a newsgroup that are part of the same conversation i.e. a reply is threaded to the original message rather than displayed as a new item.
- Sort in reverse order. This reverses the order in which messages are currently sorted i.e. if they are sorted with the latest date displayed first in a folder, this command would place it last instead.
- Sort unread before read. This ensures that unread messages are displayed above those that have been read.
- Apply time zone correction. This manages the time of received messages, for sorting purposes.
- Save messages to disc. This saves the text of the selected messages onto a disc, for back-up purposes.
- Select colour. This allows you to change the colour of the selected message(s) in a folder.
- Quick copy/move. This moves or copies the selected message into another folder.
- Annotations. This allows you to enter annotations to messages. This is like leaving a note for yourself. This includes an option for a timestamp

and annotations are identified with a green dot next to a message in a folder.
- Special. This includes various advanced options, such as verifying digital signatures and adding the sender of a message to a mailing list.
- Font. This allows you to change the font used for displaying messages within a folder.

Window

The Window menu contains the following options:

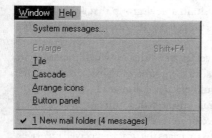

- System messages. This displays messages relating to your use of Pegasus.
- Enlarge. This enlarges the active window to fill the screen.
- Tile. This makes all open windows visible, by placing them next to each other. The more open windows there are, the smaller the size of each one.

- Cascade. This places all open windows on top of one another, so that the top bar of each is showing. Click on this to bring a specific window to the front.
- Arrange buttons. This allows you to tidy up any windows that you have turned into buttons.
- Button panel. This activates the button panel, which is a set of buttons underneath the menu bar that contains shortcuts for the most frequently used functions in Pegasus. (Also known as the toolbar.)

Help

The Help menu contains the following options:

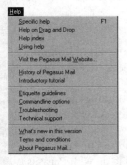

- Specific help. This provides help relating to the currently open window.
- Help on Drag and Drop. This contains hints on how best to use drag and drop techniques within Pegasus.
- Help index. This contains the full help index.
- Using help. This provides help about the help menu!

- Visit the Pegasus Mail Website. This contains a link to the Pegasus site on the Web and it is worth a visit, if only to keep up with the latest releases and developments.
- History of Pegasus Mail. This contains an informative and entertaining look at how Pegasus has developed and the ethos behind it.
- Introductory tutorial. This guides you through some of the basics of the program.
- Etiquette guidelines. This contains some dos and don'ts of using email.

The Pegasus Help files are very user friendly and definitely superior to those of more commonly used programs.

- Commandline options. This pertains to the more complicated configuration settings that can be used with Pegasus. For most users, these will not apply.
- Troubleshooting. Information on what to do if things go wrong.
- Technical support. This provides an email address for obtaining help on technical matters.
- What's new in this version. Latest information and updates.
- Terms and conditions. What you are allowed to do with Pegasus.
- About Pegasus Mail. Information about the version of Pegasus that you are using.

Creating a new message

When you want to send your first message with Pegasus you have to open up a new message window. This is done by clicking on the button at the far left hand side of the toolbar (or button panel). This is denoted by a pen and a piece of paper. The other buttons are (from left to right):

- Read new mail. This is denoted by an open envelope.
- Open/manage mail folders. This is denoted by a yellow folder and lets you arrange and organise your folders.
- Open/manage address books. This is denoted by an open book and lets you add entries to your address book and edit the ones already there.
- Open/manage distribution lists. This is denoted by a single sheet of paper and can be used to create mailing lists i.e. groups of people, and their email addresses, that are included under a single title.
- Open the local user list. This is denoted by two people standing next to each other and can be used to view other users on a network.
- New mail filtering rules. This is denoted by a blue arrow and a red funnel and can set conditions and actions for incoming messages. New rules are created in a separate dialog box, which opens when you select this option.

- Use the noticeboard system. This is denoted by a sheet of paper pinned to a board and can be used to post messages on an internal online bulletin board.
- Print. This is denoted by a printer button and can be used to print the contents of the currently active window.
- Select font. This is denoted by a red 'f' and can be used to change the default font. This will apply to all new messages that are subsequently begun, unless specified otherwise.
- Send all queued messages. This is denoted by a globe with a blue arrow pointing into it and can be used to connect to the Internet and send messages that you have written.
- Check for new mail. This is denoted by a globe with a red arrow pointing away from it and can be used to connect to your email server and download any new messages.
- Check and send mail. This is denoted by a globe with a blue and a red arrow and performs both of the above tasks in one operation.

Once you have opened a new message window, select the Message tab to enter the contents of your email. At the top of this are boxes for the recipient (To), anyone it is being copied to (Cc) and the Subject. The first two of these can have an email address typed directly into them or you can choose an address from an address book that has been created (see later for information on creating address book entries.) Directly below these boxes are half a dozen options that can be selected for your message:

- Confirm reading. If this is checked on, you will be notified when the message has been read.
- Confirm delivery. If this is checked on, you will be notified when the message has been delivered successfully.

- Copy self. If this is checked on, you will have a copy of the message placed in one of your own folders.
- Urgent. If this is checked on, the message will be sent with an urgent tag, usually a red exclamation mark, which will be displayed when the recipient receives the message.
- Encrypt. If this is checked on, the message will be encrypted so that only someone with the correct password will be able to read it. Obviously, the recipient will need to have the password.
- Rich text. If this is checked on, the message can be created with a more varied range of formatting techniques.
- There is also a box for selecting a signature and this is looked at later. Underneath this is a toolbar for basic formatting and alignment of text. Enter the text for your message in the area underneath this toolbar.

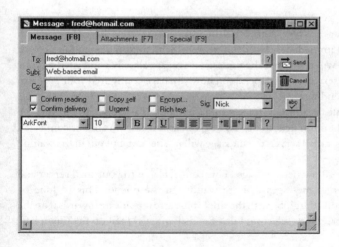

Adding attachments

If you want to add an attachment to a Pegasus email message, this is done by clicking on the Attachments tab, next to the message one. To add an attachment:

1. Click on the Add attachment button in the bottom right hand corner of the message window.
2. Select an attachment from your computer or a form of removable storage such as a digital camera or a Zip disc.
3. Select Open. This will attach the file to your email message.
4. Underneath the area for inserting attachments are two options, one to specify the file type and the other for the method of encoding. By default, Pegasus decides both of these, but it is possible to make your own selections for each, and there are dozens to choose from, particularly for the file type.

Sending

Once a message has been completed there are a few options that can be applied:

- Send immediately by clicking on the Send button next to the To box. This will only send the message if you are already connected to your mail server. (This depends on how you have configured your program for sending mail.)
- Queue the message for sending later. This is also done by clicking the Send button next to the To box, but as long as you are not connected to your mail server, the message will not be sent, but put in the waiting queue.
- Send all queued message. This connects you to your mail server and sends all messages that are waiting in the queue. This is done by selecting the globe with the single blue arrow pointing towards it on the toolbar, or by selecting File > Send all queued mail on the menu bar.

- Send queued messages and download any ones that are waiting for you on your mail server. This is the same as above, but it also retrieves your messages. This is accessed by selecting the globe with the blue and red arrows next to it on the toolbar, or by selecting File > Check and send mail from the menu bar.
- Review and edit messages that have yet to be sent, but have been queued. This is done by selecting File > Review queued mail from the menu bar. This will display the messages that have been queued, which can then be opened and edited by double clicking on them, or deleted by selecting the delete button.

Address books

If you have a lot of email contacts the quickest way to access them is via an address book within your email program. Pegasus has powerful features for creating and managing address books. To create an address book:

1. Select the Create or manage address books button on the toolbar (depicted by two white pages side-by-side) or select Addresses > Address books from the menu bar.
2. In the Select an address book dialog box, select the New button at the right hand side.
3. In the Enter name dialog box, enter a name for your new address book. There is also an optional choice for giving it a file name, but this is not necessary. Select OK.
4. Back in the Select an address book dialog box, select the Open button.
5. In the address book window, select the Add button to insert a new email contact.
6. In the Edit address book entry dialog box, enter a minimum of the person's name (this can be their full name or a nickname, which is

called an alias in Pegasus), a key on the keyboard, which can be used to enter their email address automatically when composing a message, and their email address. There are also boxes for additional items of contact information, such as a fax number.

7. Select OK to insert the new contact into your address book.

To delete a contact in an address book, select it and then select the Delete button.

To insert a contact directly into the To of an email, select the contact and then select the Paste button. This will insert the selected contact into the active email message.

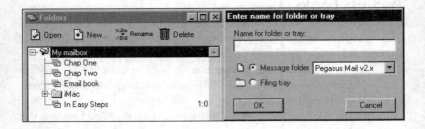

Mail folders

Folders are a convenient way to store and sort email messages and they can be created in a similar fashion to creating address books. By default, all new messages are placed in the New mail folder. However, it is good practice to create different folders for areas such as work, family and hobbies. Once you receive messages, they can then be sorted into the relevant folders. To create a new folder:

1. Select the Work with your mail folders button on the toolbar, or select File>Mail folders from the menu bar.
2. To open the contents of an existing folder, double click on it or click on it once and select the Open button.
3. To create a new folder, select the New button.
4. You can then create a new folder or a new tray in the Enter new name for folder or tray dialog box. A new tray is like a main folder and a new folder is usually a sub-folder. If a folder contains sub-folders, this is denoted by a plus sign next to it. Click on this to expand the hierarchy and then click on the minus sign that appears to minimise it again.

Once messages have been received they can be moved into folders within your Pegasus structure by using the Move to another folder or Copy to another folder buttons. Select the message, click on the relevant button and then select a folder where you want the message moved or copied to.

Signatures

Signatures are elements that can be added automatically to the end of email messages. If one is selected, it is included in the sent message, but it is not visible to the sender. Therefore, if you are using signatures, you have to be careful that you include the right one with the relevant message: you may not want to include a signature that you use to your best friend to a new business acquaintance. Pegasus allows for up to nine different signature sets to be created and each one can have different information depending on how it is being sent, i.e. over the Internet or over a local network. To create a signature:

1. Select Tools>Options from the menu bar; select the Signatures tab.
2. Next to Signature set #1 select the Edit button. In the Editing signature set #1 dialog box, enter a name for this set of signatures, such as 'For Work Contacts'. Enter the signature information for each option

within the signature set: two of them are for sending messages over a network and the other is for sending items via the Internet. The signature information can be the same for each element and it is common for it to consist of the sender's name and contact details such as email, fax and telephone.

3. Select Save and repeat for any other signature sets that you want to create.

4. Check on the Use by default button next to one of the signature sets to use this as the default for all messages, unless specified otherwise. If you want to make sure that you do not include any unwanted signatures with messages, check on the Default to no signature button at the bottom of the dialog box.

5. Select OK when you have completed all of the required signature sets.

To add a signature set when you are composing an email message (if you want to change the default, or it has been set to no signature):

1. In the Sig. box just above the Formatting toolbar, select the down pointing arrow.

2. Select a signature set from the drop down list.

This is a useful method for adding a specific signature to a particular message.

Although Pegasus has a slightly different interface to some of the better known programs, it is extremely powerful and particularly effective as a network email client.

Netiquette

Composing with care

Despite the fact that emails bear more than a passing resemblance to hard-copy letters, in that they both convey a message from one party to another, there is a considerable difference in the medium. While the message may be the same, the means of conveying it is at the opposite end of the communications scale. Although this should not make a difference to the way emails are written there is no doubt it does.

There is something about writing and sending a message on a computer, without the intervention of paper at any point, which makes people react differently to one that is created with a pen and paper. In some ways email is less structured and has fewer hard and fast rules. However, this does not mean that there is not a loose code of best practice that has grown up around email. In some circles this is known as 'Netiquette', or how not to upset other people on the Internet.

This is the type of phrase that appeared in the early days of the Internet, when the users considered the new medium to be some kind of online community. There are still individuals who yearn for a return to those days, but the Internet has grown into such a global commercial phenomenon that sometimes these phrases almost seem slightly anarchic (in Internet terms at least). But Netiquette is as good a phrase as any for an all-encompassing term for what you should, and should not, do when sending emails.

Reply promptly

Since one of the main advantages of email is the speed at which it can be sent, a lot of people expect an almost instant reply. While it may not always be possible to reply immediately in full to all messages, it is a good habit to get into if you can at least send an acknowledgement, stating that you have received the message and you will get back to the sender with a complete reply as soon as possible. This at least puts the sender's mind at rest and prevents them from sitting at their terminal waiting for your reply to appear on screen a few seconds after they have sent the original message. When sending an acknowledgement to a message, select the Reply button, but ensure you delete the original text in the message.

Replying promptly does not mean that you have to rush your reply or send a message while you are annoyed. Always check a message before you send it.

Check your Inbox regularly

To make sure you keep up to date with your messages, try and check for incoming email at least once a day. This will only take a few seconds and if you do have any new items you will be able to reply to them as above, so the sender knows they have arrived. Most people check their physical mail once a day and so it should be the same with virtual mail.

If you have just sent a message and you are expecting a reply, do not check you Inbox every couple of minutes. Be patient – just because you reply promptly does not mean that everyone else does too.

Do not hassle people for a reply

Even if you get into the habit of replying promptly to messages, other people may not be so conscientious. It can be frustrating waiting for a reply to a message, particularly if a few days have elapsed, but it is unlikely that you will get much of a response if you start sending reminder emails only a few hours after the original has been sent. If your email was urgent, in your eyes at least, wait three or four days and then send a polite reminder. You could preface it by saying that you are just checking that the intended recipient got the original message. If it is an email to a family member or a friend, you could always revert to some traditional technology and phone the person up to check if they received your message

Be concise

One of the peculiarities of email is that is does not lend itself to long, drawn out messages. Perhaps this is because it is harder to read lengthy compositions on screen, but even when they are printed out, anything over a page in length seems dauntingly long. Because of this it is best to keep you messages short and sweet. Say what you have to say and then hit Send. Remember, the recipient of your message is probably not reading it in isolation and they may have several other emails to look at. You stand a much better chance of a speedy response if you keep your original message concise and to the point.

If you are writing a long email message, use bullet points and numbered lists to break up the text and make it seem more manageable.

Avoid sending huge attachments

One of the most annoying aspects about email is waiting several minutes for a message to download, only to find that the delay was caused by a large attachment that you are not particularly interested in. Some Internet Service Providers (ISPs) will not let you send attachments over a certain size (this is more to do with reducing the strain on their own email servers than any sensitivity for the intended recipient of an enormous attachment) and so this should be blocked. If you do want to send a large email then there are a few steps to follow:

- Check with your ISP what size of attachments they will accept (the figure is usually high enough to cope with most files, except those that run into several megabytes).
- Email the recipient with a plain text message, telling them that you are going to send them a large attachment. Explain what it is and ask them if they are happy to download it.
- Compress large files. This can be done with a compression program such as WinZip . This makes the file smaller so that it can be sent more quickly. However, make sure the recipient has a similar program, because they will need to uncompress the file before they can view it.

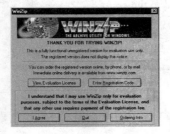

Edit your responses

If you want to reply to a message that you have received, the easiest way is to select the Reply button on the toolbar of your email program. This automatically inserts the sender's email address in the To box of the message you are composing. It also includes the whole of the original text in your message. If it is a short item then this does not pose much of a problem, but if it is a reasonably large amount of text, it is best to delete some or all of it before you send your reply. This is just to make your message more streamlined and take up less resources on the way from your computer to the recipient's. Of course, if there is a specific part of the original message that you are referring to, leave this in your reply, but remove anything that is irrelevant. If any attachments have come with the original message these will not be returned with your reply, although there will be a textual note of what the attachment was.

From: Nikki Read
Date: 31 May 2000 12:31
To: 'Nick Vandome'
Subject: RE: Permission to reproduce Commonwealth Material

-----Original Message-----
From: Nick Vandome [SMTP:nick@vandome.freeserve.co.uk]
Sent: 22 May 2000 21:04
To: nikki@howtobooks.co.uk
Subject: Fw: Permission to reproduce Commonwealth Material

Hi Nikki
Here is the reply from AusInfo about reproducing pages from the Tax Pack.
See what you think about it - it seems they want to charge A$20 (about ?8 at
the current exchange rate) per page reproduced. I have included the
contact's email address in case you want to get in touch with him directly.
Best wishes
Nick
----- Original Message -----
From: Gillson, Bill <Bill.Gillson@dofa.gov.au>
To: <nick@vandome.freeserve.co.uk>
Sent: 22 May 2000 04:56
Subject: Permission to reproduce Commonwealth Material

Avoid shouting

One of the most common reasons for misunderstandings with email messages is the inability for an electronic message to convey the mood of author. Again, this should be no different from a hard copy letter but it seems to be the case. With words on a screen there seems to be less scope for following the subtleties and nuances in a message and so an innocuous phrase can easily be misinterpreted. One way some users try and put more meaning into emails is to place words, phrases and sentences in uppercase type. This is often intended to add emphasis, but to the recipient it can look like the sender is shouting at them. (Uppercase type can be used deliberately to shout at people, but it is not considered to be a good thing to do to win friends and influence people.) In general, steer clear of uppercase type and use bold or italics if you want to emphasis a point.

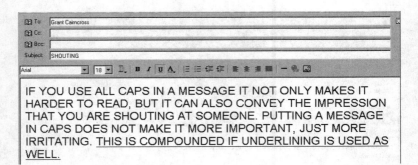

Do not expect confidentiality

Once you have sent an email it is no longer your exclusive property and it could end up anywhere if the recipient decides to forward it on. You can ask that something is kept confidential but this does not guarantee it will be so. If there are sensitive matters that you do not want to risk being made public, even to a limited audience, then do not commit them to an email. Conversely you should do your best to respect the confidentiality of people who send emails to you. If you are told something that is obviously in confidence then you should appreciate this and not forward it on to everyone in your email address book. If you treat other people with this type of courtesy then, hopefully, they will do the same for you. Remember though, there is no such thing as truly confidential email.

Be careful with humour

Humour is another contentious area in email circles. What may seem uproariously funny in your head, may not have the same effect when transferred to email. In some respects it depends on who you are emailing as to the degree to which you use humour. If you are sending a message to your best friend, there is a good chance that they will understand your sense of humour and so you will be able to write what you like. However, if you are contacting someone you do not know so well, such as a business contact, it is best to leave the humour aside. Or perhaps wait until they make the first move in this department. There is definitely a place for humour in emails (indeed there are numerous humorous items that circulate around the Internet, many of which are genuinely funny, although no-one ever seems to know where they originated from) but use it with discretion.

Take your time to respond

When we see something that annoys us, it is human nature to get upset or angry. Nine times out of ten our anger recedes fairly quickly and when we look at things in the cold light of day they are not as bad as maybe we first thought they were. This is usually the case if we receive a letter or similar piece of correspondence that riles us. Initially we are intent on firing off a stinging reply, possibly based on our frustration rather than good judgement. But by the time we have written the letter, found an envelope and a stamp we have usually had time to reflect and come to the conclusion that perhaps our response would benefit from being toned down a notch or two. Unfortunately, due the speed and ease with which an email can be replied to, there is not this built in breathing space that you have with a hard copy letter. If you receive an email that upsets you, it is possible to draft and send a reply in less than a minute. Then, after only a few minutes' reflection, you may decide that you did not really want to say what you did to your in-laws. But by this time it is too late and the damage has been done. To avoid replying in haste and repenting at leisure, always give yourself a cooling off period between when you write an email under stressful conditions and when you send it. Leave a minimum of half an hour and preferably longer. Then go back to your message and see if your burning retort is really what you want to send. Even with emails that were not created out of anger it is always a good idea to set them aside for a few minutes before you send them, just so that you can give them a proper double-check.

Sometimes the tone of an email can be misinterpreted. If you are in any doubt or confusion, use the old standby of the telephone to check with the sender what they mean.

Avoid flame wars

Flame wars occur if you ignore the earlier advice and send emails while your blood is boiling. This will probably enrage the recipient equally and if they reply to you in kind then you could become engaged in a flame war, where insults are traded freely and frequently. Of course, this does no-one any good and it is generally a huge waste of time. If you can bring yourself to do it, while you are in the middle of a flame war, try and diffuse the situation by simply not replying to the latest message you receive. Hopefully that should give both parties enough time to cool off. Always try and avoid flame wars in a work environment as this could be kept as a permanent reminder of a volatile characteristic.

Flame wars also occur in newsgroups, usually when an individual takes exception to something someone else has posted on the site. This can take the form of some fairly vitriolic personal abuse and although there is a great temptation to reply in kind, try and resist. That is probably what the person wanted in the first place and it will annoy them more if you turn the other cheek. Some people can become very possessive about newsgroups they contribute to so tread carefully if you are unsure of the territory. For a more detailed look at newsgroups see the 'Mailing Lists and Newsgroups' chapter.

There are several Web sites dedicated to the art and history of Internet flaming. Try: www.mcs.net/~jorn/html/flamers.html

Using emoticons

In the early days of the Internet, when it was inhabited mainly by computer enthusiasts and their quirky habits, a form of online sign language was developed to inject more meaning and variation into email messages. This consisted of little icons that where created from letters and symbols on a computer keyboard. The main limitation of this is that you have to tilt your head to the side to view the icons properly. These emotional icons became known as emoticons and there are literally hundreds of them, for those who like this sort of thing. Feelings are generally mixed about the usefulness of emoticons: some people think they are humorous and add character to otherwise lifeless text; while others see them as childish and representing the cliquish tendencies of early Internet users. Make up your own mind, but some common emoticons are:

:-)	Smiling
:-D	Laughing
:-{)	Smiling and moustache
8-)	Smiling and glasses
:-(	Frowning
:-O	Surprise
:-I	Indifferent
:-/	Puzzled
:'-)	Crying
;-)	Winking
:*	Kissing
$-)	Greedy
:-X	I'll not say anything
:->	Sarcastic

If you are a fan of emoticons (or smileys as they are also sometimes known) try looking at the following Web site: (or enter 'emoticons' or 'smileys' into a search engine)

www.pop.at/smileys/

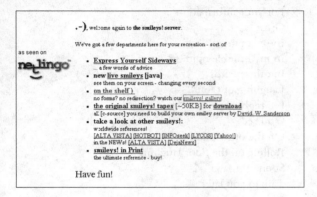

Using abbreviations

Similar to emoticons are Internet abbreviations. These are acronyms that have been developed by the Internet community and they are most frequently used in emails that are posted with newsgroups. As with emoticons, some people love them and others see them as an immature obsession. If you do use them in your own email, do so sparingly since the recipients of your message may not be clued up on the latest Internet shorthand lingo. Some abbreviations that you may come across are:

AFAIK	As far as I know
BBL	Be back later
BD	Big deal
BTW	By the way
CU	Goodbye
FYI	For your information
GR8	Great
IMO	In my opinion
IMHO	In my humble opinion
IOW	In other words
LOL	Laughing out loud
NRN	No reply necessary
OIC	Oh I see
OTOH	On the other hand
ROTFL	Rolling on the floor laughing
SOL	Sooner or later
TTYL	Talk to you later

Email on the Move

WAP

One of the traditional drawbacks of the Internet and all of the elements associated with it, including email, has been its lack of mobility. If you have a connection via your computer then you have to be at that computer to gain access. The advent of the laptop computer helped to alleviate this problem in that you could take it with you, but you still needed a physical connection to a telephone line, which restricted mobility once you were online.

However, the development of WAP, and other similar technologies, promises to transform the way in which we use the Internet. WAP stands for Wireless Application Protocol and it can provide access to the Internet through mobile phones or personal organisers. No wires or cables, no modems; just a completely portable device that can be used to gain information from the Web and send and receive emails on the move. These devices are already on the market and in use and although they are fairly basic compared with Internet access through a desktop or a laptop computer, the technology is developing at break-neck speed and WAP devices are improving constantly. Predictions abound about the future usage of WAP technology (and not all of them from the telecommunications companies: the respected research company Forrester have conducted some research in this area) and the only thing that is certain is that we are currently at the beginning of the next stage of the Internet revolution. Some of the predictions that have been made for WAP include:

- In 2001 there will be 72 million WAP mobile phones sold in the USA, compared with 45 million PCs.

- By 2004, 1/3 of people in Europe will be using WAP-enabled mobile phones to access the Internet. This is in excess of 219 million users.
- By 2005, 830 million mobile phone users worldwide will be connected to the Internet through WAP technology.
- By 2005, 14 billion e-commerce transactions a year will be conducted using WAP mobile phones, accounting for goods and services to the value of $200 billion.

Although WAP phones are still something of a novelty, they seem destined to become, in time, as ubiquitous as the current standard mobile phones.

The beginnings of WAP

Unlike some technological developments, there has been a considerable amount of co-operation and agreement during the development of WAP. Both Internet and telecommunications companies have been quick to appreciate the value of having wireless access to the Internet and so they have worked together to create a global specification with an agreed standard protocol. This means that users can buy WAP devices, safe in the knowledge that all of them will be able to access the same services. This is not to say that there is not fierce competition between companies such as BT, Orange, Ericsson and Nokia in selling their WAP products and services, but the users benefit from the fact that they are all using the same standard. There is even a forum that is used to develop WAP and this is supported by most of the key players in this area. To view the WAP Forum on the Web, look at the following site:

- *www.wapforum.org/*

How WAP works

Since a mobile phone or a personal organiser is a lot smaller than a desktop computer it means that the available space for viewing content from the Internet is reduced considerably. This has resulted in the current WAP services only being produced in a text format. This is not much of a problem for email, since this is generally text only anyway. However, for Web pages it presents a new challenge. This has currently been overcome by creating pages that are specifically designed for viewing with a WAP device. Instead of using HTML as the code for authoring the pages, a new code, WML (Wireless Markup Language), is used. This is like a simplified version of HTML that does not contain some of the more advanced formatting features or the use of graphics. In some ways this is an interim measure, since as the technology progresses more varied content will be available online. The current WAP sites on the Internet can only be viewed using a WAP device and they cannot be seen through a browser such as Internet Explorer or Netscape Navigator. There are currently approximately 40,000 WAP sites available from within the UK but this number is rising on a daily basis as more and more organisations realise the importance of getting in at the beginning of the WAP revolution. Most of these sites cover areas such as online banking, stock market reports, shopping, entertainment and sports results. In theory, it is now possible to organise large parts of your business and your social life through a WAP-enabled mobile phone or a personal organiser.

Although email can be sent and received over WAP devices, the one drawback is the limitations of the keyboard. At present they are acceptable for keying in short messages, but for anything too lengthy they are a little bit fiddly. This is one area that the developers are looking closely at, mindful of the fact that in the not too distant future some people will only be using a WAP device for sending and receiving their emails. It is also possible to send images using WAP devices, but only if they are reasonably small in size. Anything too big and it just becomes a blur when it reaches the recipient.

Drawbacks of WAP

Since it is still an emerging technology there are a number of drawbacks associated with WAP mobile phones and personal organisers:

- Cost of devices. At present WAP devices are still reasonably expensive (approximately £100 and above in the UK). This will not put off the early adopters (technology junkies who have to have every latest piece of technology that hits the shops, whether they need it or not) but it could be a barrier to immediate acceptance by a mass audience. If someone has a standard mobile phone and they are not too concerned about using the Internet, then it could be a struggle to convince them to part with more money for a higher specification device. Having said that, people said that mobile phones would not catch on in a big way and they are now an ubiquitous part of society. The cost of WAP devices is likely to fall considerably and quickly, to the point where users will buy them as standard whenever they need to upgrade their existing mobile. Also, this type of innovation has a habit of snowballing and once people see their friends and work colleagues using WAP mobiles and personal organisers, they will conclude that they have to have one too. At least that is what the telecommunications companies are hoping, as they have invested billions of pounds in WAP.

- Cost of calls. Using a WAP device is not the cheapest way to connect to the Internet, with access currently costing approximately 5 pence per minute or above. As with the devices, this will come down in the next couple of years fuelled largely by a greater number of users. This is because if more people use the WAP network then more advertisers can be attracted to it and so the companies offering the services can cut their costs because of their increased advertising revenue. There is no reason why the cost of access to the WAP network will not come in line with the cost of accessing the Internet through desktop and laptop computers.

Some consumers seem to be under the impression that the current range of WAP devices can offer a full multimedia Internet experience. This is not true, as the Web surfing is text based and emails are not capable of carrying attachments. However, this is likely to change with the next generation of WAP devices.

- Network coverage. If you want to check stock market prices while you are hiking up the top of a Scottish mountain you may be thwarted by the fact that the network coverage for WAP devices is not as extensive as it could be. This is another area that is being developed actively by telecommunications companies as they are aware that there could be a credibility problem if WAP technology only extended to certain areas. If you are worried about the network coverage in the area where you will be using a WAP device, try borrowing one to test it before you take the plunge of buying one. Also check with the companies offering these services (currently BT and Orange) to see what their advice is about network coverage and their plans for extending it.

- Memory. One of the main challenges for the developers of WAP devices is to increase the amount of information that they can process. At present, this is limited by the physical size of the devices, but as the demand for more varied content grows, so the need to increase the memory of the devices will become more urgent. This is one area that is being very actively pursued by the designers of WAP technology.

- The speed of technology. When is a good time to buy a WAP mobile phone or personal organiser? This is a common question regarding new technology and if you are worried about it becoming out of date quickly, the answer is probably never. Even with the current crop of WAP devices offering email and textual WML Web sites, there are new ranges waiting in the wings to take over and offer cheaper, faster and more varied services. However, if you wait until these appear in the shops, there will be yet more devices appearing on the horizon, eager to take WAP to the next level again. If you keep waiting for the next big thing, then may never join the WAP generation. It is best to decide on the specifications you want from a WAP device and then buy that when it comes along. But at the same time, be prepared for it to be superseded very quickly and accept that you will have to upgrade regularly to keep up with the latest developments.

WAP resources

General Web sites with WAP information and resources:

- *www.wap-resources.net/*
- *www.wap.net/*
- *www.anywhereyougo.com/ayg/ayg/Index.po?*
- *www.gelon.net/*

Two of the companies that are currently leading the development of WAP mobile phones in the UK are:

- BT at *www.bt.com/* and
- Orange at *www.orange.co.uk*

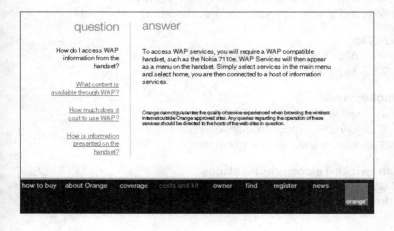

Some of the following WAP sites are located around the world and so give a global perspective of the subjects they cover. Most of these organisations have a traditional Web site and also a WAP one.

Business sites

Wapetite

Wap: *http://www.rlwap.com/*
Web: *http://www.wapetite.com/*

WAP NAWEß

Web: *http://come.to/naweb*
Wap: *http://www.naweb.pt/*

ßlueCycle Auctions

Wap: *http://www.bluecycle.com/wap/bluecycle.wml*
Web: *http://www.bluecycle.com/home/wap.html*

VipWap

Wap: *http://www.vipwap.dk/vipwap.wml*
Web: *http://www.systematic.dk/*

Hughesmedia

Professional Web design.
Wap: *http://www.hughesmedia.co.uk/wap/*
Web: *http://www.hughesmedia.co.uk/*

ßandwidth Telecommunications

Wap: *http://www.bandwidth.ie/wap/index.wml*
Web: *http://www.bandwidth.ie/*

ITIL

Wap: *http://www.itil.com/index.wml*
Web: *http://www.itil.com/mobile.htm*

Agilic

Web design and e-commerce.

Wap: *http://www.agilic.com/mobile/index.wml*
Web: *http://www.agilic.com/*

If a company has recognised the importance of WAP then there is a good chance that they will offer a good service for Web and e-commerce products.

Minutehand.com

Web/WAP development.

Wap: *http://www.minutehand.com/wap/*
Web: *http://www.minutehand.com/*

Uplands

Mobile communications, in-car entertainment, satellite navigation. Links to several useful WAP sites.

Wap: *http://www.uplands.co.uk/wap/index.wml*
Web: *http://www.uplands.co.uk/*

Vesti Mobile Service

Wap: *http://www.vesti-rtr.com/wap/i.wml*
Web: *http://www.vesti-rtr.com/*

Computing sites

Corpex

Registers domain names.

Wap: *http://wap.corpex.com/index.wml*

Web: *http://www.corpex.com/*

LCI Technology Group

General WAP news and information.

Wap: *http://wap.lcigroup.com/*

Web: *www://wap.lcigroup.com/*

JumpingDuck

Wap: *http://www.wapdrive.net/jumpingduck/*

Web: *http://www.jumpingduck.co.uk/*

Siteloft Wireless AS

Wap: *http://wap.siteloft.com/*
Web: *http://www.siteloft.com/*

Haloplayers.com

Wap: *http://wap.haloplayers.com/*
Web: *http://www.haloplayers.com/*

Wap Planet

Send email, read WAP news, and visit WAP links. Needs registration.

Wap: *http:// www.wap-planet.net/wap/*
Web: *http://www.wap-planet.net/*

xebec mediafactory

Wap: *http://wap.xebec.de/*
Web: *http://www.xebec.de/*

Mdj's Computer Guide

Information on games, news and the Internet.

Wap: *http://www.mdj.dk/wap/*
Web: *http://www.mdj.dk/*

WAP sites i.e. those with a '–.wap' extension can only be viewed via a WAP device and not through a normal Web browser.

Email sites

Quick Access E-mail
Wap: *http://hicon.nl/wap/*
Web: *http://www.hicon.nl/qa.htm*

Mail and News
Wap: *http://www.mailandnews.com/*
Web: *http://www.mailandnews.com/*

WAP 0
Wap: *http://wap0.com/*
Web: *http://wap0.com/*

WAP Machine
Wap: *http://www.wapmachine.com*
Web: *http://www.wapmachine.com*

M-Minimail
Wap: *http://m-minimail.com*
Web: *http://www.m-minimail.com/*

E-Search
Wap: *http://www.esearch.ie/wap*
Web: *http://www.esearch.ie/wap*

Financial sites

Mobile Invest
Financial and technology information
> Wap: *http://www.mobile-invest.co.uk/*
> Web: *http://www.mobile-invest.co.uk/*

Finance is predicted to be one of the growth areas for WAP. It will enable people to keep up-to-date with share prices and financial information when they are away from their computer.

Jagnotes
Financial reports
> Wap: *http://www.jagnotes-euro.com/premium/pda*
> Web: *http://www.jagnotes-euro.com/*

UBS Quotes
> Wap: *http://wap.ubs.com/quotes*
> Web: *http://www.jagnotes-euro.com/http://www.ubs.com/quotes*

money.pl
> Wap: *http://wap.money.pl*
> Web: *http://www.jagnotes-euro.com/http://www.money.pl*

Wiener Börse
Read your indices.
> Wap: *http://www.wbag.at/wap.wml*

Web: *www.jagnotes-euro.com/http://www.wbag.at/index_english.html*

moneyeXtra

Latest share prices and other WAP services.

Wap: *http://wap.moneyextra.com/*

Web: *http://www.moneyextra.com/*

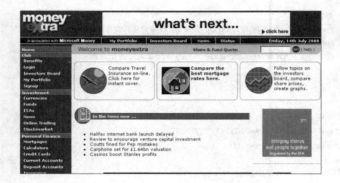

Stock Smart

Stock market reports and prices.

Wap: *http://agsub.stocksmart.com/ss.wml*

Web: *http://www.stocksmart.com/*

Stockpoint

Stock quotes from world markets.

Wap: *http://www.stockpoint.com/*

Web: *http://www.stockpoint.com/*

Entertainment sites

UK Entertainment Centre

Details of live music, clubs, comedy and theatre throughout the UK.

Wap: *http://www.ents24.com/index.wml*

Web: *http://uk.ents24.com/*

Sessami

Services for eating out.

Wap: *http://wap.sessami.com/*

Web: *http://www.sassami.com/*

Breathe

General entertainment.

Wap*: http://wap.breathe.com/*

Web: *www.breathe.com/*

Rock Nights

Pubs and nightclub information.

    Wap: *http://wap.rocknights.co.uk/index.wml*

    Web: *http://rocknights.co.uk/*

Hitchhiker's Guide to the Galaxy

    Wap: *http://wap.h2g2.com/*

    Web: *http://www.h2g2.com/*

Games sites

BetMart

Online betting.

    Wap: *http://www.betmart.com/wap.wml*

    Web: *http://www.betmart.com/*

Hangman

Online version of he popular game.

    Wap: *http://www.topstudy.com/wap/game/hang*

    Web: *http://www.zenith.ie/*

wapscallion.net

Play Battleship and Pontoon games and generate Lottery numbers.

    Wap: *http://wap.wapscallion.net/*

    Web: *http://www.wapscallion.net/*

WAPCasino

On-line casino with poker, slot machine and black jack. For fun rather than profit.

    Wap: *http://www.fantastock.com/casino/index.wml*

    Web: *http://www.fantastock.com/casino*

Space

A text-based adventure game utilising WAP.

    Wap: *http://www.greatelephant.co.uk/wap/space.asp*

    Web: *http://www.homepages.co.uk/http://www.greatelephant.co.uk/*

News sites

BBC

    Wap: *http://www.bbc.co.uk/mobile/mainmenu.wml*

    Web: *http://www.bbc.co.uk*

News organisations have identified the importance of WAP technology and they are working to ensure that the latest headlines are always at your fingertips.

Newsvendor

Wap: *http://wap.newsvendor.com/i.wml*
Web: *http://www.newsvendor.com*

News Unlimited

Wap: *http://www.newsunlimited.co.uk/wml/*
Web: *http://www.newsunlimited.co.uk/*

CNN

Wap: *http://www.cnn.com/mobile*
Web: *http://www.cnn.com/mobile*

The Tuck Shop

Wap: *http://www.thetuckshop.com*
Web: *http://www.thetuckshop.com*

Interpuntonet.it news

Wap: *http://www.interpuntonet.it/wap*
Web: *http://www.interpuntonet.it/*

Shopping sites

Homepages.co.uk
Online property services.
>   Wap: *http://wap.homepages.co.uk/*
>   Web: *http://www.homepages.co.uk/*

1-800-MOBILESInc.
>   Wap: *http://wapSN.com/360wireless*
>   Wap: *http://wapSN.com/1800mobiles*

Battery Outlet
>   Wap: *http://wapSN.com/BatteryOutlet*

Camera Sound
>   Wap: *http://wapSN.com/CameraSound*

Candlescape.com
>   Wap: *http://wapSN.com/Candlescape*

Cellpoint Corporation
>   Wap: *http://wapSN.com/cellpoint*

Cool Sports Equipment, LLC
>   Wap: *http://wapSN.com/coolsports*

Flowers On Command
>   Wap: *http://wapSN.com/flowersoncommand*

Gadget Universe
   Wap: *http://wapSN.com/Gadgets*

Getcellular
   Wap: *http://wapSN.com/Getcellular*

Pinelli's Flowerland
   Wap: *http://wapSN.com/PINELLISFLOWERLAND*

Metrolabels
   Wap: *http://wapSN.com/Pricelabels*

D M Merchandise Company
   Wap: *http://wapSN.com/Scentsations*

Top Dog Entertainment
   Wap: *http://wapSN.com/tickets*

A-1 T-Shirts
   Wap: *http://wapSN.com/T-SHIRTZ*

Young Pharmaceuticals, Inc.
   Wap: *http://wapSN.com/Young*

Sport sites

WAP a Result
Sports Results – Football, Rugby, Formula 1
   Wap: *http://www.waparesult.com/index.wml*
   Web: *http://www.waparesult.com*

Arsenal Wapsite

The latest online news about Arsenal FC.

Wap: *http://www.waparesult.com/http://arseweb.com/wap/*

Web: *http://arseweb.com/*

Manchester United Wapsite

The latest online news about Manchester United FC.

Wap: *http://www.europewap.com/manutd/manmenu.wml*

Web: *http://www.wapprofit.com/*

 Most English and Scottish Premiership football clubs have their own Web sites but, at present, they do not all have WAP sites

I Golf The World

General worldwide golfing news and information about courses.

Wap: *http://www.igolftheworld.com/phone*

Web: *http://www.igolftheworld.com/*

Travel sites

CitiKey

News, information and maps for cities around the world.

Wap: *http://wap.citikey.com/*

Web: *http://www.citikey.com/*

Italy Hotel Reservation Online

Wap: *http://wap.venere.it/*
Web: *http://www.venere.it/*

The Hotel Catalogue

Find hotels world-wide – More than 550,000 accommodations in 215 countries.

Wap: *http://wap.hotelcatalogue.net/*
Web: *http://www.hotelcatalogue.net/*

Personal Travel Mart

You can book flights and hotels from a number of sources.

Wap: *http://peseta.ecomm.bt.co.uk/wap/facts/start.wml*
Web: *http://peseta.ecomm.bt.co.uk/wap/facts/index.html*

BCN WAP

A general tourist guide to Barcelona.

Wap: *http://artbites.com/bcn.wml*

GIN

Information on European weather and tourist information.

Wap: *http://wap.gin.nl/pub/hhotel.wml*

IRLWap

Tourist information concerning Ireland.

Wap: *http://www.irlwap.com/i.wml*

Malaysia Search

News and tourist information for anyone wanting to visit Malaysia.

Wap: *http://www.malaysiasearch.net*

Shefon.com
Tourist information about Sheffield.
  Wap: *http://www.shefon.com/s1.wml*

Wonderful Copenhagen
Tourist attractions and where to eat and sleep in Copenhagen.
  Wap: *http://www.copenhagenpictures.dk/wap/*

worldroom.com
Tourist information relating to Manila, Hong Kong, Singapore, Sydney and Taipei.
  Wap: *http://wap.worldroom.com/*

Giroscopio
A search facility for tourist accommodation in Italy.
  Wap: *http://www.giroscopio.com/wap/*

Hotelguide.com
A general search engine for hotel accommodation and similar.
  Wap: *http://wap.hotelguide.com/*

2PL
Information about hotels around the world.
  Wap: *http://wap.2pl.com*

UK miscellaneous sites

These sites are proof that the eclectic nature of the Web is alive and well and living on a mobile phone near you.

Advanced Telecom PLC

Mobile telephone and computing services.

Wap: *http://www.advanced.co.uk/wap/index.wml*

All The Recipes

Ideas for in the kitchen.

Wap: *http://www.wapdrive.net/recipe/*

Alternative QPR Wapsite

Proof that it is not only top flight football clubs that can embrace the new mobile revolution.

Wap: *http://www.altQPR.freeserve.co.uk/wap/index.wml*

Autolocate

Offers a list of used cars and car dealers.

Wap: *http://wap.autolocate.co.uk*

Bigger Deffer

Caters for those interested in hip-hop in the London area.

Wap: *http://www.wapdrive.net/biggerdeffer/*

BlueSky

Web development with WML and HTML.

Wap: *http://wap.bluesky.co.uk/index.wml*

BookBrain.co.uk

Books at bargain prices.

Wap: *http://www.bookbrain.co.uk/bbwap/wmenu.asp*

Brighton and Hove Albion FC

Another lesser light of the footballing world breaks onto the mobile Web.

Wap: *http://wappy.to/seagulls*

Bullivants Garages

Derby based importer of Japanese cars.

Wap: *http://www.got2wap.co.uk/bullivants/*

Chess Corner

For chess buffs around the country.

Wap: *http://www.chesscorner.com/*

Clockwork Orange

Not the film, but mobile phone services.

Wap: *http://wappy.to/orange/*

Curryhouse.net

A searchable index of curry houses around Britain.

Wap: *http://www.curryhouse.net/wap/*

CurryPages

Similar to above.

Wap: *http://wap.currypages.com/*

E Loan

Offers loans for mortgages and similar products.
  Wap: *http://wap.eloan.com/uk*

ents24.com

Information about what's on around the country.
  Wap: *http://www.ents24.com/index.wml*

Flowerwap.co.uk

A flower and gift delivery service within the UK.
  Wap: *http://www.flowerwap.co.uk*

Frazer and Orr

WAP design services within Northern Ireland.
  Wap: *http://www.frazerandorr.com/index.wml*

Freedom Phones

Everything to do with buying a new telephone.
  Wap: *http://wap.wirefree.com/*

Gillingham Football Club

WAP is alive and well at Gillingham FC.
  Wap: *http://wappy.to/gills*

Handspace

General transportation information for in and around London.
  Wap: *http://www.handspace.com*

Interactive Investor

The latest from the stock markets.

Wap: *http://mobile.iii.co.uk*

Leek Computers and Comms

Provides telecommunications and computing equipment.

Wap: *http://wap.lcc.co.uk*

Limahl

The 80s star returns on the mobile Web.

Wap: *http://www.limahl.co.uk/index.wml*

Loot

An online version of the classified ads magazine.

Wap: *http://wap.loot.com/*

Mapquest

Directions for getting around on the roads.

Wap: *http://wl.mapquest.com/gb/*

Mobile Invest

Stock quotes and global financial and investment information.

Wap: *http://www.mobile-invest.co.uk*

NCB Direct

News and information from the financial world.

Wap: *http://telecom.ncbdirect.com/wap/index.wml#ncbhomepage*

News Unlimited

News and updates from around the globe.

Wap: *http://www.newsunlimited.co.uk/wml*

PR Newswire

Similar to above.

Wap: *http://wap.prnewswire.co.uk/*

Rebus Electronic Business

Developing services for the WAP world.

Wap: *http://www.rebusebusiness.com/home.wml*

Rishworth School, Yorkshire, UK

A forward-thinking school that appreciates the value of using the Internet for displaying contact details and timetables.

Wap: *http://www.rishworth-school.co.uk/wap/index.wml*

Scoutnet

Scouting details from around the UK.

Wap: *http://www.scoutnet.org.uk/wap/*

Search UK

A search tool looking for advertisements placed by specific companies, according to localised criteria.

Wap: *http://www.getlocal.co.uk/WAP/*

Sedbergh School, Cumbria, UK

Another school which publishes its details on the mobile Web.

Wap: *http://www.sedbergh.sch.uk/wao/index.wml*

Swanage Lifeboat Crew

Details about the local lifeboat.

Wap: *http://www.swanagelifeboat.co.uk/wap.wml*

Swindon Town FC

News, results and interviews for the devoted followers of Swindon FC.

Wap: *http://wappy.to/stfc/*

TV2000

Rents a variety of telephones.

Wap: *http://www.wapdrive.net/richardb/index.wml*

Under One Roof

Property service.

Wap: *http://wap.underoneroof.co.uk/*

United Kingdom Music Coverage (UKMC)

Music charts, news and band details.

Wap: *http://wappy.to/ukmc*

Unmissable TV

TV listings for the UK.

Wap: *http://www.unmissabletv.com/txw/wap.wml*

Wolverhampton Warriors FC

A local football team WAP the ball.

Wap: *http://wappy.to/wolves*

Worldof.net

Holiday offers in Europe.
　　Wap: *http://mobile.worldof.net/*

4 Clubbers

Clubbing details and news from throughout the UK.
　　Wap: *http://www.wapped-out.co.uk/wap/4clubbers/index.wml*

WAP search directory sites

Ajaxo

Financial, general and sporting information.
　　Wap: *http://phone.ajaxo.com/*

AusWAP

An Australian based WAP search engine.
　　Wap: *http://www.auswap.com.au/wap/*

Babelserver

WAP search services and also the conversion of HTML Web pages into a format that can be displayed on a WAP device.
　　Wap: *http://babelserver.com/*

FAST Search

General WAP search engine.
　　Wap: *http://wap.fast.no/*

M-Central

General WAP search engine.
　　Wap: *http://m-central.com*

Oracle Mobile

Information on travel, finance and eating out.

Wap: *http://www.oramobile.com*

Pinpoint

General WAP search engine.

Wap: *http://wap.pinpoint.com/*

wannaWAP.com

General WAP search engine.

Wap: *http://www.wannaWAP.com/wap/index.asp*

WAPAW

Search engine for all WAP devices.

Wap: *http://www.wapaw.com*

Wap.com

List of all major WAP sites.

Wap: *http://wap.com/*

WAPJAG

Search engine for travel, news and entertainment.

Wap: *http://wapjag.com*

WAPjump

General WAP search engine.

Wap: *http://www.wapjump.org/*

Wapmore

General WAP search engine.

Wap: *http://www.wapmore.com/links/index.wml*

WAPscan

General directory and email services.

Wap: *http://mmm.wapscan.com/*

Wapwag.com

General search through a mini browser.

Wap: *http://wapwag.com/wap*

Webcab

General WAP directory.

Wap: *http://webcab.de/wwe/i.wml*

Yahoo!

An extension of the popular search engine.

Web: *http://www.yahoo.com/*

2thumbsWAP.com

General WAP search engine.

Wap: *http://wap.wapwardlymobile.com/home.wml*

Junk Email

What is junk email?

Whenever you receive any items of email from an unknown source or company there is a good chance that it will be unsolicited i.e. something that you did not ask to be sent to you. This is known as junk email, or spam, and it even has its own acronym: UCE, which stands for Unsolicited Commercial Email. This accounts for a vast amount of email traffic and it is a major problem for the companies running email accounts (usually Internet Service Providers, known more commonly as ISPs) and also email users. Some of the problems that are associated with junk email are:

- Cost. Even if there is no direct cost to the user when they receive an item of junk email, there are a number of hidden costs involved in the sending and receiving of these items.
- Time. Time is money on the Internet and ISPs waste a lot of time processing junk email, that could be better spent on dealing with legitimate messages.
- Credibility. Junk email is an annoyance to all email users, but it can be a particular turn-off to people who are new to email and the Internet. If someone opens up a new email account, only to be bombarded by numerous junk email messages, they may conclude that this new technology is more of a hindrance that a help.

There are ways that email users can try and filter out unwanted emails but, due to the unregulated nature of the Internet, it is impossible to stamp them out completely. As soon as someone open a new email account they are in a position to start receiving junk email and they probably will very soon. The best way to deal with this problem is to understand what it involves and then try and take some preventative steps. Luckily, help is hand and there are numerous Web sites dedicated to all aspects of junk email. As with many things connected to the Internet, the USA is leading the way in terms of both junk email and efforts to combat it. However, it is spreading throughout the global online community and it is a situation that is likely to become more troublesome and widespread as the profits available on the Internet increase.

Types of junk email

It is easy to associate junk email with the paper type of junk mail that falls through our doors with monotonous regularity, advertising the latest credit card or double-glazing offer. By and large these items are nothing more that annoying marketing leaflets that can be thrown away and forgotten about. However, although some junk email is similar to its paper counterpart, there are other types of junk email that have more serious implications. Some of the items that can be classified as junk email are:

- Marketing items. These will be familiar to most people, even if they have never had email before. These are advertising messages from companies who have managed to get hold of your email address. They can be for virtually any product that is available on the Web. Some of these emails are very slick and sophisticated and they frequently contain a link to the Web site of the company involved. If you are involved in business and are interested in email clients then it is worth looking at the format and style of these messages to see if you think they are effective or not. If you have bought goods or services over the Internet, the companies you have dealt with will probably send you marketing material via email from time to time. (When you make online purchases, you invariably have to fill in a registration form, that includes your email address. This is then stored by the company and used for marketing purposes, unless you expressly tell them that you do not want them to do this.) Since you have already used this company, the information may be of interest to you. Other items of marketing email may appear from companies you have never dealt with. This is usually as a result of organisations selling lists of email addresses, one of which will be yours. The companies that receive these lists then use them for mass email marketing. This practice is highly questionable and in general it is best to delete items from unknown sources.

Do not take it personally if you receive junk email marketing. The company has just got your name from a list and they are only interested in you as a potential Inbox location.

- Money making schemes. Everyone likes to think that they can become a millionaire overnight and this enthusiasm has been fuelled by the Internet and stories in the media of dotcom millionaires popping up at every second computer terminal. This has resulted in some genuine money-making ventures but also thousands of scams, frauds and cons. Unfortunately, most of these are perpetrated by email. The most common ones are alleged money-making schemes through pyramid selling, where people buy a list of names and then pass it on, in the hope that eventually there will be a huge number of people on the list, all paying them money. This has been going on for years before computers were around, but email is now a popular platform for this type of con trick. However, it never worked when it consisted of letters, and it will never work via email. Steer clear of this type of message and also any other that claims to be able to give you untold wealth at the click of a mouse button. There is no such thing as a free lunch on the Internet and at least 99% of these money-making schemes are frauds.

Never participate in any get-rich-quick schemes on the Internet. They may have extravagant claims for them but this is all pure fabrication.

- Advertisements for pornographic material. Like it or not, pornography is one of the most popular items on the Internet. The anonymity of the Web gives pornographers the opportunity to distribute their material to a global audience and it is consistently one of the most searched for topics. Whatever the morals of this, one fact is indisputable: pornography on the Web is big business and there is a lot of money being made from it. For the average email user this means one thing: people running pornography on the Web are going to try and contact as wide an audience as possible to try and attract them to their sites. The end result is more junk email, but this time of a more disturbing nature. Pornographers on the Web are not concerned with limiting their marketing to people who have used their services in the past: they want to reach as many Inboxes as possible and they will use any means possible to obtain lists of email addresses. If yours is on one of these lists then you could be subjected to messages for pornographic Web sites, or phone sex sites. This type of material can be extremely offensive and are certainly not the type of message that would be suitable for children to see. Most ISPs try and filter out any junk email that contains pornographic material, but the perpetrators of this type of item have methods of disguising the content of their messages, so there is always a chance that it will get through any safety nets that are in place. One important fact to remember is that receiving this type of email message is not an indication of the Web sites you access: they can be sent to anyone.

Pornography is huge business on the Internet: if children are using the Web or email, make sure that they have some form of supervision.

- Offers of health care. Health is another massive area on the Web and there are thousands of sites dedicated to giving out information about health care. In addition, numerous sites also selling pharmaceutical drugs, some of which are legal and others that are not. This is a difficult area because it can be hard to differentiate between sites that are offering genuinely useful medical advice (and there are a lot of these) and the ones that are offering unsuitable or untested cures. But due to the desire to find information and also miracle cures, there are Web sites devoted to virtually every disease known to mankind. This has led to the inevitable deluge of junk email messages that claim to offer cures for everything from the common cold upwards. These messages should be treated with extreme care as they may be trying to sell you something that will actually harm your health. In addition, some products may be illegal in some countries, or only obtainable with a prescription from a doctor. As with get-rich-quick schemes, there are no miracle cures on the Internet and anyone emailing you to tell you differently should be treated with the utmost caution. This is not to say that valuable health advice cannot be found on reputable Web sites, but buying health products online is a risky business that should be avoided. If in doubt, the best course of action is to speak to your own, real-life, doctor.

A lot of junk emails offering medical products are not run, or sanctioned, by any official medical organisation. In some cases, they may have no medical connections at all.

- Advice on junk emailing. Some items of junk email are from companies that offer to let you do exactly what they are doing to you: sending large volumes of email to customers on mailing lists. These types of emails usually take two forms. The first type is companies offering to send junk email for you. This involves paying them a fee so that, in effect, they do your dirty work for you. The second type of unsolicited mail service is one where a company offers you the means, for a fee naturally, for collecting email addresses and sending your own messages to them. If you are involved in business there could possibly be some merit in pursuing either of these avenues if you are interested in sending high volumes of unsolicited email. However, you have to determine the effectiveness of this and also the moral issue of whether it is right to contribute to what is generally viewed as the scourge of the Internet. Perhaps a more important issue is whether you feel confident doing business with any organisation that is in the habit of sending you junk email.

If you are thinking of undertaking email marketing do it responsibly. Target a specific audience and send them information they want, rather than random, blanket, coverage.

- Stock market tips. The stock market is another area that has benefited greatly from the Internet. It has given a wider audience access to dealing in stocks and shares since users can now sit at their computers and trade at the touch of a button. There are dozens of online share dealing companies, some of which are traditional stockbrokers who developed an online service, while others have sprung up as purely online organisations. This has increased share-dealing activity considerably and it has demystified the process for a lot of people. The junk email marketers are well aware of this and they have not been slow to exploit this heightened interest in stocks and shares. This manifests itself in junk email that offers share tips for existing companies, or the chance to buy shares in companies that are about to float on the stock market. It is conceivable that some people have taken up these offers in the past and made money from them. However, in general, they are merely attempts by individuals who have a vested interest in a company to bolster its value. Dealing in shares in technology companies is a risky business at the best of times and this risk is heightened considerably if you take the advice of anyone who sends you an unsolicited email on the subject. Sometimes, these messages can be very persuasive and include the names of several well-known and successful companies. However, the only people who are likely to make any money if you respond to these messages are those that distribute them.

Treat emails claiming to offer shares in new companies extremely cautiously, even if they come from a known source. At best these can be described as risky investments.

- Pirate software. Software companies hate pirated software because it dilutes their profits and can lead to a product of inferior quality being on the market and bearing their name. Alternatively, some computer users believe that it is reasonable enough to use pirate software rather than pay what can be hundreds of pounds for the official versions. But piracy is a fact of life in the world of computing and most computer users know where they can buy it, whether it is at a local market or from a Web site. The danger in this is that there is no guarantee with the software and it is a popular way for programmers to spread viruses. Therefore there is a much greater chance of having your computer or its files damaged if you use pirated software. Despite this, illegal software is widely available and used and much of it is distributed through junk email. On the surface, some of these offers may look enticing for the user, as they will show a considerable saving over the genuine price for the product. However, on the downside, it should be remembered that it is illegal to use unauthorised software and that if people are trying to sell it through junk email then they may not be the most scrupulous individuals in the first place, so it is a risky business.

If you are worried about software piracy, either from a personal or a corporate perspective, contact the Federation Against Software Theft on their Web site at: www.fast.org.uk/

The cost of junk email

On the surface, it would appear that there is no actual cost incurred by the user as a result of junk email. The argument most frequently put forward by the junk emailers, or spammers, is that users can simply delete any unwanted messages and so the problem is removed. Unfortunately, it is not that simple and there are a number of real, if hidden, costs associated with junk email. Most of these costs fall on the company that is managing your email account, your ISP, and this is then detrimental for the user in that the costs are passed on to them or the ISP cannot offer an improved service because so much of its time it taken up dealing with junk email.

The easy part about junk email is sending it. Anyone with a modem and an Internet connection can send literally thousands of messages in a matter of seconds. However, once they are out in the global email network the problems can begin. Initially this will be with the mail servers of the ISPs. Junk email has to be processed in just the same way as any other messages and this takes time, which is a precious commodity on the Internet. So if a mail server has to process several thousand items of junk email, this is holding up the processing of other messages. And considering that some estimates put the amount of junk email being sent over the Internet at between 20–30% of the total volume of email traffic it is easy to see how this is putting an unnecessary strain on email servers. The problem is compounded by the fact that one batch of junk email will pass through dozens of different email servers on its way to the Inboxes of the unsuspecting recipients. The time spent dealing with junk email could be used much more productively by the ISPs to improve services, cut down costs and speed up the processing of non-junk email.

Another problem for ISPs in dealing with junk email is the amount of bandwidth that they consume. This is a tangible cost because every ISP has to purchase a certain amount of bandwidth; based on their calculations of how much email traffic they will be dealing with. Bandwidth is an ISP's link to the Internet and the amount of it determines the amount of information they can process. It is like a large cable: the larger the cable then the more information that can be sent down it at any one time. Obviously, if bandwidth is busy with junk email then it will not be able to process other items until it has finished with the spam. This means it can take longer to send and receive messages and so each user is paying more in the way of telephone charges because their ISP has to spend valuable time dealing with junk email.

One of the cumulative effects of junk email is that some ISPs can become so overwhelmed that they have to shut down completely for a period of time to deal with the problem. This can happen if there is a surge of junk email and some companies are well known for their tendency to send batches of unsolicited mail that are so large that mail servers cannot cope. This is particularly true for small ISPs, but it has also happened to some of the major players such as AOL. In order to combat this, most ISPs employ full-time staff to deal with junk email and its associated problems. This adds another cost into the equation, which is directly attributable to unsolicited mail.

The cost to the user

Even though email users do not see a monthly bill as a result of the efforts of junk emailers, they do experience various everyday problems. The most obvious one is the annoyance factor. One or two items of junk mail are mildly irritating, a dozen is annoying and several dozen can be a considerable imposition. All of these messages take time to be downloaded (thus passing on a real cost to the user) particularly as some of them may contain sizeable attachments. Then they at least have to be scanned through to make sure there is nothing important or that may actually be of any use, before you delete them.

This all takes time and effort and this is time that could be more profitably spent doing something productive, particularly if you are running a business or are a freelancer. The first time you receive a large number of junk emails you may just shrug your shoulders and be grateful that anyone has contacted you. However, this novelty will soon wear off and if it continues you will realise what a serious problem junk email is becoming on the Internet.

If you know about junk email, and can take some steps to combat it, then you may accept that it is part (albeit an annoying one) of life on the Internet. However, for the Internet novice (and approximately 200 new users come online every second) a flood of spam when they first get connected may be enough to convince them that the scare stories they have heard about the Internet being an unregulated mass of pornography and con artists are true and that they should avoid it at all costs.

Of course, experienced users know that this is not the case, but it can undermine the credibility of the Internet if people are turned away from it as a result of their initial experience with spammers.

Spam and newsgroups

Spam is now widely circulated through email on the Internet, but this is not its only outlet. Bulletins boards that link users on the Internet (known as newsgroups or Usenet — see the 'Mailing list and Newsgroups' chapter for more details) are also regularly bombarded by unwanted messages. Since each of these bulletin boards, and there are over 30,000 of them, has a specialist area of interest those people who subscribe to them become extremely annoyed if large numbers of junk emails start appearing. This can lead to protracted online arguments, known as flame wars, which only serve to waste more time and resources. Users of bulletins boards tend to be more vociferous in their condemnation of spammers and they greatly resent their newsgroups being misused. In order to combat this menace, a number of newsgroups have been created specifically to deal with issues relating to spam (see later for addresses).

Combating junk email

Junk email is recognised as such a problem on the Internet that there are now numerous Web sites and newsgroups that have been created to look at the issue and ways of combating it (see later). In addition to this, every individual can take their own steps to try to limit the amount of spam they receive and identify the worst culprits. Some of these include:

- Setting up filters within your own email program. The method of doing this is looked at in greater detail in the 'Organising Emails' chapter and this is a way of trying to block unwanted emails before they reach your Inbox. To create a filter you set criteria and actions. The criteria are a set of circumstances that have to be met for the action to be performed. This could include a certain name in the To box or a particular subject heading. So if you are getting a lot of email from one particular company you can enter their name as the criteria that have to be met. Similarly, subjects such as 'money' or 'free' that appear in the subject heading can be set as the criteria for the filter. Once the criteria has been specified, an action can then be assigned to be performed on any emails that match it. This could include message management tasks, such as placing items into a specific folder when they arrive, or forwarding them to other individuals. In the case of junk email the action to be performed is usually putting it into the Wastebasket folder, or, preferably, not downloading it from the server in the first place. In addition to individual users being able to set up filters, ISPs also spend a lot of time trying to create filters to combat junk email. In some cases people are employed specifically for this task. Unfortunately the junk emailers are well aware of this fact and therefore sometimes try and disguise their messages to get past the filters. This can be done by sending spam through a third party's server (therefore doubling the load on the system) and then forwarding this on to the intended recipients. This is an ongoing battle; if each user can use filters to block out a few items of email then this will help in the long run.

Update and amend your filter system regularly. You will not be able to stop all junk email but you should be able to cut down the amount that you receive.

- Emailing the spammers. If you receive an item of unwanted mail one solution could be to contact the sender (using the Reply function on your email program) and ask to be removed from their mailing list. This may seem like an idealistic approach and it is not one that is guaranteed to bring dramatic results, particularly as junk emailers are adept at hiding their identity by disguising their header information. However, some of the less unscrupulous operators may agree to your request while others will probably just ignore it, and even use the fact that you have contacted them to exaggerate the situation (see next point). If you do contact a sender of junk email, make sure you keep copies of any correspondences. This could be useful if you want to take any further action as it shows that you have made a reasonable effort to solve the problem.

- Using the spammer's own offer of removing you from their list. With some unsolicited email there is a sentence that offers to remove you from the sender's mailing list if you reply to the message and enter a certain word in the subject box of your email. While this may seem like a simple and straightforward way to avoid receiving spam the reverse may be true. Some companies take the fact that you have replied at all as an admission of interest and use it as an excuse to bombard you with even more messages. To compound matters, some of them also pass on your email address to other companies, telling them that you have replied to one of their unsolicited messages. The result can be a deluge of spam into your Inbox.

In a junk email message, the offer to remove your name from the company's mailing list is sometimes a complete con. They have no intention of doing this and it is just a ploy to generate more communication.

- Contacting your ISP. If your individual attempts to stop spammers sending you unwanted messages fail, you could then turn to your own ISP. Contact them explaining the problem and, if necessary, send them copies of the unwanted messages you have received, particularly if they contain offensive material. Your ISP may then be able to take any action that they deem necessary particularly if they have received other complaints about the same organisation. If spammers can be identified, then it is possible to have them disconnected from the Internet and there are several examples of this having happened in the USA.

- Take the spammers to court. Again, the USA leads the way in court action against companies who persistently send large quantities of unsolicited email. Most of these are taken by large ISPs and AOL has won a few court cases against spammers. However, it is debatable whether many individuals will want to go to the trouble of pursuing companies through the courts. Always consult a lawyer if you intend taking this course of action and make sure they are aware of the latest legislation concerning online issues.

- Create a junk email account. Since a lot of unsolicited mail is sent to email addresses that are collected from users entering them into registration forms on the Web, it is good sense to give an address other than your own everyday email one. This applies when you are buying goods or services online or if you are registering on a Web site for any reason. Your junk email address could be completely fictitious (just change a few letters in your actual address), or you could use a Web-based email address such as HotMail. However, some online companies do not accept Web-based email addresses, since these email providers do not want to have thousands of accounts that are being bombarded with junk mail. If you do create a junk email address, bear in mind that you may not be able to get any genuine messages from the company to whom you have given this address. This may be of little concern, but it is worth remembering if you think there are some useful items that could be sent to you.

Opt-in emailing

Known in some circles as responsible bulk mailing, opt-in emailing is a genuine attempt to try and match up companies selling goods and services and people who are interested in buying them. In order to receive this type of email, you register with a site and then, according to your stated preference, you will be sent messages from companies who are affiliated to the opt-in emailing site. On some of these sites, you are given points for reading messages, which can then be redeemed in whole or in part for other goods and services. Some opt-in emailing sites to look at are:

- BonusMail at *www.bonusmail.com/*
- Choose Your Mail at *www.chooseyourmail.com/*
- Infobeat at *www.inofbeat.com/*
- Postmasterdirect at *www.postmasterdirect.com/*

CAUCE

There are hundreds of Web sites and organisation that are dedicated to fighting unsolicited email and the most prominent one is CAUCE, which stands for Coalition Against Unsolicited Commercial Email. Their Web site can be viewed at:

- *www.cauce.org/*

CAUCE is primarily an information and lobbying site whose aim is to promote fair and reasonable use of the Internet. It is a voluntary organisation that does not accept any donations and exists solely on the Web. People can become members of CAUCE and contribute information about unsolicited email. It is a creation of the Internet and it serves the majority of users who use it in a responsible fashion.

One of the main successes of CAUCE has been to support a bill in the USA aimed at cracking down on organisations sending bulk junk emails. These have included issues such as giving users a legitimate means of asking to be removed from mailing lists and of imposing financial penalties on organisations that try and hide the location of where an email has come from. This is a complex area and although some headway is being made the nature of the Internet makes it very hard to catch and penalise people who are intent on sending large quantities of junk email, and clever enough to avoid detection.

In addition to its main site, CAUCE also has sites for other locations around the world:

- EuroCauce at *www.euro.cauce.org/*
- CAUBE.au at *www.caube.org.au/* (This is the Australian site and CAUBE stands for Coalition Against Unsolicited Bulk Email.)
- CAUCE in India at *www.india.cauce.org/*

Other Web sites

There are hundreds of Web sites dedicated to removing junk email from the Internet. One way to find them is to use a search engine and enter words such as 'spam', 'junk email' or 'UCE'. Alternatively, try looking at some of the following Web sites and newsgroups:

- Boycott Internet Spam – *http://spam.abuse.net/*. This has a lot of general information and links to other sites about spam.
- Stop Spam FAQ – *www.qsl.net/spamfaq.html*. Information about spam and how to take action against it. Some of the advice is a bit on the technical side.
- Filter Spam Out! – *http://www.sunworld.com/sunworldonline/swol-12-1997/swol-12-spam.html*. Information about stopping unwanted messages getting into your Inbox.
- Spamlaws.com – *www.spamlaws.com/* Laws in the USA that cover the distribution of unwanted email.

Checking a message has been sent
  106–110
Checking for new messages 94
Connecting options 95–96
Hanging up 96
Playing sound 93
Writing offline, sending online 103
Servers 19, 26
Signatures. *See also* Formatting:
    Signatures
  Naming 263
  Usage 240
Simple Mail Transfer Protocol. *See*
    SMTP
SMTP 27, 266
Spam. *See* Junk email
Spelling. *See* Formatting: Spelling
Stationery
  Applying 126
  Creating 125
  Defined 124
  Guidelines 128
  Obtaining more 126
  Styles 124
  Template 125
  Usage 250
Status bar 71
Sub-folders. *See* Folders: Creating
Switchboard 87

Telephone line
  Second 96
Television
  For receiving email 37
Telewest 38
TescoNet 29
Toolbar 68
Toolbars 65–69
  Check Mail 68
  Defined 30
  Delete 69
  Find 69
  Forward 68
  New message 68
  Next 68
  Previous 68
  Print 69
  Reply 68
  Reply To All 68
  Send and Receive 68
TWAIN 161
Twigger. *See* Forwarding services:
    Defined

Ulead
  PhotoExpress 159
  PhotoImpact 159
Underlining

T

U

Signatures 357–358
   Creating 357–358
System requirements 56
Tools menu 335
Window menu 348–349
Personal Computer. *See* PC
Photo CDs 162
PhotoDeluxe. *See* Adobe: PhotoDe-
   luxe
PhotoDraw. *See* Microsoft: Photo-
   Draw
PhotoExpress. *See* Ulead:
   PhotoExpress
PhotoImpact. *See* Ulead: PhotoImpact
Photoshop. *See* Adobe: Photoshop
Picture CD-ROM. *See* CD-ROM:
   Picture
Plain Text 101
POP3 26
Portable Document Format. *See*
   Attachments: PDF files
Post Office Protocol. *See* POP3
PowerPoint. *See* Microsoft: Power-
   Point
Preview pane 70
Proof reading 135

QUALCOMM 44

Recipient 30
Remote access 22
Removable storage 166
Reply to All. *See* Replying: Reply to All
Reply to Sender. *See* Replying: To
   sender
Replying
   Reply to All 109
   To a group 109
   To sender 108
Rich Text Format. *See* RTF
RTF 100, 113
Rules. *See* Email: Rules

Scanners 21, 121
   Flatbed 162
   Sheet feed 162
   Types 161–162
Security
   General 423
   FAQ sites 424
   Hoaxes 425
Sending and receiving 34, 89
   Basics 89–91

Q

R

S

Web-based email
  Accessing an account 203–204
  Creating an account 200–202
  Defined 195–197
  Filters 208
  Finding 197–206
  Forgotten password 203
  Forwarding services 209
  Functions 196
  HotMail 198
  Information misuse 205–206
    Policy statements 205
  Providers 199
  Registration 201
  Restrictions 197
  Terms and conditions 202
  Testing 203
Wideband code division multiple
    access. See WCDMA
Windows 151
WinPMail. See Pegasus
WinZip 362
Wireless Application Protocol. See
    WAP
Wireless Markup Language. See WML
WML 373
  Web sites 376
Word. See Microsoft: Word
World Wide Web 19

Writing offline, sending online 103–
    104

Yahoo 200

Zip
  Disc 166, 180
  Drive 167
Zoom 29

Y

Z

Use of 116
Uniform Resource Locator. *See* URL
Universal Serial Bus. *See* USB
UNIX 20, 35
URL 119
USB 167

vCard. *See* Formatting: vCard
Verisign 138
Video clips 21, 142
Viruses 24, 281. *See also* Attach-
        ments: Viruses
    Anti-virus products 430–434
    Articles 434–435
    Chain Letters 425–427
    Databases 427–429
    Denial of service 423, 436–438
    FAQ sites 424
    Filters 149
    Hoaxes 425–427
    Mac 424
    Mailing lists 436
    Newsgroups 436
    Organisations 430
    Resources 423

WAP 35, 371–402
    Background 372
    Browsing the Web 375
    Business sites 378–379
    Computing sites 380–382
    Developments 376–377
    Devices
        Cost 374–375
        Memory 376
    Drawbacks 374–377
    Email sites 382
    Entertainment sites 385–386
    Explained 373–374
    Financial sites 383–384
    Games sites 386–387
    Introducing 371–372
    Network coverage 376
    News sites 387–388
    Predictions 371–372
    Resources 377
    Shopping sites 389–390
    Sport sites 390
    Travel sites 391–392
    UK miscellaneous sites 393
    Viewing WAP sites 381
    WAP search directories sites 399
WCDMA 36
Web pages
    Creating 100

W

V

- Scambusters – *www.scambusters.com/*. Information on the types of cons and frauds that happen on the Web.
- Unsolicited E-mail Cases – *www.jmls.edu/cyber/case/spam.html*. A collection of court cases dealing with unsolicited email.
- The Email Abuse FAQ – *http://members.aol.com/emailfaq/emailfaq.html*
- How to Get Rid of Junk Mail, Spam, and Telemarketers – *www.csn.net/~felbel/jnkmail.html*
- The Netizen's Guide to Spam, Abuse, and Internet – *http://com.primenet/spamking/*
- Netizens Against Gratuitous Spamming – *http://axxis.com/~ian/nags*
- Stop Unsolicited Mass E-Mail Advertisements – *www.coyotecom.com/stopjunk.html*
- Information covering a wide range of disreputable email practices – *www.emailabuse.org/*

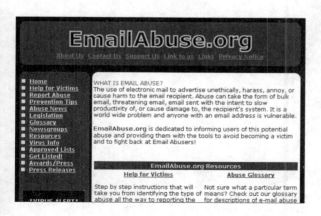

- The Forum for Responsible and Ethical E-mail – *www.spamfree.org/*
- Server software to help combat spam – *www.mailessentials.com/*

Newsgroups:

Some of the spam related newsgroups are:

- news.admin.net-abuse.policy
- news.admin.net-abuse.sightings
- news.admin.net-abuse.usenet
- news.admin.net-abuse.email
- news.admin.net-abuse.bulletins
- news.admin.net-abuse.misc

Security and Viruses

Security

Despite the advantages associated with email in terms of speed of delivery and cost, there are also some drawbacks, the most serious of which is the ease with which email can be used to disrupt computers and computer networks and destroy data. This is usually done in two ways:

- Through the use of viruses, which can be attached to emails and then activated when the user opens the attachment.
- Denial of service (DoS) attacks, which are attempts to block users from using specific computer networks.

Computer virus resources

Given the havoc that computer viruses can cause it is not surprising that there is a wealth of information about them on the Web and how to combat them. A lot of this is concerned with viruses that can be contained within emails. It is also worth visiting some of these sites for general information about viruses and the damage they can cause.

A lot of ISPs have information about viruses on their home pages. Look for any links to technical information or Frequently Asked Questions.

Frequently Asked Questions (FAQs) sites about computer viruses

Computer Virus FAQ for New Users

www.faqs.org/faqs/computer-virus/new-users/
Virus-L/comp.virus FAQ v2.00
www.faqs.org/faqs/computer-virus/faq/

Viruses and the Mac FAQ

www.faqs.org/faqs/computer-virus/macintosh-faq/
alt.comp.virus Mini-FAQ
www.faqs.org/faqs/computer-virus/mini-faq/
alt.comp.virus FAQ Part 1/4
www.faqs.org/faqs/computer-virus/alt-faq/part1/
alt.comp.virus FAQ Part 2/4
www.faqs.org/faqs/computer-virus/alt-faq/part2/
alt.comp.virus FAQ Part 3/4
www.faqs.org/faqs/computer-virus/alt-faq/part3/
alt.comp.virus FAQ Part 4/4
www.faqs.org/faqs/computer-virus/alt-faq/part4/

Although Macs are not generally as susceptible to viruses as PCs, partly because hackers write more PC-based virus programs, they can still be attacked. They are equally at risk from a lot of viruses carried by email.

Hoax and chain letters

Charles Hymes' New Hoaxes

www.nonprofit.net/hoax/newhoax.html

CIAC (Computer Incident Advisory Capability)

http://ciac.llnl.gov/ciac/CIACHoaxes.html

Internet chain letters: how to recognize a new chain letter, what to do

http://ciac.llnl.gov/ciac/CIACChainLetters.html

Command Software–Virus Hoaxes

www.commandcom.com/virus/virus_hoaxes.html

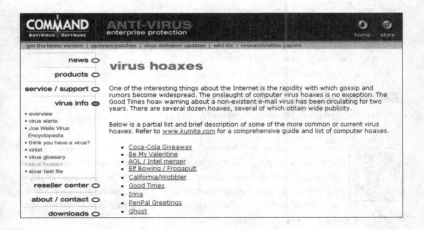

Computer Virus Myths home page

Rob Rosenberger's links to computer virus myths, hoaxes, urban legends.
www.kumite.com/myths/

Data Fellows–Hoax warnings

www.datafellows.com/virus-info/hoax/
www.europe.datafellows.com/virus-info/hoax/

IBM antivirus online–hype alerts!

www.av.ibm.com/BreakingNews/HypeAlert/

A hoax virus email is one that claims that there is a new virus in circulation and advises you to forward the email to all of your contacts in your address book. It may quote various high-profile companies who are aware of the virus, but in reality you would not get this type of warning about a real virus.

ICSA–Hoax Information
www.icsa.net/html/communities/antivirus/hoaxes/

iRiS Software's Virus Lab–Virus Hoaxes
www.irisav.com/lab/hoax.htm

McAfee–Virus Information Library–Virus Hoaxes
http://vil.mcafee.com/hoax.asp

Network Associates–Virus Library–Hoaxes
www.nai.com/asp_set/anti_virus/library/hoaxes.asp

Sophos Virus info–hoaxes and scares
www.sophos.com/virusinfo/scares/

Symantec AntiVirus Research Center (SARC)–Virus Hoaxes
www.symantec.com/avcenter/hoax.html

Virus Databases
These are databases that contain information about specific viruses.

Central Command–AntiViral Toolkit Pro Virus Encyclopedia
www.avpve.com/

CIAC Virus Database
www.ciac.org/ciac/CIACVirusDatabase.html

Command Software–Virus Alerts
www.commandcom.com/virus/virus_alerts.html

The Joe Wells Virus Encyclopedia

www.commandcom.com/virus/joe_wells.html

Computer Associates–Virus Encyclopedia

www.cai.com/virusinfo/encyclopedia/

Data Fellows F–Secure Virus Info Center

www.datafellows.com/vir-info/

Dr. Solomon's Virus Central

www.drsolomon.com/vircen/index.cfm

IBM antivirus online–virus information

www.av.ibm.com/InsideTheLab/VirusInfo/

McAfee–Virus Information Library

http://vil.mcafee.com/

Proland Software–Virus Information
   www.pspl.com/virus_info/

Trojan Horses
   www.pspl.com/trojan_info/

Sophos Virus Information
   www.sophos.com/virusinfo/

Symantec AntiVirus Research Center
   www.symantec.com/avcenter/index.html

Trend Micro–Virus Encyclopedia
   www.antivirus.com/vinfo/virusencyclo/default.asp

Virus Bulletin–The Project VGrep Home Page
   www.virusbtn.com/VGrep/

IBM antivirus online
   www.av.ibm.com/

Virus Bulletin list of anti-virus web sites
   www.virusbtn.com/AVLinks/sites.html

The Original J and A Computer Virus Information Page
   www.bocklabs.wisc.edu/~janda/

Virus organisations

EICAR (European Institute for Computer Anti-Virus Research)

www.eicar.com/

ICSA (International Computer Security Association)

www.icsa.net
www.icsa.net/html/communities/antivirus/

Virus Bulletin

www.virusbtn.com/

The WildList Organization International

www.wildlist.org/

Anti-Virus Products

Anti-virus companies offer products for protecting computer systems from attacks from viruses. New viruses appear all the time so it is important to keep anti-virus software up-to-date. The following companies have their own Web sites and also sites where updates and patches can be obtained. In addition, a lot of them have mailing lists to which you can subscribe to obtain the latest virus information.

Aladdin Knowledge Systems

www.esafe.com/
Virus definition file: *www.esafe.com/download/virusig.html*
Product patches: *www.esafe.com/update.html*
Support: *www.esafe.com/support.html*

Central Command, Inc.

www.avp.com/
Product updates: *www.avp.com/new_updates.html*
Support: *http://avp.custhelp.com/*
Mailing lists: *www.avp.com/*

Command Software Systems, Inc.

www.commandcom.com
Virus definition file: *www.commandcom.com/downloads/virus_definition_updates.html*
Product patches: *www.commandcom.com/downloads/components.html*
Support: *www.commandcom.com/service/index.html*

No anti-virus software is foolproof and it should be updated regularly by visiting some of the sites listed here to find the latest additions to the programs.

Computer Associates International, Inc.

http://www.cai.com
Virus definition file: *http://support.cai.com/Download/virussig.html*
Product patches: *http://support.cai.com/Download/patches/techptch.html*
Support: *http://support.cai.com/*

Data Fellows Corporation

www.datafellows.com
www.europe.datafellows.com

Virus definition database: *www.datafellows.com/support/av-workstation/ generic/updating.html*

Product patches: *www.datafellows.com/support/av-workstation/generic/ updating.html*

Support: *www.datafellows.com/support/*

Mailing lists: *www.datafellows.com/virus-info/index.html*

Dr. Solomon's Software Inc.

www.drsolomon.com

Product updates: *www.nai.com/asp_set/download/dats/find.asp*

Support: *www.drsolomon.com/support/index.cfm*

iRiS Software Ltd.

www.irisav.com

Product update: *www.irisav.com/shop/upgrade.htm*

Support: *www.irisav.com/supp/index.htm*

McAfee

www.mcafee.com
Virus definition file: *http://download.mcafee.com/updates/updates.asp*
Product upgrades: *http://download.mcafee.com/upgrades/upgrades.asp*
Support: *http://support.mcafee.com/*

Network Associates, Inc.

www.nai.com
Virus definition file: *www.nai.com/asp_set/download/dats/find.asp*
Product patches: *www.nai.com/asp_set/download/upgrade/login.asp*
Support: *www.nai.com/asp_set/services/technical_support/tech_intro.asp*

Norman Data Defense Systems

www.norman.com
Virus definition file: *www.norman.com/local/support/deffiles.htm*
Product patches: *www.norman.com/local/support/index.htm*
Support: *www.norman.com/local/services.htm*

Proland Software

www.pspl.com
Virus definition file: *www.pspl.com/download/download.htm*
Product patches: *www.pspl.com/download/download.htm*
Mailing lists: *www.pspl.com*

Sophos

www.sophos.com
Virus definition file: *www.sophos.com/downloads/ide/*
Product patches: *www.sophos.com/downloads/full/*
Support: *www.sophos.com/support/*

Symantec Corporation

www.symantec.com
Virus definition file: *www.sarc.com/avcenter/download.html*
Product patches: *www.symantec.com/nav/index_updates.html*
Support: *www.symantec.com/techsupp/*
Mailing lists: *www.symantec.com/avcenter/newsletter.html*

Trend Micro, Inc.

www.trendmicro.com
Virus definition file: *www.antivirus.com/download/pattern.htm*
Product update: *www.antivirus.com/download/engines/default.asp*
Support: *www.antivirus.com/support/index.htm*
Mailing lists: *www.antivirus.com/support/subscribe.htm*

Online articles

There are numerous online articles on computer viruses, chain letters and hoaxes. A lot of these are not only very informative but entertaining as well.

Flash in the Pan?

This paper is a technical discussion of the CIH virus.
www.virusbtn.com/VirusInformation/cih.html

The NORMAN Book on Viruses

By Norman Data Defense Systems
www.norman.com/local/virusbook.htm

Various Papers at Command Software Systems

www.commandcom.com/virus/research_and_writings.html

Various Papers at Dr. Solomon's

www.drsolomon.com/vircen/vanalyse/index.cfm

Various Papers at SOPHOS

www.sophos.com/virusinfo/articles/

Various Papers at Symantec Antivirus Research Center (SARC)

www.symantec.com/avcenter/refa.html

Don't Spread that Hoax!

By Charles Hymes
www.nonprofit.net/hoax/

How to Hoax-Proof Yourself

By Walt Howe and Delphi Internet Services Corp.
www.delphi.com/navnet/legends/legends.html

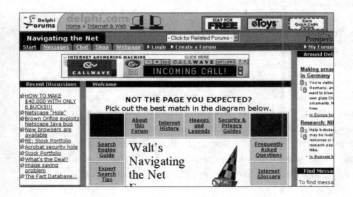

Newsgroup sites for viruses

comp.virus
alt.comp.virus

Mailing lists

VIRUS—L is a moderated mailing list with a focus on computer virus issues. To be added to the mailing list, send mail to listserv@lehigh.edu

Denial of service

A denial of service attack is a deliberate and malicious attempt to close down a computer network. This can be done in a number of ways:

- Sending such high volumes of email to one location that the company's server cannot cope and closes down, thus denying legitimate users access to this location.
- Corrupting the link between two or more computers in a network. This usually requires some programming and networking knowledge.
- Physical attempts to disable computer equipment.

While denial of service attacks do occur as a result of the second and third factors, the most common reason for a network to be closed down is because of the huge volume of email being sent to a specific server. There have been some high profile instances of this, including such Internet giants as Yahoo and eBay, who have both suffered as a result of this 'mail-bombing' technique. Since reliable Web and email links are crucial for companies who operate online, it can be very expensive if they suffer a denial of service attack and have to close down their servers for any length of time.

Unfortunately, the amount of disruption that can be caused by a denial of service attack is not proportional to the amount of effort that has to be put into one. Anyone with a medium specification PC and a modem could, in theory,

instigate a denial of service. If you know where to look, and have the inclination, there are sites on the Web that offer software that can be used to create a denial of service attack by sending frequent and bulk email messages to one specific server. However, this is an illegal activity and there are very severe penalties for anyone caught perpetrating a denial of service attack. Even hackers who have tried to cover their tracks very carefully have been apprehended in the past and it is considered one of the most serious abuses of email that there is.

If you run a business that is dependant on its Web site and email link there are some steps that can be taken to try and prevent a denial of service attack. (Unless you are a large corporation it is unlikely that you will be deemed high profile enough to have a denial of service attack launched at you, though. The people who undertake this type of activity seem to get a perverse pleasure from attacking the most high profile companies on the Web, thus gaining maximum publicity. However, it only takes one disgruntled employee, with the know-how to launch a denial of service attack, for serious damage to be done.) Before putting any preventative measure in place against a denial of service attack you should consult an IT security expert or consultant to make sure you are doing what is best for your business. Some measures that can be taken are:

- Use software that is designed to lessen the threat of denial of service attacks. This comes in a variety of formats, depending on your own needs, but it all serves the same purpose: to try and prevent your server being flooded with email messages. This will not necessarily cut out the risk altogether, but it will certainly make it harder for anyone who is attempting a denial of service attack.

- Make sure you are only using the parts of your network that are needed. If you have areas that are lying idle, disable them. If there are less active areas of a network this will decrease the opportunities of anyone trying

to enter it illegally. It is a bit like reducing the size of the target for someone shooting at it.

- Keep a record of what your average network usage is, in terms of email traffic and disc activity. This can be used to compare against any rogue usage figures, which could indicate some form of illegal activity such as an attempted denial of service attack.

- Be aware of the physical security of your network. If people can physically gain unauthorised access to any of the items within your network, they may be able to tamper with equipment so that it makes it easier for a denial of service attack to be perpetrated.

- Have a robust back-up procedure. This should include backing up the settings for the configuration of the network and also spare machines, such as servers, that can be used as a substitute if the one in use is disabled as a result of an attack or a malfunction. A computer network is only as secure as its weakest link, so make sure you cover all eventualities.

- Set passwords for access to the network and make sure that they are used where required and that the users are aware of the security risks inherent in giving out passwords to third parties. It is good practice to change passwords regularly in order to lessen the threat of unauthorised access. However, if someone is determined enough they will probably be able to enter a network illegally sooner or later, even if a robust system of passwords is in place.

Mailing Lists and Newsgroups

Options

Everyone who is online likes to get email messages; there is nothing worse than looking at an empty mailbox for days, or weeks, on end. Thankfully you do not have to just rely on your friends and family to send you messages as there are two ways of guaranteeing that you receive enough emails to satisfy even the most voracious online appetite. These are:

- Mailing lists
- Newsgroups

Mailing lists

Mailing lists are set up by special interest groups (these interests can be, and are, virtually anything) and they then send out email messages and updates to everyone who has subscribed to the list. Members can also send their own messages, which are then forwarded on to everyone else on the list. Some mailing lists are moderated, which means the content of messages is checked before they are sent out to all of the members of the list, while on others it is a free-for-all with no form of regulation. In addition, some lists send out messages as soon as they are received from the users. Others offer a digest service, whereby messages are collected and sent out at specific intervals, usually once a day. Messages can be sent to and from mailing lists with standard email programs.

Finding mailing lists

There are literally tens of thousands of mailing lists on the Internet, usually connected to a specific Web site. This could be a fan club for a pop band or a form of online journal for the scientific. Whatever your interests there will almost certainly be a selection of mailing lists to support them.

The easiest way to find a mailing list relating to your favourite subject is to go to your regular search engine on the Web and type in 'mailing lists'. You will then be faced with various topic headings which you can drill through until you find something that interests you. Click on the link to go to the site that is offering the mailing list.

When searching for a mailing list, add a + sign before the topic you are looking for i.e. 'mailing list +cookery' in order to make your search more specific.

Subscribing to a mailing list

Before you can receive messages from a mailing list, you have to subscribe to it. This involves sending an email message to the list's administrative address, or filling in a simple online form. The administrative address is one of two addresses connected with mailing lists and it is used for tasks such as subscribing and unsubscribing to a list. The other address is the mailing one, which is used to send messages to the list's members. It is important that you do not get the two addresses muddled up, or else you will end up sending your subscription request to everyone else on the list. This does not do any real harm, but it could make you look a bit foolish.

Although the idea of administrative and mailing addresses can sound a bit complicated, most mailing lists make things fairly straightforward by offering links directly to their administrative address when you want to subscribe. This involves sending an email to the relevant address, with the word 'Subscribe' as the subject of the message. To remove yourself from the mailing list, send a message to the same email address, with the word 'Unsubscribe' as the subject. (Since mailing lists are run by a variety of online companies, subscribing to them is not an exact science. Almost all of them use the word subscribe, but some of them use additional words too.)

When you receive your first message from the mailing list, this will contain the mailing address, and this can be used if you want to send your own messages to the list. Make sure that you save the instructions on the Web site where you first located the mailing list, as you may want to refer back to these at some point. One way to do this is to bookmark the site or add it to your list of favourites.

Quality of lists

The quality of information and postings on mailing lists varies enormously. Some of them are very factual and straight-laced, while others are more anarchic. The best way to sort through the good, the bad and the downright appalling is to subscribe to a number of lists and see if the quality of information is what you are looking for. If you feel that there is nothing that really suits your taste, you could create your own list. This can be done for free through the following Web sites:

- Coolist at *www.coolist.com/*
- Topica at *www.topica.com/*
- OneList at *www.onelist.com/*

Newsgroups

In many ways, newsgroups, also known as Usenet groups, adhere the most closely to the early days of the Internet. They are like online communal notice-boards, where people with a shared interest discuss the burning issues of the day via email messages that are posted to the group. This clings to the slightly anarchic community spirit that prevailed on the Internet before the commercial giants began to realise the worth of this new creature. There are over 60,000 newsgroups, covering every subject known to mankind – if you want to discuss the mating habits of the African fruit bat, there is probably a newsgroup that will accommodate you. It is free to subscribe to a newsgroup and you can then read messages that other people have posted and also add your own comments. This can be done as part of an existing conversation that is taking place (known as a thread), directly to one of the participants of the newsgroups who has posted a message, or as an entirely new message.

People who read messages in newsgroups but do not participate themselves are known as 'lurkers', although this is not necessarily a derogatory term.

Newsreaders

The first thing you need to participate in a newsgroup is a newsreader. This is a program that locates and manages the newsgroups so that you can view them and post messages to them. Different newsreaders access different sets of newsgroups, but whichever one you use you should still have access to tens of thousands of groups. If you are using Outlook Express and Internet Explorer 4 or later, or Messenger and Netscape Communicator 4 or later, then you will

not have to worry about a separate newsreader as both of these email programs contain powerful and efficient readers. If you are using an email program that does not come packaged with a newsreader, or you do not like the one you currently have, you could look at the ones on the following Web sites:

- Forte at *www.forteinc.com* (PC)
- MT NewsWatcher at *www.best.com/~smfr/mtnw/* (Mac)

Configuring a newsreader

Before you start accessing newsgroups you may have to configure your newsreader. In most cases this will have been done automatically when you registered with your Internet Service Provider (ISP), but it is always useful to know where these details are stored. Also, there are some preference settings that you may want to change, to determine functions such as how many messages are downloaded at a time. Most newsreaders have different configurations, so it may be necessary to contact your ISP if you are unsure of any settings. The configurations for the newsreaders with Outlook Express and Messenger can be set as follows:

Outlook Express

1. Select Tools>Accounts from the main menu bar.
2. In the Internet Accounts dialog box, select the News tab.
3. Select the Add>News to create a new newsgroup list. A connection wizard will appear, into which you can enter details about your newsgroup account.
4. Enter your name as you want it to appear when you communicate with newsgroups. This can be your actual name, a nickname or an alias, depending on how much recognition you want. Select Next.
5. Enter an email address which people can reply directly to. Do not include your regular email address. Select Next.
6. Enter the name of your news server. This will probably consist of part of your ISP's own email address, prefixed by 'news' e.g. *news.btclick.co.uk.* (If you are unsure about your news server address, contact your ISP). Select Next.
7. Select Finish to complete the configuration of your news server.

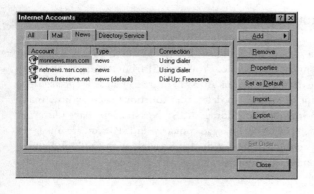

Since some newsgroups may have thousands of messages to deliver at any one time, it is a good idea to limit the number of headers that are downloaded at a time.

In Outlook Express, this can be done as follows:

1. Select Tools>Options from the main menu bar.
2. In the Options dialog box, select the Read tab.
3. Under News, enter a number for Get headers e.g. Get 100 headers at a time.

Headers are the subject lines of newsgroup postings and they appear in the newsreader along with the sender's name. Double click on a header to read the message.

Messenger

1. Select Edit>Preferences from the main menu bar.
2. Under the Preferences Category, select Mail and Newsgroups>Newsgroup Servers.
3. Select Add, to add a new newsreader.
4. In the Newsgroup Server Properties dialog box, enter the address of your news server. Select OK.
5. In the Newsgroup Servers dialog box, enter a number in the Ask me before downloading more than xx messages, box. This will save you from being inundated with thousands of messages at once.

Accessing newsgroups

Once you have configured your newsreader, it should appear at the bottom of your folder list in your email program, together with an icon that varies from those next to any of your mail folders. (These icons also vary between programs.) The next step is to download all of the available newsgroups for that particular newsreader. This is known as building a group list and it can be done in Outlook Express and Messenger as follows:

Outlook Express

1. Double click on the newsgroup server icon in your list of folders.
2. If this is the first time you have accessed any newsgroup, a message will appear asking if you want to view a list of the available newsgroups. (These will be the newsgroups that are available through your newsreader. Although there will be several thousands of these, they will not be all of the newsgroups in existence.) Select Yes.
3. The newsgroups will then be downloaded from your news server. This may take a few minutes to complete, because of the sheer number of newsgroups involved. However, they only need to be downloaded once.
4. Once the newsgroups have been downloaded, the Newsgroup Subscription box appears. To find newsgroups on specific subjects, enter a topic in the Display newsgroups which contain box. A list of relevant newsgroups will then appear.
5. To subscribe to a newsgroup i.e. join it so that you can read and post messages, select the name of the relevant group and select subscribe. This is completely free and does not include any fee. It just means that you have access to that particular newsgroup.
6. Select the Go To button

7. The selected newsgroup will appear as a subfolder from your main newsgroup folder. Double click on the new newsgroup icon to view the latest messages in the group.

Messenger

1. Select the newsgroup server icon in your list of folders by clicking on it once.
2. Select File > Subscribe from the main menu bar, or right click and select Subscribe to Newsgroups, from the contextual menu.

A contextual menu is one with options specific to the item that has been selected. These are accessed by right clicking on the item, or Ctrl click on a Mac.

3. The newsgroups will be downloaded from your news server. This could take a few minutes.
4. To look for newsgroups on specific subjects, select the Search tab in the Subscribe to Newsgroups dialog box and enter a topic in the Search for box and select the Search Now button. Alternatively, you can look through the list of all the available newsgroups by clicking the All tab.
5. When you have located a newsgroup in which you are interested, select it by clicking on it once and select the Subscribe button. Select OK. This will then appear as a subfolder from your main newsgroup folder. Double click on the new newsgroup icon to view the latest messages in the group.

Removing yourself from a newsgroup

If you decide that you do not want to continue to participate in a certain newsgroup you can unsubscribe from it, so you are not sent any more messages from it. This is a straightforward process and you can subscribe and unsubscribe from the same newsgroup countless numbers of times. To do this:

It is also possible to unsubscribe from a newsgroup by selecting it in the Newsgroup Subscription dialog box and selecting the Unsubscribe button.

Outlook Express

1. In the folder list, right click on the newsgroup from which you want to unsubscribe.
2. Select Unsubscribe from the contextual menu.
3. A warning dialog box will appear asking if you are sure you want to unsubscribe from the selected newsgroup. Select OK.

Messenger

1. In the folder list, right click on the newsgroup from which you want to unsubscribe.
2. Select Remove Newsgroup from the contextual menu.
3. A warning dialog box will appear asking if you are sure you want to remove this newsgroup. Select OK.

Participating in newsgroups

It is perfectly possible and allowable to subscribe to hundreds of newsgroups and never post a single message to them, just read the ones that other people send. In fact, when you first start using newsgroups it is best to look rather than

Novice newsgroups users are known as newbies. There are even newsgroups dedicated to this group, where you can put test postings without fear of being flamed.

participate, just so you can pick up on the tone and the level of certain newsgroups. Some newsgroup users can get very protective about their groups and do not take kindly to people misusing them (See 'Flame wars', later). Resist the temptation to plunge straight in there: look around and see what other people are doing. In a lot of cases you will soon see that some newsgroups are full of little more than unsolicited junk mail (spam) and people with chips firmly on both shoulders. Since most newsgroups are unmoderated i.e. no one checks what is put on them, the quality of the content of many of them is questionable to say the least.

Most newsgroups have a list of Frequently Asked Questions (FAQs) which is a good way to find out about the group and the type of standards which are expected.

Once you have decided you want to participate in a newsgroup, you post a message in a similar way to sending a regular email message:

1. In the folder list, select the newsgroup to which you want to post a message.
2. In Outlook Express, select the New Post button on the toolbar. This will open up a new email message box, with the address pre-inserted as going to the selected newsgroup. In Messenger, the same process is achieved by selecting the New Message button on the toolbar.
3. Write your message and send it in the same way as a normal email.
4. Check on the newsgroup to see that it has been posted.

Newsgroup messages

When you look at the messages in a newsgroup, you will see a variety of different symbols next to them. This denotes various types of messages. The most common symbol to see is a plus sign. This indicates that there are more messages attached to the one that is on view. If you click on the plus sign, the rest of the messages that are related to this will be displayed. This is known as a threaded message and is the way in which numerous people can have a conversation about a specific topic without each individual message appearing as a new header in the newsgroup folder.

There are several ways in which you can post messages to a newsgroup:

- Start a new thread, which is the first message of a brand new topic. (Remember to put a clear entry in the subject line of the message so that

Be careful when you are replying directly to an individual in a newsgroup. You have no idea who they are, although a number of friendships have started this way.

other people can quickly see what the posting is about. This is the same as creating a new email message.)

- Reply to an entry in an existing thread. This is done by opening the message to which you want to reply and selecting Reply to Group from the toolbar in Outlook Express and Reply > to Newsgroup in Messenger.

- Reply directly to the personal email address of the person who posted the message. This can be useful if you want to have a one-to-one conversation, without involving the rest of the newsgroup. This can be done by selecting Reply from the toolbar in Outlook Express and Reply > to Sender Only in Messenger. (There is also an option in Messenger for replying to the newsgroup and the sender together: select Reply All.)

Flame wars

If you spend much time looking around a range of newsgroups you will soon discover that it is an eclectic mixture of the good, the bad and the downright rubbish. However, within the approximately 60,000 newsgroups there will be plenty that take your interest and which you will probably want to participate in at some point. This is where newsgroup Netiquette comes into play. This a convoluted way of saying, use good manners on the Internet when posting messages. In many ways, newsgroups have clung the most closely to the original concept of the Internet: an online community that is linked to share information and ideas. Because of this, a lot of newsgroup contributors get very irate if they think people are misusing their group. This could be for a variety of reasons:

- Spam. The scourge of the Internet. This is bulk unsolicited junk email that is becoming part and parcel of life on the Internet. It infiltrates not only personal mail boxes but also newsgroups, with mass emailings of

items that have no relevance to the subject of the group. There is nothing more guaranteed to annoy the dedicated members of a newsgroup than a pile of spam appearing.

- Inexperienced users posting to the wrong site. If someone is new to the world of newsgroups they may be unsure about some of the unspoken conventions of newsgroups. If they then post an inappropriate question (e.g. asking about Honda guitars on a site for Honda motorbikes) they will probably be met with derision by some of the members in the group. In reality this is just a form of cyber-snobbery but it certainly happens.

- Simple disagreement. If there are a lot of people expressing their opinions in a newsgroup, it is human nature that some of them are going to disagree with each other. In some cases this can be dealt with by a simple online correspondence, but sometimes it can spiral out of control.

If a member of a newsgroup takes exception to something that was posted in the newsgroup they sometimes express their feelings in very forceful, and very personal, terms. This in turn can generate more negative responses and before you know it, you have a cyber squabble, or flame war, on your hands. This involves two or more members of a newsgroup conducting an online slanging match, with no holds barred. Although these can sometimes be entertaining to watch unfold (there are some newsgroups specifically dedicated

Sometimes a polite enquiry about being redirected to a more relevant site will bring better results than trying to post inappropriate questions in a specific group.

to flame wars) they are generally hugely counterproductive and should be avoided if at all possible.

Some guidelines for trying to avoid being 'flamed' or drawn into a flame war are:

- Take the time to find out the correct subject matter of a newsgroup and the style and tone of the users who post messages. Note if they use any email shortcuts (e.g. emoticons or abbreviations) and try and follow suit if possible.

- If it is a specialist group, try not to ask too many simple questions, but rather find a group at your own level.

- Do not use a specialist group to send test messages when you first start using newsgroups.

- Never try and sell any unsolicited items in a newsgroup, unless it is specifically for this purpose. Newsgroup members do not like to think people are trying to take advantage of them.

- If you disagree with something in a newsgroup, try and be measured and constructive in your reply. But be careful: even constructive criticism is like a red rag to a bull to some people.

- Never use all capital letters when you post to a newsgroup. This is equated with shouting and is considered bad form in cyber circles.

Most newsgroup postings expire after a certain period of time and are removed. To view an archive of newsgroup messages visit Deja at 'www.deja.com' and click on the Discussions link on the home page.

- If you are flamed in a newsgroup i.e. someone posts something derogatory about you or something you have said, resist the temptation to immediately fire back a stinging response. This is how flame wars start. Take some time to reflect on the situation and leave at least an hour before you send a reply.
- If possible, turn the other cheek and do not get involved in flame wars. They are not worth the bother and nothing constructive comes out of them. Best to leave them to the people who have too much time on their hands.

Finding newsgroups

With so many newsgroups to choose from it is perhaps surprising that anyone ever finds what they are looking for. The search facilities in newsreaders are a good starting point as they can narrow down the groups in relation to a word or phrase.

There are also several sites on the Web which offer directories of newsgroups:

- *www.liszt.com/news/*
- *www.cyberfiber.com/index.html*
- *http://uk.dir.yahoo.com/Computers_and_Internet/Internet/Chats_and_Forums/Usenet/Newsgroup_Directories/*

Types of newsgroups can also be identified by the prefix at the beginning of their address. These either identify a newsgroup according to its subject matter or by its geographical location. Some of the newsgroup prefixes that are used are:

- alt – alternative Groups. The creation of these groups is not moderated.
- bionet – biology.
- biz – commercially oriented (business).
- comp – computing. Many groups, on all aspects.
- eunet – European Usenet newsgroups.
- misc – miscellaneous newsgroups (small ads. etc.).
- news – about the news system itself.
- pubnet – public access systems.
- rec – recreation.
- sci – science.
- soc – society.
- talk – gossip and discussion about current affairs.

Most messages in the 'biz.' newsgroups revolve around email marketing schemes and scams.

Newsgroups directory

The following is a selection of some of the newsgroups that are, or have been, active on the Internet. Not all newsreaders will be able to access all of these groups but it shows the diverse range that is on offer:

Alternative groups

alt.3d
> Discussions of 3 dimensional imaging.

alt.activism
> Activities for activists.

alt.alien.visitors
> Space creatures ate my modem.

alt.amateur-comp
> Of interest to the Amateur Computerist.

alt.angst
> Anxiety in the modern world.

alt.aquaria
> The aquarium and related matters as a hobby.

alt.archery
> Discussion of archery.

alt.architecture
> Building design/construction and related topics.

alt.artcom
> Artistic community.

alt.astrology
> Discussion about all aspects of astrology.

alt.atheism
> Discussions of atheism.

alt.atheism.moderated
Atheism and related topics. (Moderated)

alt.autos.antique
Discussion of all facets of older automobiles.

alt.bacchus
A newsgroup for the non-profit 'BACCHUS' organization.

alt.bbs
Computer BBS systems and software.

alt.beer
Good beer guide.

alt.binaries.multimedia
Sound, text and graphics data rolled in one.

alt.binaries.sounds.d
Sounding off.

alt.binaries.sounds.misc
Digitised audio adventures.

alt.bonsai
Bonsai gardening.

alt.boomerang
Technology and use of the boomerang.

alt.cable-tv.re-regulate
Re-regulation of the cable television industry.

alt.cad
Computer Aided Design.

alt.cad.autocad
CAD as practiced by customers of Autodesk.

alt.california
The State and the state of mind.

alt.cd-rom

Discussions of optical storage media.

alt.censorship

Discussion about restricting speech/press.

alt.child-support

Raising children in a split family.

alt.chinese.text

General postings of Chinese in a standard form.

alt.co-ops

Discussion about co-operatives.

alt.cobol

Use of the programming language COBOL.

If you are interested in any form of computer programming, then newsgroups are an excellent place to further your knowledge and discuss problems.

alt.comedy.british

Discussion of British comedy in a variety of media.

alt.comp.acad-freedom.news

Academic freedom issues related to computers. (Moderated)

alt.consciousness

Discussions of all aspects of the essence of human consciousness.

alt.conspiracy

Be paranoid – they're out to get you.

alt.conspiracy.jfk

Discussion of the JFK assassination.

alt.cult-movies

Movies with a cult following.

alt.culture.us.asian-indian

Asian Indians in the US and Canada.

alt.culture.usenet

The USENET community.

alt.dcom.catv

Discussion of Cable TV technology.

alt.dcom.telecom

Discussion of telecommunications technology.

alt.dreams

What do they mean?

alt.drumcorps

Drum and bugle corps discussion (and related topics).

alt.education.disabled

Learning experiences for the disabled.

alt.education.distance

Learning over nets etc.

alt.emusic

Ethnic, exotic, electronic, elaborate etc. music.

alt.fan.disney.afternoon

Any and all cartoons in the Disney Afternoon.

alt.fan.douglas-adams

Author of "The Meaning of Liff", and other fine works.

alt.fan.frank-zappa

Fans of Frank Zappa and Zappa related bands.

alt.fan.holmes

Elementary, my dear Watson.

alt.fan.howard-stern
Fans of the radio and TV personality.
alt.fan.letterman
Fans of David Letterman.
alt.fan.madonna
Fans of Madonna

Most major celebrities, and a lot of minor ones too, have newsgroups dedicated to their activities.

alt.fan.monty-python
Electronic fan club for those wacky Brits.
alt.fan.pratchett
Discussions about Terry Pratchett's works.
alt.fan.q
Fans of Q from Star Trek: The Next Generation.
alt.fan.shostakovich
Classical music composer.
alt.fan.tom-robbins
Fans of author Tom Robbins.
alt.fandom.misc
Topics for fans of various kinds.
alt.fashion
Discussions about the world of fashion.
alt.feminism
Unmoderated discussion of feminist issues.

alt.fishing

Fishing as a hobby and sport.

alt.folklore.computers

Stories and anecdotes about computers (some true!).

alt.folklore.ghost-stories

Ghost story folklore, personal experiences, etc.

alt.folklore.science

The lore and folklore of science.

alt.folklore.urban

Urban legends.

alt.galactic-guide

Hitch Hiker's Guide to the Known Galaxy Project Group.

alt.games.mornington.cresent

Mornington Cresent.

alt.good.news

A place for some news that's good news.

alt.gopher

Discussions of gopher-news servers, clients, protocols.

alt.gourmand

Recipes and cooking info. (Moderated)

alt.graphics

Discussion of drawings.

alt.great-lakes

Discussions of the Great Lakes and adjacent places.

alt.guitar

Guitar enthusiasts.

alt.guitar.bass

Bass guitars.

alt.hypertext
Discussion of hypertext.

alt.individualism
Philosophies where individual rights are paramount.

alt.internet.access.wanted
Information about connecting to the Internet.

alt.internet.services
Information about services available on the Internet.

alt.irc
Internet Relay Chat material.

alt.lang.cfutures
Discussion of the future of the C programming language (not C++).

alt.magic
For discussion about stage magic.

alt.models
Model building, design, etc.

alt.motorcycles.harley
Harley Davidson motorcycles.

alt.msdos.programmer
For the serious MS/DOS programmer.

alt.music.alternative
Discussion of "alternative" music.

alt.music.enya
Discussion of Enya's music.

alt.music.progressive
Progressive rock, e.g., Genesis, RUSH, Yes, et cetera.

alt.mythology
The understanding of human nature through the discussion of mythology.

alt.net.personalities
About those who post a lot.

alt.paranormal
Phenomena which are not scientifically explicable.

alt.parents-teens
Discussions about raising teenagers.

alt.pcnews
Discussions about PCNews software.

alt.personals.ads
Personal ads only, no discussions.

alt.planning.urban
Urban and regional planning concepts.

alt.politics.british
Discussions about the British political world.

alt.politics.clinton
Discussions about Bill Clinton.

alt.politics.correct
For discussing the issue of political correctness.

alt.politics.ec
European Community politics.

alt.politics.reform
Political reform.

alt.privacy
Privacy issues in cyberspace.

alt.prose
Postings of original writings, fictional and otherwise.

alt.rap
For fans of rap music.

alt.rock-n-roll
  Traditional rock music.
alt.rock-n-roll.metal
  For the headbangers on the Net.
alt.romance
  Discussion about the romantic side of love.
alt.save.the.earth
  Environmentalist causes.
alt.sci.physics.new-theories
  Scientific theories you won't find in journals.
alt.sci.planetary
  Studies in planetary science.
alt.security
  Unmoderated security discussions.
alt.self-improve
  Self-improvement in less than 14 characters.
alt.sewing
  Working with needle and thread.
alt.skate
  Rollerskating and skateboarding.
alt.skate-board
  Skateboarding.
alt.society.civil-liberties
  Individual rights.
alt.society.futures
  Events in technology affecting future computing.
alt.sources.wanted
  Requests for source code.

alt.sport.bungee

For those who like to hang upside down from rubber bands.

alt.startrek.creative

Stories and parodies related to Star Trek.

alt.stupidity

Discussion about stupid newsgroups.

alt.supermodels

The discussion of famous and beautiful models.

alt.surfing

Riding the ocean waves.

alt.sustainable.agriculture

The study and practice of sustainable agriculture.

alt.tv.muppets

Fans of the Muppets, TV shows and movies.

alt.tv.prisoner

The Prisoner television series from years ago.

alt.tv.red-dwarf

For the British sci-fi comedy Red Dwarf.

alt.tv.simpsons

Bart, Homer and company.

alt.usage.english

English grammar, word usages and related subjects.

alt.uu.lang.esperanto.misc

Learning Esperanto.

alt.uu.virtual-worlds.misc

Learning about virtual worlds and virtual reality.

alt.war.civil.usa

The US Civil war of 1861-1865.

Recreation groups

rec.antiques
>Discussing antiques and vintage items.

rec.aquaria
>Keeping fish and aquaria as a hobby.

rec.arts.animation
>Discussion of various kinds of animation.

rec.arts.anime
>Discussion about all aspects of Japanese animation.

rec.arts.bodyart
>Tattoos and body decoration discussions.

rec.arts.books
>Books of all genres, and the publishing industry.

rec.arts.cinema
>Discussion of the art of cinema. (Moderated)

rec.arts.comics.info
>Reviews, convention information and other comics news. (Moderated)

rec.arts.comics.marketplace
>The exchange of comics and comic related items.

rec.arts.comics.misc
>Comic books, graphic novels, sequential art.

rec.arts.dance
>Any aspects of dance not covered in another newsgroup.

rec.arts.disney
>Discussion of any Disney-related subjects.

rec.arts.drwho
>Discussion about Dr. Who.

rec.arts.fine
Fine arts and artists.

rec.arts.movies
Discussions of movies and movie making.

rec.arts.movies.reviews
Reviews of movies. (Moderated)

rec.arts.poems
For the posting of poems.

rec.arts.sf.misc
Science fiction lovers' newsgroup.

rec.arts.theatre
Discussion of all aspects of stage work and theatre.

rec.arts.tv
The tube, its history and past and current shows.

rec.arts.tv.soaps
Postings about soap operas.

rec.arts.tv.uk
Discussions of telly shows from the UK.

rec.arts.wobegon
About the popular Lake Wobegon series.

rec.audio
High fidelity audio.

rec.audio.car
Discussions of automobile audio systems.

rec.audio.high-end
High-end audio systems. (Moderated)

rec.audio.pro
Professional audio recording and studio engineering.

rec.aviation

Aviation rules, means, and methods.

rec.aviation.homebuilt

Selecting, designing, building, and restoring aircraft.

rec.aviation.misc

Miscellaneous topics in aviation.

rec.aviation.simulators

Flight simulation on all levels.

rec.backcountry

Activities in the Great Outdoors.

rec.bicycles

Bicycles, related products and laws.

rec.bicycles.misc

General discussion of bicycling.

rec.bicycles.racing

Bicycle racing techniques, rules and results.

rec.birds

Hobbyists interested in bird watching.

rec.boats

Hobbyists interested in boating.

rec.boats.paddle

Talk about any boats with oars, paddles, etc.

rec.climbing

Climbing techniques, competition announcements, etc.

rec.collecting

Discussion among collectors of many things.

rec.crafts.brewing

The art of making beers and meads.

rec.crafts.misc
General handiwork.
rec.crafts.textiles
Sewing, weaving, knitting and other fibre arts.
rec.equestrian
Equestrian issues.
rec.folk-dancing
Folk dances, dancers, and dancing.
rec.food.cooking
Food, cooking, cookbooks, and recipes.
rec.food.drink
Wines and spirits.
rec.food.recipes
Recipes for interesting food and drink. (Moderated)
rec.food.veg
Vegetarians.
rec.gambling
Articles on games of chance and betting.
rec.games.misc
Games and computer games.
rec.games.video
Discussion about video games.
rec.gardens
Gardening, methods and results.
rec.heraldry
Discussion of coats of arms.
rec.humor.funny
Jokes that are funny, allegedly (Moderated).

rec.juggling

Juggling techniques, equipment and events.

rec.kites

Talk about kites and kiting.

rec.martial-arts

Discussion of the various martial art forms.

rec.models.rc

Radio-controlled models for hobbyists.

rec.motorcycles

Motorcycles and related products and laws.

rec.music.afro-latin

Music with Afro-Latin influences.

rec.music.beatles

Postings about the Fab Four and their music.

rec.music.bluenote

Discussion of jazz, blues, and related types of music.

rec.music.cd

CDs – availability and other discussions.

rec.music.classical

Discussion about classical music.

rec.music.compose

Creating musical and lyrical works.

rec.music.country.western

CandW music, performers, performances, etc.

rec.music.dylan

Discussion of Bob's works and music.

rec.music.folk

Folks discussing folk music of various sorts.

rec.music.funky

Funk, rap, hip-hop, house, soul, r&b and related.

rec.music.indian.classical

Hindustani and Carnatic Indian classical music.

rec.music.info

News and announcements on musical topics. (Moderated)

rec.music.makers

For performers and their discussions.

rec.music.marketplace

Records, tapes, and CDs: wanted, for sale, etc.

rec.music.video

Discussion of music videos and music video software.

rec.org.mensa

Talking with members of the high IQ society Mensa.

rec.outdoors.fishing

All aspects of sport and commercial fishing.

rec.pets

Pets, pet care, and household animals in general.

rec.photo

Hobbyists interested in photography.

rec.puzzles

Puzzles, problems, and quizzes.

rec.radio.amateur.misc

Amateur radio practices, contests, events, rules, etc.

rec.roller-coaster

Roller coasters and other amusement park rides.

rec.running

Running for enjoyment, sport, exercise, etc.

rec.scouting

Scouting youth organisations worldwide.

rec.scuba

Hobbyists interested in SCUBA diving.

rec.skate

Ice skating and roller skating.

rec.skiing

Hobbyists interested in snow skiing.

rec.skydiving

Hobbyists interested in skydiving.

rec.sport.cricket

Discussion about the sport of cricket.

rec.sport.golf

Discussion about all aspects of golfing.

rec.sport.hockey

Discussion about hockey.

rec.sport.olympics

All aspects of the Olympic Games.

rec.sport.rugby

Discussion about the game of rugby.

rec.sport.soccer

Discussion about soccer (Association Football).

rec.sport.swimming

Training for and competing in swimming events.

rec.sport.tennis

Things related to the sport of tennis.

rec.travel

Travelling all over the world.

rec.windsurfing

Riding the waves as a hobby.

rec.woodworking

Hobbyists interested in woodworking.

Society groups

soc.culture.african

Discussions about Africa and things African.

soc.culture.australian

Australian culture and society.

soc.culture.bangladesh

Issues and discussion about Bangladesh.

soc.culture.bosna-herzgvna

The independent state of Bosnia and Herzegovina.

soc.culture.brazil

Talking about the people and country of Brazil.

soc.culture.british

Issues about Britain and those of British descent.

soc.culture.canada

Discussions of Canada and its people.

soc.culture.caribbean

Life in the Caribbean.

soc.culture.celtic

Group about Celts

soc.culture.china

About China and Chinese culture.

soc.culture.czecho-slovak

Bohemian, Slovak, Moravian and Silesian life.

soc.culture.esperanto
   The neutral international language Esperanto.
soc.culture.europe
   Discussing all aspects of all-European society.
soc.culture.filipino
   Group about the Filipino culture.
soc.culture.french
   French culture, history, and related discussions.
soc.culture.german
   Discussions about German culture and history.
soc.culture.greek
   Group about Greeks.
soc.culture.hongkong
   Discussions pertaining to Hong Kong.
soc.culture.indian
   Group for discussion about India and things Indian.
soc.culture.indian.american
   Discussions of Asian Indian-American issues.
soc.culture.indian.telugu
   The culture of the Telugu people of India.
soc.culture.iranian
   Discussions about Iran and things Iranian/Persian.
soc.culture.italian
   The Italian people and their culture.
soc.culture.japan
   Everything Japanese, except the Japanese language.
soc.culture.jewish
   Jewish culture and religion. (cf. 'talk.politics.mideast')

soc.culture.korean

Discussions about Korean and things Korean.

soc.culture.latin-america

Topics about Latin-America.

soc.culture.lebanon

Discussion about things Lebanese.

soc.culture.magyar

The Hungarian people and their culture.

soc.culture.mexican

Discussion of Mexico's society.

soc.culture.misc

Group for discussion about other cultures.

soc.culture.nepal

Discussion about Nepal and Nepalese society.

soc.culture.netherlands

People from the Netherlands and Belgium.

soc.culture.new-zealand

Discussion of topics related to New Zealand.

soc.culture.nordic

Discussion about culture up north.

soc.culture.pakistan

Topics of discussion about Pakistan.

soc.culture.polish

Polish culture, Polish past, and Polish politics.

soc.culture.portuguese

Discussion of the people of Portugal.

soc.culture.romanian

Discussion of Romanian and Moldavian people.

soc.culture.soviet

Topics relating to Russian or Soviet culture.

soc.culture.spain

Discussion of culture on the Iberian peninsula.

soc.culture.sri-lanka

Things and people from Sri Lanka.

soc.culture.taiwan

Discussion about things Taiwanese.

soc.culture.tamil

Tamil language, history and culture.

soc.culture.thai

Thai people and their culture.

soc.culture.turkish

Discussion about things Turkish.

soc.culture.usa

The culture of the United States of America.

soc.culture.vietnamese

Issues and discussions of Vietnamese culture.

soc.culture.yugoslavia

Discussions of Yugoslavia and its people.

soc.feminism

Discussion of feminism and feminist issues. (Moderated)

soc.history

Discussions of things historical.

soc.men

Issues related to men, their problems and relationships.

soc.misc

Socially-oriented topics not in other groups.

soc.penpals

In search of net.friendships.

soc.politics

Political problems, systems, solutions. (Moderated)

soc.rights.human

Human rights and activism (e.g., Amnesty International).

soc.roots

Genealogical matters.

soc.singles

Newsgroup for single people, their activities, etc.

soc.women

Issues related to women, their problems and relationships.

Talk groups

talk.bizarre

The unusual, bizarre, curious, and often stupid.

talk.environment

Discussion on the state of the environment and what to do.

talk.philosophy.misc

Philosophical musings on all topics.

talk.politics.china

Discussion of political issues related to China.

talk.politics.drugs

The politics of drug issues.

talk.politics.guns

The politics of firearm ownership and (mis)use.

talk.politics.mideast

Discussion and debate over Middle Eastern events.

talk.politics.misc

Political discussions and ravings of all kinds.

talk.politics.space

Non-technical issues affecting space exploration.

talk.politics.theory

Theory of politics and political systems.

For the posting of rumours.

Computer groups

Computer newsgroups can be some of the most in-depth and intense around. However, the amount of knowledge in them is immense.

comp.answers

All your problems answered, in theory.

comp.apps

Computer applications.

comp.arch

Computer architecture.

comp.archives

Archive material on the computing world.

comp.benchmarks

Discussion on areas against which to test your own applications.

comp.cad

Discussions on Computer Aided Design.

comp.compilers

For program makers

comp.compression

The art of making things smaller.

comp.databases

Everything you ever wanted to know about the humble database.

comp.editors

Program editors

comp.fonts

Creating fonts and typefaces.

comp.forgery

The darker side of computer programming.

comp.games

Time to have some fun.

comp.graphics

Discussion on images and the wired world.

comp.groupware

Discusions on computer groupware products.

comp.hardware

The ins and outs of what goes around the software.

comp.home

Computers in the home.

comp.jobs

Working with computers.

comp.mail

Discussion on mailing with computers.

comp.misc comp.object

Object orientated programming.

comp.os comp.parallel

Getting things connected.

comp.periphs

All the extras connected with computing.

comp.programming

Everything you ever wanted to know about programming – and a lot more besides.

comp.protocols

Discussion on the numerous computer protocols in existence, such as TCP/IP on the Internet.

comp.publish

Publish computer related items.

comp.realtime

Computers and video technology meet.

comp.robotics

Handing over to the machines.

comp.security

Trying to keep it all safe and sound.

comp.soft-sys

Computer systems.

comp.software

Discussion about those vital pieces of computer code that make the whole thing tick.

comp.software-eng

Creating software.

comp.sources

Where to find out more.

comp.specification

Discussion about all aspects of computer and program specifications.

comp.speech

Let the computer do the talking.

comp.std
Getting connected.
comp.sys
Computer systems.
comp.human-factors
Where man meets machine.
comp.infosystems
Discussion on computer based information systems.
comp.internet
The world's biggest computer network.

UK groups
uk.adverts.computer
Buying and selling computer equipment.
uk.announce
General announcements.
uk.announce.events
What's going on.
uk.comp.misc
News and comment from the music world.
uk.comp.training
Discussions on training programs.
uk.education.16plus
Further education.
uk.education.misc
General education.
uk.education.schools-it
Discussions about the state of our schools.

uk.education.staffroom
  The teacher's viewpoint.
uk.education.teachers
  More from the teacher's desk.
uk.environment
  Green and environmental issues.
uk.finance
  Money makes the newsgroup go round.
uk.net.news.announce
  Latest news.
uk.net.news.config
  News from the net.
uk.rec.birdwatching
  For twitchers everywhere.
uk.rec.boats.paddle
  Discussions for everyone who likes messing around on boats.
uk.rec.caravanning@
  Caravanners of the world unite.
uk.rec.cars.classic
  The allure of the classic car.
uk.rec.competitions
  Views and tips from people obsessed with competitions.
uk.rec.crafts
  Arts and crafts.
uk.rec.cycling
  For the enthusiast on two wheels.
uk.rec.fishing.sea
  Discussion on deep sea fishing.

uk.rec.fishing.game
Discussions on game fishing.

uk.rec.fishing.coarse
Discussion on coarse fishing.

uk.rec.gardening
For those who like to potter around in the shed.

uk.rec.motorcycles
Revving up the discussion.

uk.rec.motorsport.misc
General motorsport.

uk.rec.naturist
For those who like to let it all hang out.

uk.rec.scouting
Baden Powell would have been proud.

uk.rec.sheds
More for the gardeners.

uk.rec.walking
These discussions were made for walking.

uk.rec.waterways
Getting around on the water.

uk.rec.youth-hostel
Discussions over a backpack.

uk.religion.buddhist
About Buddhism.

uk.religion.christian
About Christians.

uk.religion.hindu
About Hinduism.

uk.religion.islam
About Islam.
uk.religion.jewish
About Jews.
uk.religion.misc
General religion.
uk.religion.other-faiths
General religion.
uk.sci.weather
The great British obsession.
uk.local.geordie
Regional discussion around Tyneside.
uk.local.london
Regional discussions around London.
uk.local.midlands
Regional discussions around the Midlands.
uk.local.nw-england
Regional discussions around the north-west of England.
uk.local.southwest
Regional discussions around the south west of England.
uk.local.thames-valley
Regional discussions around the Thames Valley.
uk.local.yorkshire
Regional discussions around Yorkshire.

Miscellaneous groups

misc.books.technical
Discussion of books about technical topics.

misc.consumers
Consumer interests, product reviews, etc.
misc.consumers.house
Discussion about owning and maintaining a house.
misc.education
Discussion of the educational system.
misc.emerg-services
Forum for paramedics and other first responders.
misc.entrepreneurs
Discussion on operating a business.
misc.fitness
Physical fitness, exercise, etc.
misc.forsale
Short, tasteful postings about items for sale.
misc.forsale.computers
Computers and computer equipment for sale.
misc.handicap
Items of interest for/about the handicapped. (Moderated)
misc.headlines
Current interest: drug testing, terrorism, etc.
misc.int-property
Discussion of intellectual property rights.
misc.invest
Investments and the handling of money.
misc.invest.real-estate
Property investments.
misc.jobs.contract
Discussions about contract labour.

misc.jobs.misc

Discussion about employment, workplaces, careers.

misc.jobs.offered

Announcements of positions available.

misc.jobs.offered.entry

Job listings only for entry-level positions.

misc.jobs.resumes

Postings of resumes and situation wanted articles.

misc.kids

Children, their behaviour and activities.

misc.legal

Legalities and the ethics of law.

misc.legal.computing

Discussing the legal climate of the computing world.

misc.misc

Various discussions not fitting in any other group.

misc.news.southasia

News from Bangladesh, India, Nepal, etc. (Moderated)

misc.rural

Devoted to issues concerning rural living.

misc.taxes

Tax laws and advice.

misc.wanted

Requests for things that are needed

misc.writing

Discussion of writing in all of its forms.

Jargon Buster

Abbreviations
Used mostly by users of newsgroups, abbreviations are used to lessen the amount that has to be typed in a message. Some items consist of little more than a string of abbreviations.

Address book
A small database within an email program that can be used to store contact details of your email correspondents. This includes their name and email address and it can also include items such as their home address and their fax number.

Attachments
Items that are sent with an email as a separate document. This can be anything from a word processed document, to a graphics file. Attachments give more versatility to emails but they do create bigger file sizes, which can be an issue when sending and receiving.

Auto-completion
The method by which email programs recognise an email address just from the first few letters that are entered.

Auto-responders
Automated programs which are established to return a pre-written message upon receipt of email. This can be used by people who are going on holiday and

also by e-commerce companies – when a customer makes a purchase an auto-responder message is automatically sent to them.

Blind copy

To send a copy of a message to another recipient, without the original recipient knowing about it. This can be used to keep different people informed but it can also make you look secretive.

Contacts

Details of people who you communicate with via email. These can be individuals or groups and contact details are stored within one or more address books.

Copy

To send a copy of a message to another recipient. This is usually for information or a courtesy.

Ecards

Electronic greeting cards, communicated by email. They are created on a Web page and then an email is generated to the recipient. When they receive the message it will contain the relevant hyperlink – clicking this takes them to the location of the ecard.

Emoticons

Also referred to as smileys, these symbols help convey the tone or emotion of an email. Short for 'emotional icon', there is a huge range of emoticons that can be used.

Email account

This is the location where your email messages pass through and where your email details are kept.

Email address

The electronic address for sending and receiving emails. It will be made up of your user ID, usually a combination of your own name and your ISP's domain name (such as 'freeserve.net').

Email client

See 'Email program'.

Email program

The software program that you use to compose, send and receive email messages. It contains your address book and also has the capability to sort and organise your messages. All ISPs provide an email program (usually Outlook Express) when you register with them. However, there are other programs that can be found on the Web; these include Netscape Messenger, Eudora and Pegasus.

Encoding

A method of sending non-text files with email messages. Common encoding options include: Mime, BinHex and UUencode. If two computers are communicating with each other, they must both have the same method of encoding in order for them both to read attachments sent from the other.

Eudora

A popular and successful email program that can be downloaded from the Web for free.

Flame

An angry or rude email message, often posted as a public response on a discussion group. If you become the target of a flame, avoid responding or you might incite a flame war.

Forward

Sending on an email you have received to another person.

Forwarding services

Online companies that let you access your email account from another computer.

Groups

Several email addresses that are created under one address. This way you only have to select the single address and everyone in the group will be included as recipients of the message.

Header

The first part of a received email message which contains information about the route of the message while it was making its way to your mail server. Much of this may not be displayed if the email software program keeps it hidden. However, there is usually an option for showing these details (though there is usually little reason for doing so).

IMAP

Internet Message Access Protocol. A method to access and manipulate email that is stored remotely on another computer.

Inbox

All email programs provide an Inbox, a special mail folder or mailbox that holds your incoming mail messages. Your email program will allow you to read, reply to, save, or delete the messages in your Inbox.

Internet

The infrastructure of computers, cables, modems and other peripheral devices that enable a global network of computers to be connected. The elements that make up the Internet are the World Wide Web (WWW), email, newsgroups and chat rooms.

Internet Service Provider

See ISP.

ISP

A company which gives you access to the Internet and provides you with an email account. There are dozens of ISPs to choose from and they differ in terms of charges for registration and also online call charges.

Junk email

See Spam.

Lurker

Someone who reads newsgroup discussions without contributing. This is a perfectly acceptable practice.

Mail bomb

Hundreds or thousands of email messages sent to the same address, sometimes to the central posting address of a discussion group, causing an avalanche effect and perhaps bringing down a server with the heavy load it causes.

Mail folders and mailboxes

Places where your mail program stores email messages. Some programs call them mail folders while others call them mailboxes. Most people save their mail in different mail folders depending on topic, correspondent, date, or other categories. Modern email programs provide the same services (read, reply, save, or delete) to other mail folders that they provide for the Inbox.

Mailing List

A collection of email addresses of people who have asked to receive regular mail discussions on a particular topic, and for which they can sometimes submit messages for disbursement to the entire group.

Mailing list manager

An automated program which handles the administrative functions of adding/removing subscribers, disseminating the message postings and generally administering a mailing list. Example of mailing list managers are Majordomo, Listserv, ListProc, Mailbase, etc.

Messenger

Netscape's email program that comes bundled with its popular Communicator package.

MIME

Multipurpose Internet Mail Extensions. The format used to encode attachments so that they can be sent via email.

Moderator

Someone who controls the postings of messages in a newsgroup or mailing list to ensure conformity with the topic and list policies.

Netiquette

Good practice for sending email and participating in newsgroups. Some users can get very protective about their newsgroups in particular and if you breach the Netiquette then you could end up being flamed i.e. attacked verbally via email.

Newbie

A novice user in a newsgroup.

Newsgroup

An electronic bulletin board that is accessed by people with a shared interest. There are tens of thousands of newsgroups, covering every subject imaginable. Using a newsreader it is possible to subscribe to newsgroups and then read the messages that have been posted or join in yourself. It is free to subscribe to newsgroups and it is also easy to unsubscribe.

Newsreader

The software that is used to access newsgroups. Several email programs, such as Outlook Express and Messenger, have built-in newsreaders.

Outlook

The business-orientated version of Outlook Express. It includes extra features such as a calendar and a tasks manager.

Outlook Express

The widely used Microsoft email program. It comes bundled with the Internet browser and email package provided by most ISPs.

Pegasus

An alternative email program to those more widely used, such as Outlook Express.

POP/POP3

Post Office Protocol. This is an email protocol that has become the standard for sending email.

Postmaster

The person to contact at a particular server/site to get help, or information about that server/site. Also the person to contact to register a complaint about a user's behaviour.

Reply

To send an email directly back to the person who sent it to you. This means you do not have to enter their email address details.

Reply to All

If you are sent an email as part of a large group, this can be used to reply to all of the members of the group, not just the sender of the message.

Server

A computer that processes incoming and outgoing email messages. The bigger the ISP then the larger the server should be. If a server is asked to handle too many messages it may crash i.e. close down.

Signature

Text placed at the end of a mail message to provide the reader with the author's contact information, Web site address, etc. The signature line is composed and placed into the email software's signature file for automatic appending.

Smileys
Another name for emoticons.

SMTP
Simple Mail Transfer Protocol. The most common protocol used for transferring email across the Internet.

SPAM
This is slang for unsolicited commercial email (UCE), also known as junk email. This is indiscriminate mass marketing and it can cover a multitude of sins: selling items; get-rich-quick schemes; health care; offers of stocks and shares; pornography; pirated software; and offers to set up your own junk email operation. To be avoided at all costs.

Stationery
Pre-formatted designs that can be added to emails to give them an added design dimension. Stationery can be added to individual messages, or used as a default for all messages.

Thread
A written conversation on a particular topic in a larger group discussion. People can reply to a specific thread.

Usenet
The network of newsgroups on the Internet.

Unsolicited Commercial Email (UCE)
The official name for spam or junk email. There are organisations and Web sites which are dedicated to fighting UCE and there is even some legislation in progress in different countries designed to combat this growing menace.

However, given the nature of the Internet, it is unlikely that it will be removed completely.

Viruses
Programs that are designed to corrupt data on a computer or jam a mail server by generating huge volumes of messages. Viruses are frequently spread in email messages as attachments, but they cannot be activated unless the attachment is opened.

Web-based email
An email account that is run through a Web browser such as Internet Explorer or Navigator rather than an email program. The most well-known provider of Web-based email is Hotmail, but there are numerous other companies that offer the same service.

World Wide Web (WWW)
The collection of pages of individual and corporate information that are distributed on the Internet and connected by hyperlinks.

Index

Acrobat. *See* Adobe: Acrobat
Acrobat Reader. *See* Adobe: Acrobat
    Reader
ActiveShare. *See* Adobe: ActiveShare
Address book 30–31
    Adding contacts 76–77
    Backing up 82
    Groups 31
    Individuals 31
    New contact
        Contextual menu 82
    Viewing details 77
Address fields
    Blind copy 32
    Copy to 31
    Message 32
    Subject 32
    To 31
Adobe
    Acrobat 164
    Acrobat Reader 164
    ActiveShare 158
    PageMill 119
    PhotoDeluxe 158
    Photoshop 157

Web site 165
Animated cards 142
AOL 29
Apple Mac 20, 35, 147
Attachments 33–34
    Benefits 141–143
    Compatibility issues 146–148
    Compressing files 362
    Defined 141
    Digital images
        Cropping and sizing 156
        Editing 155
        Special effects 157
        Touch-up techniques 156
    Image files 143
        Creating 151
    Long documents 143
    PDF files
        Distribution issues 165
        Features 163
        Uses 164
    Printing
        Print Preview 169
        Print Styles 170
    Program files 150

Saving 166
Size issues 144–145
Use 144
Viruses 148–150
  Activating 150
  Defined 148
Automatic invitations 22

Background colours 124
BBC 28
Bigfoot 87
Blocking senders. *See* Email: Rules:
  Blocking senders
British Telecommunications. *See* BT
BSkyB 29, 38
BT 372, 377
BT ClickFree 28
BT Internet 29
Business contacts 239

B

Cable and Wireless 29
Canon 160
Cascading and tiling 72
CD-ROM 56
  Picture 121
Chat rooms 19

C

Communicator. *See* Netscape:
  Communicator
Composer. *See* Netscape: Composer
Composing with care 359
Computer
  For receiving email 34
Contact groups
  Creating 78–79
  Editing 83
Contact information 80
  Editing 81–83
Contacts
  Email addresses
    Obtaining 74
  Editing 81
  Pane 71
  Searching for 77–78
  Setting up 73
  User details 85–86
Contextual menus 179, 447
Copy and paste. *See* Formatting:
  Copy and paste
Cut. *See* Formatting: Copy and paste

Deja 453
Demon Internet 29
Denial of service 423, 436–438

D

Digital camera 21, 121
  Explained 152–153
  LCD panel 153
  Resolution 153–155
    dpi 154
Digital Certificates. *See* Formatting:
    Digital Certificates
Digital ID. *See* Formatting: Digital
    Certificates
Digital signing. *See* Formatting: Digital
    Certificates
Dots per inch. *See* Digital camera:
    Resolution: dpi
Dr. Solomon 166
Draft 34
Drafts
  Folder 104
  Messages 104–106
Dreamweaver. *See* Macromedia:
    Dreamweaver

Ecards. *See* Electronic cards
Electronic cards 212–216
  Accessing 213
  Creating 215
  Providers 212
  Topics 213
Electronic invitations 218

Electronic mail 19
Email
  Account 27
  Attachments 33
  Blind copy field (Bcc) 32
  Business uses 23–24
  Copy to field 31–32
  Defined 30
  Disadvantages 23
  Formatting 361
  Good practice 206–208
    Password security 206
  Growth of 19
  Message field 32
  Misuse 24
  Opening and closing conventions
    130
  Organising 171–194
    Reasons 171
  Receiving 34–38
  Rules 182–189
    Actions 185
    Applying 183
    Blocking senders 189–190
    Conditions 183
    Descriptions 187
    Filtering for children 188
    Naming 189
  Servers 26
  Services 195–218

E

Size 33
Subject field 32
The future 39–40
To fax 216–217
    Providers 217
Uses 21
WAP sites 382
Email accounts 59
Changing 60–61
With a new identity 194
Email addresses 73
Automatically completing 99
Extensions 30
Format 30
Obtaining 74–77
    From business cards 75
Record keeping 80
Recording 74
Email directories 75. *See also* Finding:
    Contacts: On the Internet
Email messages
Properties 80
Email programs
Changing 60–61
Installing
    From the Web 58
    Through ISP 56
    With a CD-ROM 57
Setting a default 61–63

Upgrading 58–59
Using different programs 63–64
Emoticons. *See* Netiquette: Emoticons
Encryption. *See* Formatting:
    Encryption
Ericsson 372
Eudora 44–47
Creating a new mailbox 300
Creating a new message 296
Creating signatures 302
Displaying 293
Edit menu 252–254
Encoding 276
Features 46, 248
File menu 249–251
Filters 260
Folders 300–301
    Creating 300
Formatting text 284
Help menu 294–295
History 44
Importing 251
Light mode 46, 248
Mailbox menu 255
Mailboxes 300–301
    Creating 300
Menu bar 249
Message menu 256–258
Messages
    Creating 296

New Message toolbar 297–298
Options 265
  Advanced Network 291
  Attachments 275–276
  Auto configure 291
  Auto-completion 286–287
  Automation 290
  Background tasks 289
  Checking Mail 266–267
  Date Display 287–288
  Display 278–279
  Extra Warnings 290
  Fonts 277–278
  Getting attention 288
  Getting started 265–266
  Incoming Mail 267–269
  Internet Dial-up 273–274
  Kerberos 291
  Labels 288
  Mailboxes 282–283
  MAPI (Messaging Application Program Interface) 290–291
  Miscellaneous 291–292
  Replying 274–275
  Sending Mail 270–273
  Spell checking 285–286
  Styled text 284–285
  Viewing Mail 279–281
Paid mode 45, 248
Queuing messages 298

Receiving mail 299–300
Registering 295
Signatures
  Creating 302
Special menu 259–261
Sponsored mode 45, 247
Stationery 263
System Requirements
  Macintosh 47
  Windows 47
Toolbar tips 278
Tools menu 262–265
Transfer menu 258–259
Viewing messages 279
Window menu 293
Evite 218. *See also* Electronic invitations
Excel. *See* Microsoft: Excel
Excite 200
Executable files 281
Explorer. *See* Microsoft: Explorer

Fax. *See* Email: To fax
File formats 33
File size 127
Finding
  Contacts 83–85
    On the Internet 86–88

F

Messages 83–85
Flame wars. *See* Netiquette:
    Flaming; Newsgroups: Flame
    wars
Flash. *See* Macromedia: Flash
Floppy disc 166, 180
Folder bar 71
Folder list 71
Folders
    Archiving 180–182
    Backing up 180–182
        Storage 181
    Creating 174–175
    Deleted Items 173
    Deleting 176
    Drafts 105–106, 173
    Inbox 109, 172
    Local 106
    Moving 178
    Notation 173–174
    Outbox 172
    Renaming 177
    Rules for incoming email 182
    Sent Items 106, 172
    System 177
Fonts
    Monospaced 345
Formatting 111–140
    Background 123

Copy and paste 136–137
Default font 129
Digital Certificates 138–140
Encryption 140
Font size considerations 129
Grammar 135–136
HTML 113–114
Importing text 137
Issues 111–112
Opening and closing conventions
    130–132
Plain text 112
RTF 113–114
Signatures
    Defined 132–133
Spelling 135–136
Toolbar 114–123
    Alignment 117
    Bold 116
    Bulleted list 117
    Font 115
    Font size 115
    Horizontal Line 118
    Hyperlink 119
    Indentation 117
    Insert picture 121
    Italics 116
    Numbered list 117
    Paragraph style 115

Text colour 116
Underlining 116
Uppercase type 364
vCard 134–135
Attaching 135
Creating 134
Forwarding 109
Forwarding services
Defined 209–210
Providers 211
Using 209
Four11 87
Free-Online 28
Freeserve 28
FrontPage. *See* Microsoft: FrontPage

GIF 122, 151
Grammar. *See* Formatting: Grammar
Graphical Interchange Format. *See*
GIF
Groups. *See* Contact groups: Creating
Replying to 257

Handheld computers
For receiving email 37
Hewlett Packard 160

Hotmail 242
HTML 33, 100, 113
Designing with 124
Templates 124
Hyperlinks 116
Creating 119
HyperText Markup Language. *See*
HTML

iBook 147
iMac 147
Image editing
Programs 157
Image formats 122
Images
Alternate Text 122
Layout 122
IMAP 26
iMode wireless technology 36
Importing
Addresses and messages 62
Importing text. *See* Formatting:
Importing text
Infospace 87
Internet
Development 19
Disconnecting 273

Free access 28
Wireless 35
Internet Explorer. *See* Microsoft:
    Internet Explorer
Internet Message Access Protocol. *See*
    IMAP
Internet Service Providers. *See* ISPs
Intranets 23, 226
ISPs 25, 28, 56, 73, 80, 96,
    195, 443

Japan 36
Joint Photographic Experts Group. *See*
    JPEG
JPEG 122, 151
Junk email 110, 184, 208, 403
    Blocking 110
    Cost of 411
    Fighting 414
    Marketing 110
    Online transactions 110
    Types of 404

Kodak 160

LINUX 35
Love Bug. *See* Attachments: Viruses
Lurkers. *See* Newsgroups: Lurkers

Mac 151
    Outlook Express 72
    Viruses 424
Macromedia
    Dreamweaver 119
    Flash 142
Mailboxes
    Identities 192
    Switching between identities 193
Mailing lists
    Defined 439
    Finding 440
    Quality 441
    Subscribing 440
    Viruses 436
Menu bar
    Defined 30
Menus 69
    Edit 65
    File 65
    Help 67
    Mailbox 65
    Message 67

Special 67
Tools 66
Transfer 66
View 65
Message icons 101–103
Messages
Copying 179–180
Deleting 179–180
Moving 179–180
Organising 190–192
Messaging services 22
Messenger. *See* Netscape: Messenger
Microsoft 139, 147
Excel 33
Explorer 195
FrontPage 119
Internet Explorer 43, 73
Office 2000 159
Outlook 42, 57
Actions menu 233
Adding a new note 246
Adding a new task 245
Address book 239
Attributes 219
Calendar 223, 241–243
Calendar views 241–242
Composing email 235–236
Contacts 223, 244
Creating calendar appointments 242–243
Creating contacts 244
Customising 231
Deleted Items 224
Edit menu 227–228
Email 234–240
Features 220–222
File menu 225
Formatting 235
Go menu 230–231
Help menu 233
Inbox 234–240
Journal 223, 246
Menu bars 224–233
Notes 223, 246
Other user's calendars 243
Out of Office Assistant 233
Outlook Bar 223–224
Outlook Today 223
Preview Pane 220
Sending and receiving email 236–238
Signatures 240
System requirements 222
Tasks 223, 245
Toolbar 234
Tools menu 231–233
View menu 229–230
Viewing calendar options 241
Outlook Express 43, 57
Accessing newsgroups 446

Configuring 89
Configuring the newsreader
444–445
On the Mac 72
Unsubscribing from newsgroups
448
PhotoDraw 159
PowerPoint 142
Word 33, 146
MIME 113, 275
Mobile telephones
For receiving email 35
Modems 19, 25
Modulator/Demodulator. *See* Modem
Multipurpose Internet Mail
Extensions. *See* MIME

Navigator. *See* Netscape: Navigator
Netiquette 359. *See also* News-
groups: Netiquette
Abbreviations 369
Attachments 362
Being concise 361
Checking your mail 360
Confidentiality 365
Defined 359
Editing responses 363
Emoticons 368

Flaming 367
Humour 365
Replying promptly 360
Responding with care 366
Seeking a reply 361
Shouting 364
Netscape
Communicator 48, 303
Composer 316
Messenger 48–49
Accessing newsgroups 447
Advanced preferences 318
Appearance preferences 309–
310
Checking messages 326
Communicator menu 322–323
Composer preferences 317
Composing messages 326
Composition menu bar 326–
330
Configuring the newsreader 445
Creating a user profile 303–305
Edit composition menu 327–328
Edit menu 308–323
Features 49
File composition menu 326–327
File menu 305–307
Format composition menu 330
Formatting 315–316

Go menu 320
Importing 307
Insert composition menu 329
Mail and Newsgroup preferences 311–317
Menu bar 305
Message menu 321–322
Navigator preferences 310
Offline preferences 317
Preferences 309
Return receipts 317
Roaming Access preferences 317
Sending messages 306
Standard toolbar 323–324
Text wrapping 313
Unsubscribing from newsgroups 448
View composition menu 328–329
View menu 318–320
Viewing options 325
Navigator 195, 310
Newbies. *See* Newsgroups: Newbies
Newsgroups 228, 442–486
Accessing 446–447
Alternative groups 456–466
Computer groups 478–481
Defined 442
Directory 456–486

Expiry of postings 453
FAQs 449
Finding 454–455
Flame wars 451–454
Avoiding 453–454
Lurkers 442
Messages 450
Replying 450
Miscellaneous groups 484–486
Netiquette 451
Newbies 449
Newsreaders 442–443
Configuring 443–445
Messenger 442
Outlook Express 442
Participating 449–450
Recreation groups 466–473
Society groups 473–477
Talk groups 477–478
Threads 450
UK groups 481–484
Unsubscribing 448
Viruses 436
Newsgroups directory 456–486
Newsreaders 228. *See also* Newsgroups: Newsreaders
Nikon 160
Nokia 372
Norton's 166

NTL Internet 29
NTT DoCoMo 36

Office 2000. *See* Microsoft: Office
    2000
OnDigital 29, 38
Online transactions 110
Options
    Connection 96
        Internet Connection 98
    Send 98
        Formatting 101
    Send/Receive Messages 92–101
Orange 372, 377
Outlook. *See* Microsoft: Outlook
Outlook Express. *See* Microsoft:
    Outlook Express
Outlook Bar 223–224

Packets 26
PageMill. *See* Adobe: PageMill
Paint Shop Pro 159
Parallel port 167
Password security. *See* Email: Good
    practice: Password security
Passwords 267

PC 20, 35, 147
PDF 33
Pegasus 50–56
    Address books 355–356
    Addresses menu 334–335
    Attachments 354
    Creating a new message 351–353
    Edit menu 333
    Features 54–56
    File menu 331–332
    Folder menu 346–348
    Folders 356–357
    Help menu 349–350
    History 50
    Installing 52–54
    Menu bar 331
    Message menu 344–346
    Message toolbar 351
    Obtaining 51–52
    Options 337
        General 337–338
        Hyperlinks 339
        Message settings 341–343
        Reader settings 338
        Reporting 340
        Sending mail 340–341
        Signatures 340
        Toolbars 343–344
    Sending options 354–355